OCEAN CRUISING ON A BUDGET

OCEAN CRUISING ON A BUDGET

Anne Hammick

Illustrations by the Author

 International Marine Publishing
Camden, Maine

Published by International Marine Publishing. First
Published in Great Britain by Adlard Coles, 1990.

10 9 8 7 6 5 4 3 2 1

Copyright © 1991 by Anne Hammick.
Published by International Marine Publishing, an
imprint of TAB BOOKS. TAB BOOKS is a division of
McGraw-Hill, Inc.

TAB BOOKS offers software for sale. For information and
a catalog, please contact TAB Software Department, Blue
Ridge Summit, PA 17294-0850.

Questions regarding the content of this book should be
addressed to:

International Marine Publishing
P.O. Box 220
Camden, ME 04843

Library of Congress Cataloging-in-Publication Data

Hammick, Anne.
    Ocean cruising on a budget / Anne Hammick ; illustrations by the
author.
        p.   cm.
    Reprint. Originally published: London : Adlard Coles, 1990.
    Includes bibliographical references and index.
    ISBN 0-87742-300-8
    1. Yachts and yachting.   2. Ocean travel.   3. Seamanship.
I. Title.
GV813.H33   1991
797.1'246—dc20   91-14501
                                                          CIP

CONTENTS

The lights begin to twinkle from the rocks:
The long day wanes: the slow moon climbs: the deep
Moans round with many voices. Come, my friends,
'Tis not too late to seek a newer world.

(Alfred, Lord Tennyson, *Ulysses*)

ACKNOWLEDGEMENTS

I would like to take the opportunity to thank all those who have been involved with the writing of this book and without whose encouragement and practical help it would have remained no more than an idea. In chronological order: Oz Robinson, Janet Murphy, Des Sleightholme, my parents, my sister Liz, Christopher and Elizabeth Dawson, and last but by no means least all those anonymous cruising friends who may experience feelings of *déjà vu* on meeting themselves in these pages.

PREFACE

This book will not show you how to start with a tree (or a steel sheet or a concrete mixer) and end up with an ocean-going yacht. It will not explain how to navigate across an ocean, though I hope it might encourage you to learn. It will not tell you how to repair your electronics, your engine or your relationships — plenty of books already cover all those admirably. It probably won't even impress your friends.

What I hope it will do is guide the newcomer to ocean cruising through some of the many decisions involved when planning a blue water cruise on the sort of budget which turns counsel of perfection into a bad joke, and help him or her to avoid expensive and unnecessary mistakes when choosing and equipping the yacht herself. Much of what follows is personal opinion and open to disagreement, but in the course of eight Atlantic crossings, the latter four as skipper of an elderly but much-loved 31-footer, nearly all of it has, in the traditional surveyors' phrase, been tested and found to be good.

AUTHOR'S NOTE

I hope I don't need to point out that the word 'man' and its derivatives are used in the sense of 'human being'. It's good to see the growing number of women owners and skippers around, but I suspect we shall be in the minority for a long time to come.

PUBLISHER'S PREFACE
TO THE U.S. EDITION

The publisher thanks Roger C. Taylor for his skillful and careful substitution of North American production boats, brand names, prices, and equipment sources throughout this book. *Ocean Cruising on a Budget* remains Ms. Hammick's book, of course, but Mr. Taylor's efforts will ensure that her advice is not only heard but can be readily followed in North America. Fair winds and following seas.

FOREWORD

Blue water voyaging requires a certain level of funding. This volume is based on the author's own considerable practical experience of making up for a minimum of funds by applying common sense and skill, and from these pages a basic level of capital and running costs can be estimated. Many ways of making funds stretch are shown which maintain that essential approach to all seafaring: safety.

The interest of the Pilotage Foundation of the Royal Cruising Club in this matter lies in its brief to promote safety at sea. The Foundation is anxious to promote cruising, but at the same time it recognizes that many who would like to cruise face a shortfall in cash compared with what they might wish. Through the ideas presented here it is possible to sort out the essential from the desirable and the economical from the extravagant. Thinking along these lines will, the Foundation believes, lead to the reduction of worries, to better standards afloat and a consequent increase in safety.

O.H. Robinson
Director, RCC Pilotage Foundation

1 WHAT IS A BUDGET?

A. KEEPING YOUR FEET ON THE GROUND

Different budgets and different priorities

> Any man who has to ask about the annual
> upkeep of a yacht can't afford one.
> (Attributed to John Pierpont Morgan)

The *Supplement* to the *Oxford English Dictionary* defines a budget as, among other things, '... the money available for domestic spending; so *on a budget*, with a restricted amount of money. Budget-wise ... making full use of limited resources.' I have taken a budget to be the amount of money available to cover certain necessities, certain semi-necessities, and perhaps a few of the luxuries associated with a long-distance cruise of limited duration. Being on a budget means constant awareness of very little room for error in both the planning and the sailing stages, since a poor decision may have to be lived with rather than corrected. This increases the potential for stress and argument or, as we have seen more than once, large debts which take years to clear after arriving home.

While no two people's idea of a budget is the same, very few of us are without financial limitations of some kind and everybody wants to see the best value return on money spent. A budget means priorities, in order to get the maximum ocean sailing and general enjoyment out of whatever money is available. Unfortunately in the sailing world as much as anywhere, the higher the price tag on a particular piece of equipment the keener a good salesman will be to sell it, irrespective of its actual importance. Few of those on the marketing side are experienced ocean yachtsmen, and many genuinely believe that their product is absolutely vital simply because they are ignorant of the alternatives. They are also unlikely to have first-hand knowledge of the conditions under which it may have to function — particularly true of electronics.

Budget ocean sailing is not about cutting corners. Rather it means recognizing the necessities, particularly in terms of safety, as against the luxuries in their descending order of importance. Not only is the line between necessities and luxuries different for everyone, but the order of priorities will also vary drastically. If something is so important to you that you will genuinely not enjoy sailing without it, it has crossed that line and the fact that another person might think it not worth its own space is irrelevant. This is a particularly important point to remember where crew are concerned. Their scale of necessities will almost certainly be different from yours, so unless you want to sail singlehanded — particularly if your crew is also your partner — encourage as much cooperation and discussion at the planning and equipping stage as possible. This is also an ideal opportunity for the less experienced to widen the knowledge they will be relying on once afloat, and to build up the very important feeling of involvement and joint enterprise which is one of the hallmarks of the happy ship. At worst, if a decision or compromise is agreed which later turns out to be wrong, it's much easier to live with the outcome if everyone feels they had a hand in it rather than one person being entirely to blame.

The budget philosophy — capital outlay v. running costs

> If you wish to know how I think, you must
> endeavor to put yourself in my place. If you
> wish me to speak as if I were you, that is
> another affair.
>
> (Henry David Thoreau, *Walden*)

At the end of this book are some suggestions for further reading — books full of valuable and often fascinating information, representing the considered views of at least two dozen different authors, many with much more ocean sailing experience than I. Even so there isn't one among them that I agree with totally, and by the same token no one is likely to agree with everything I say. However, my viewpoint may make better sense if I outline the circumstances and principles which have shaped many of our decisions over the past seven years.

My sister and I have sailed all our lives, and both crewed aboard (different) blue water cruising yachts in the mid 1970s. Together we had a limited brush with sponsored racing in 1981, and late the following year reached the stage of acquiring our own boat capable of extended passagemaking. Since then we have twice cruised the Atlantic circuit — the standard 'Leave the UK in autumn, take the Trade Wind route to the West Indies for Christmas, stay there until late spring, and return home about a year after departure.' Hundreds, perhaps thousands, of yachts follow this track every year, while others turn left into the Mediterranean or perhaps limit their horizons to the Atlantic islands. To venture through into the Pacific in your own boat demands an entirely different commitment in terms of both time and money, one which we have never been able to make.

When we bought our Rustler 31, *Wrestler of Leigh*, she was already fourteen years old, had been laid up ashore for the previous five years, and was distinctly tatty. Her purchase was funded by a mixture of savings and loan, and including the installation of a diesel engine to replace the original gas engine she cost us something like $25,000. We have always regarded that sum as invested rather than spent (though, admittedly, her current value is not as great as the accumulated amount had we actually invested the money), and have attempted to protect and even increase our investment by looking after *Wrestler* as carefully as her active life and our limited funds permit, and by keeping her fully insured.

Day-to-day running expenses have always been viewed in a quite different light, however. Major items such as replacement spars or sails help to keep a yacht's value from dropping, but $2,000 spent on new sails will not increase the resale value of the boat by more than half that amount — less if they've been well used. Thus, while attempting to keep to the 'Nothing but the best for *Wrestler*' maxim, we have always kept an eagle eye on outlay, trying to prolong the life of gear until a satisfactory replacement (either new or second-hand) could be found at an acceptable price. We've always kept meticulous accounts — necessary for two individuals who have no intention of pooling income — and calculate that we've saved between 25% and 40% of possible expenditure by habitually devoting time and effort to looking for the best option at the cheapest price. Examples include the replacement Canpa forehatch — half price because the colour was being discontinued; a used 35lb CQR anchor — not an item which comes up in second-hand chandlery shops too often, but after four months it did, at less than 50% retail price; additional parachute flares at 33% discount because they were one year into their three-year period — not too important for a cruise of less than two years' duration. The list is endless.

We quickly worked out a scale of priorities where running costs are concerned, priority going to safety — both ours and *Wrestler's* — and to items such as engine servicing which help to 'protect the investment'. Every expenditure is scrutinized not only from the value-for-money aspect but to be sure it's really necessary in the first place. One lesson learned the hard way is that good quality fittings are often a better buy in the long term than cheaper substitutes, even if it means foregoing less important items completely. The trick is to seek out the good stuff when its going cheap!

This accumulated knowledge was put to the test in 1987, while preparing *Wrestler* for her second Atlantic circuit. With a total of nine Atlantic passages between us we'd not been novices in 1984, but that had been our first experience of equipping our own boat for blue water cruising and inevitably we made mistakes. Knowing that an inescapable aspect of a limited budget is that errors in judgement usually have to be lived with rather than rectified, we were extremely careful the second time around. Our efforts were rewarded, both in terms of getting maximum enjoyment from limited funds, and in a trouble-free cruise with no major financial crises along the way other than a lost dinghy, hardly the fault of inadequate pre-planning.

Perhaps illogically, it upset me to find that many other crews with little more money than we had might be loaded with unnecessary or even downright useless equipment, but were sometimes lacking the basics. What do you do when you meet a yacht with almost no charts or coast pilots on board, cruising where there's no chart agent? Do you say 'too bad', or do you lend them yours and tell them where to find the nearest photocopier? It's happened to me twice now. We've met others with expensive roller furling genoas but totally inadequate self-steering, or the most common, a satnav but no sextant or tables.

Even though my opinions are nearly all the result of personal experience, I would never claim to have either all the answers or the only answers. However, I have tried to avoid generalizing and theorizing in an attempt to stick to the facts and costs as the would-be blue water cruiser will face them. I'm also quite convinced that there are limits to economy below which no sane person should venture. These include the 'circumnavigation in an 18-footer' and 'navigation by world atlas' schools. I don't say that people haven't lived to tell the tale, but if that is the only financial alternative I'd advise either crewing or staying at home. Each person must decide their own individual necessities v. luxuries scale (see Section 3A) and then decide whether they can afford to sustain it. If there's a gap, take another look at both the scale and your pocket. If there's *still* a gap turn to Section 1D — Crewing for Others, or take up cycling while you get the money together. Accept that going cruising will probably mean working overtime or even taking a second job, and almost certainly mean sacrifices. I have been accused of single-mindedness, one-track-mindedness and even eccentricity, but if you're really determined to go ocean cruising other things may just have to go by the board.

People occasionally ask how we can afford to spend so much time cruising — in my case an average of about one month in three since buying *Wrestler* seven years ago. The straight answer is that we spend very little, and always cruise with one eye on the budget. Fortunately it's a remarkably cheap way to live once away from home waters and $10 to lie to your own anchor' areas, but only so long as one accepts it as a way of life, with no more excursions, meals out, new clothes or souvenirs than one would normally have at home. As soon as one falls into the trap of treating a blue water cruise as an extended holiday the budget is doomed. (This can be a particular problem if friends are flying out to visit, unless they understand the situation and pick up most of the additional bills.) Most people who repeatedly take off for bluer seas and warmer waters have to earn money at other times to finance it, and we are no exception. Some people work along the way (see Section 8D), while others return to base camp at intervals to replenish the kitty. Whether one views it as taking time off from working to cruise, or time off from cruising to work, is a moot point.

Though the vast majority of blue water yachtsmen either do, or have, worked hard to support their chosen lifestyle, it's not unknown for people (usually singlehanders in very small boats) to rely on scrounging, borrowing and even begging. The more common fault of always accepting a beer but never buying, or scrounging for spares when something breaks with no offer of payment or a swap, is not calculated to win many friends and is unlikely to add to the enjoyment of a cruise. This is not to imply that we haven't occasionally been at the receiving end of extreme generosity, and I shall never forget the American woman who was so thrilled to have met a yacht which had sailed all the way from England *without* a man aboard, with which to confront her chauvinist husband, that she insisted on breaking out the champagne and caviar . . . Others have given us surplus canned food and waved away any suggestion of payment, or contributed knowledge and occasionally brute strength to help with some practical problem.

Most cruising people are generous with what they have. The only thing we felt we had in greater quantity than most last time around was first-hand knowledge and experience, so we did our best to share it. Sometimes this was in the form of information about the next harbour and sometimes it was more roundabout, as with a depressed couple to whom we showed our most evocative Caribbean photographs. They'd spent years refitting a boat only to find it was the wrong one for the job, and discovered while still only a few hundred miles from home that they weren't enjoying the sailing much either. At least we were able to say 'Look, that's *Wrestler* anchored in the Tobago Cays', or 'That's Barbuda, the diving was terrific.' They left at the end of the evening knowing that even if the Atlantic passage might not be all roses, there was a prizewinning carrot at the end.

This brings up another point — preconceived ideas about what to expect. Too much of what is written about ocean sailing either makes it out to be all horrific, until you wonder about the author's sanity, or all fabulous, with dolphins leaping under the bow. Certainly you get both of these, but you also get an awful lot of in between. One friend remarked that 'A bad crossing is frightening, a good one merely boring', and while he may have been phrasing this for effect rather than accuracy there's a kernel of truth in it. Parts of each ocean passage will be pure heaven, parts deepest hell and parts sheer frustration, but very few people return from their first blue water cruise swearing that they'd never do it again.

The budget cruise — limiting duration and distance

> They sailed away for a year and a day,
> To the land where the Bong-tree grows . . .
> (Edward Lear, *The Owl and the Pussycat*)

Many people assume that all blue water yachtsmen are permanent live-aboards, with no home base and no time limit, but in fact this is rarely the case. Among twenty cruising yachts from the UK you might find one that falls into the above category, two or three may be on cruises of several years' duration, while the rest are expecting to be away from home for between six and eighteen months. Americans seem to be slightly different, with a higher percentage of retired couples who may spend several seasons exploring Europe, wintering aboard in the Mediterranean but often with a home in the States to which they return at intervals. There are several reasons why few people cruise for more than two or three years at a stretch — a combination of choice and necessity, of which several often apply.

Financial Even the most economical cruise costs money, and most people have to stop at intervals to earn it. With employment laws strictly enforced almost everywhere, unless one has a skill which can be plied on the water itself or at a distance, this means regular visits home to replenish the kitty. The subject of working *en route* is covered in Section 8D.

Personal Leaving family, friends and familiar surroundings is a wrench at best, and can be quite traumatic if combined with doubts about the cruise itself. Knowing that the bridges have not been burnt and that you will return within a given time will lessen the problems of departure, and make the whole undertaking more intelligible to non-sailing friends who will merely wonder at the length of your 'holiday'. Announcing that you are leaving to sail the world and may never come back will strain the firmest of friendships. A larger budget would allow occasional flights home to keep the bridges in repair, but the further one sails the more expensive this becomes.

Spatial A small yacht at sea is probably the most cramped environment most of us will ever experience unless we go to jail. Not only is there the physical problem of stowing people, food and gear, but the psychological one of long-term proximity to our fellow humans. Privacy is reduced, and even with all sides attempting to give more than take, reserves of patience can be eroded to vanishing point. A further problem which affects crews who are not couples is the partial surrender of individuality. New friends are shared, invitations of the 'Come over for a drink this evening' type naturally include the entire crew, and certainly Liz and I have noticed that, whereas we lead independent social lives ashore, when cruising we tend to be regarded as a single unit.

Practical Even for those with few possessions ashore and an efficient home agent (see Section 8C) there are a few things which are best seen to at home. These might include work on the boat herself, and particularly the installation of new equipment (guarantees may not be valid unless fitted by an approved agent) or attention to long term medical or dental problems.

Avoid being over-ambitious when planning your first long cruise. Much better to achieve a modest aim and build confidence than be forced to abandon an impractical itinerary. Many more people announce their intention to sail around the world than actually carry it through, and if all is going well and your finances will stand it you can always extend your objectives *en route*. Most circumnavigators cut their teeth on shorter cruises, often in smaller boats, return home, and apply their practical knowledge to planning the 'big one'.

Limitations of distance are closely allied to those of time, and apply for many of the same reasons. American yachtsmen can feel relatively near home while on their own seaboards or, say, in the Canadian Maritimes, the Caribbean, Mexico, British Columbia, or Alaska, with the option of immediate return should an unforeseen financial or health problem arise. Return flights home may not be cheap, but at a maximum of $500 per person or so they should fall well within the limits of the emergency reserve. Few cruising yachts circumnavigate in less than three years — I believe the record is claimed as eighteen, with the yacht still sailing! Distances are longer, the navigation more demanding, and the yacht must be self-sufficient to a much greater degree than when closer to the support system of home. There is no denying, of course, that a circumnavigation is the ultimate as far as the cruising yachtsman is concerned, but don't attempt to run until you have proved to yourself not only that you *can* walk, but that you really want to.

What am I doing and why am I doing it?

> They change their sky, not their soul, who run
> across the sea. We work hard at doing nothing:
> we seek happiness in yachts and four-horse
> coaches. What you seek is here . . . if an even
> soul does not fail you.
>
> (Horace, *Epistles*)

Ask a hundred people in distant anchorages why they decided to go ocean cruising and you'd probably get at least eighty different answers. What will be noticeably absent will be the reply 'Because I couldn't stand life at home any more.' (Unless perhaps followed by a remark about the weather!) Very few ocean sailors are aimless drifters, and those who see ocean cruising as a means of escape from their own problems generally come unstuck long before they ever reach the more distant anchorages. Problems have a nasty habit of stowing away for the voyage, much of the comforting safety net that the western world has created to protect us from our own actions is left behind, and perhaps worst of all, there's no faceless 'they' to blame when things go wrong.

The blue water life is not for everyone. There are a few who will never be confident enough of their own abilities to enjoy sailing in distant waters, there are those whose attachment to home comforts is stronger than their desire to cruise, and there are those who prefer to live at a faster pace than ocean sailing can provide.

This is as far as I intend to venture into the 'Do I really want to go ocean cruising anyway?' minefield. If still in doubt on this fundamental point, read and ponder the chapter 'Is this the life for me?' in Geoff Pack's excellent *Ocean Cruising Countdown,* published by David & Charles. However don't expect anyone else to answer this question for you. Indeed, the probability is that without actually putting it to the test you won't be able to answer it either.

B. WHAT WILL IT COST? SOME TYPICAL CRUISING BUDGETS

Yachting Monthly asked me to contribute an article on 'Cruising Costs' to their October 1989 *Blue Water Supplement,* and I would like to thank the Editor for permission to base this section on that material.

Attempting to cost up blue water cruising is not unlike trying to measure the proverbial piece of string, with the added elasticity of fluctuating exchange rates. The variables of yacht and equipment, cruising area, lifestyle and plain luck all enter into the equation, but one fact emerges as almost always true — it's cheaper than staying at home.

Before dismissing this as sheer optimism consider the built-in overheads of life ashore. While some of these regular outgoings may have to be budgeted for even while away cruising (such as mortgage and house maintenance and taxes unless selling up completely), many others disappear with the severance of shore ties. Typically these might include running a car, travel and season tickets, household utilities such as heating and telephone, winter clothes, and even such apparently minor items as newspapers and magazines. The yacht's own running costs should also be included in the tally — the annual $3,500-odd to keep a 32-footer in a marina would cover her berthing and routine maintenance for several years almost anywhere in the world.

Against this must be balanced the problem of living without a regular income (discounting those lucky few with sizeable private means), though the initial shock can be offset to some extent by equipping and storing the boat fully before leaving home. With casual work *en route* chancy at best, most people finance longer cruises out of savings or capital, but it is absolutely essential to have reserve funds in case of medical or sailing emergencies, particularly with the large insurance excesses usually imposed when cruising range is extended.

Apart from the emergency reserve, what might day-to-day outgoings amount to? Obvious necessities are routine maintenance and repairs to yacht and equipment, clearance or transit charges as applicable, marina fees where no safe anchorage exists, fuel, food, and gas or kerosene. Many will also feel happier with yacht and medical insurance. Items which, though not necessities, certainly add to the enjoyment of a cruise might include the occasional marina berth for convenience rather than safety, meals and drinks ashore, excursions by rental car or taxi, quality souvenirs, and onboard hospitality. Most people like to keep a photographic record of their cruise, and some find that international phone calls add considerably to the budget. Mail is a lesser expense, except perhaps at Christmas.

Those reaching retirement age will find that a pension has much less to cover afloat than ashore, particularly as any mortgage has probably been paid off long since. An increasingly popular option is to base the boat abroad and fly out for periods of a month or more, laying-up in different harbours as convenient. This would seem to be an ideal compromise, though laying-up charges and return flights will need to be added to the reckoning.

Of the variables affecting cruising costs the most insidious, particularly relative to its importance, is the exchange rate. The Caribbean is no problem for Americans, but in Europe, the dollar recently has gotten in the bad habit of falling against most currencies. When planning to go foreign, it's worth considering getting some friendly, expert advice on whether or not to buy into the currencies involved before leaving.

Size of yacht seems to have little bearing on day-to-day costs, except perhaps in areas where anchorages are limited and marina fees a regular item on the budget. Charges for haul-outs, antifouling etc will obviously be greater, but this may be partly offset by carrying more tools and spares and perhaps even having a fitted workbench aboard. More relevant is the yacht's equipment and the skipper's reliance on it. Electronics undoubtedly give most problems and can seldom be repaired locally, while returning them to the manufacturer often entails not only expense but long delays. Unfortunately the occasional failure of an important item is almost inevitable, and this must be budgeted for.

Cruising area can affect living costs drastically, most noticeably in terms of food and fuel. On the whole, the better known and more popular the area the more expensive it will be, until one sometimes wonders how the local people can afford to live at all. Lifestyle, if defined in terms of where the line falls between necessity and luxury, is as impossible to quantify afloat as it would be ashore. Some may return from a day's taxi tour to a steak out of the deepfreeze washed down by a chateau-bottled claret, while others stagger back from a walk in the hills to bean stew and a bottle of local rotgut. The couples who kindly agreed to pass on their experience of blue water budgeting fall somewhere between those two extremes.

Bill and Hazel returned in July 1989 from an Atlantic circuit in their 1967-built Excalibur 36. They spent a good deal on preventative maintenance and spares before leaving, plus another $800 *en route*, mainly on replacing the water-damaged VHF. Bill never uses marinas unless forced to and seldom motors. They particularly enjoyed the Bahamas, and although a fairly expensive area, found their budget of $800 per month covered a weekly meal ashore plus a drink every few days. They reckoned to spend about $35 per week on fresh food to supplement stores carried from home. Their nine-month cruise cost approximately $8,000, though they point out that it would have been more had they not stored and prepared the boat thoroughly before leaving. Incidentally they strongly advise against selling the house if planning to return home, estimating that over the last few years it would have cost them nearly $30,000 annually in inflation costs to get back into the housing market. (That may not be true in America as of this writing.)

Ted, a professional boatbuilder with over twenty years' ocean sailing experience, recently cruised Venezuela with his wife and young son. Maintenance costs on their two-year-old Nicholson 45 were fairly high, with over $2,500 spent on a damaged cylinder head in addition to electronic failures. Having her slipped — an annual expense where tidal range is slight — cost about $200. They found Venezuela very cheap, in spite of a $20 per month cruising permit, and a typical meal with drinks at only $5 per head allowed frequent meals ashore within a food budget of $65 per week. They avoided marinas and used little fuel — even though it was extremely cheap. For a family of three to sail for only $6,500 or so annually, much of that going on a major repair, would be almost impossible in many areas and emphasizes just how much location affects expenses.

John, a retired MD, and his wife Sheila cruised their 33ft (10m) Gladiateur out to the eastern Mediterranean over three seasons, reaching Turkey in 1989. Return flights at about $350 each are a regular budget item, as is $30 for altering the transit log every time crew join or leave. Laying-up afloat for three months in Marmaris cost $600 plus a $8 customs charge but otherwise marinas are seldom visited and they use little diesel.

John does all his own maintenance and other than a new VHF has had no major repair bills. Food in Turkey is cheap, with meals ashore costing from $5 plus about $35 weekly for fresh food. The vast majority of their annual cruising budget obviously goes on flights and laying-up charges, with other overheads relatively low.

Unlike the previous couples, Tim and Cathy were relatively inexperienced when they bought their 10-year-old Nicholson 31 in 1987 and left for a one-year cruise. They had hoped to live on $350 per month, but upped it to $525 in the Caribbean to cover the regular cold beers (they had no onboard refrigeration) and once or twice weekly meals ashore which they enjoyed. With few electronics repair costs were minimal, and they did all regular maintenance themselves. Like most blue water cruisers they preferred anchoring to marinas, and used little fuel. They sold their boat within weeks of returning to England, demonstrating the advantages of having chosen a popular and classic design.

Our own 21-year-old Rustler 31 is cruised on an unashamed shoestring, with little hi-tech equipment that we cannot maintain ourselves. The only major expense during two Atlantic circuits have been for a broken boom in Madeira and a lost dinghy in Barbados, the former costing about $115 for a repair which saw us round the rest of the Atlantic, but the latter costing nearly $800 to replace. We can rarely afford to eat or drink ashore in the more expensive areas, but enjoy market shopping and often try local recipes. We seldom visit marinas and fuel bills are low, partly because of minimal power drain, but ice is a regular expense. Our chief luxuries are the occasional rental car, usually shared with another yacht, and lots of film. On both year-long cruises we allowed $1,500 each for food and other necessities and $1,500 for the boat. This proved tight in 1984/5 when the pound dropped below US $1.10, but quite adequate in 1987/8, by which time it had risen by more than 50 per cent to around US $1.70 making our funds stretch, quite literally, half as far again.

It would be very easy to spend double or treble this amount, and quite possible to exist on less — much depends on the standard of living you are accustomed to ashore and the area you plan to cruise. All the inescapable costs of long distance cruising are discussed in greater detail in the following chapters.

C. THE TIME vs. MONEY EQUATION

> Life is short and so is money.
>
> (Bertolt Brecht, *The Threepenny Opera*)

There's no doubt that one can save considerable amounts of money by a careful investment of time, and I have already remarked on the savings which we reckon to have made in equipping *Wrestler* by spending time in tracking down the cheapest acceptable option whenever new or replacement gear was required. Sometimes this merely meant knowing exactly what we needed in order to avoid any hesitation when it became available, sometimes it entailed hours of poring over catalogues comparing prices or writing individual letters to manufacturers for quotations, and always it meant having enough ready money available to take advantage of the discounts for cash usually available on larger items.

Trying to prepare and equip a boat in a hurry will cost more than it would over an extended period, with between one and two years probably the ideal time span between purchasing a boat and leaving to sail long distance. This will allow at least one season of local sailing, followed by enough time to correct any minor faults or make the improvements which are sure to suggest themselves. At the very worst, it will give warning if the chosen boat is less than suitable for the task plus the possibility of a hurried sale and a second stab at getting it right. If this is not possible — perhaps you can only buy a boat after your house is sold — do your homework thoroughly before buying and make a particular effort to find a boat with a good inventory, ideally one which has already proved herself as an ocean cruiser. Suitable designs for ocean cruising on a limited budget are discussed in Section 2A.

Why this year is better than next, and next year better than the one after (the ten-year trap)

> We have no guarantee of tomorrow. If you dream
> of cruising, start today . . . Buy the small cruiser
> you can afford now and go cruising.
> (Don Casey and Lew Hackler, *Sensible Cruising*)

While months devoted to planning and preparation will more than justify themselves in financial savings and increase the likelihood of a trouble-free cruise, years spent dreaming can prove a robber in disguise. If there is no chance of your being able to go ocean sailing in the foreseeable future for reasons of work, family or other commitments there may be little you can do about it, but do not fall into the trap of allowing the boat herself to become the cause of your delay. Do not save for years to be able to afford your dream yacht if you could buy a more modest boat and depart next season. Do not wait for retirement if there is the remotest chance of taking a sabbatical, and if this proves impossible weigh up the likely damage to your career of simply stepping off the ladder for a while. For a couple with two careers to consider the equation gets more complicated, but it all boils down to the same question — what do you want to do most?

If the unequivocal answer is 'go cruising' there is only one correct time to start planning the project, and that is now. Some calculated risks may have to be taken and hard-headed decisions made, and this is the stage at which the old fashioned virtues of determination, hard work, practicality, self-discipline and single-mindedness (some might say pig-headedness) are at a premium. To be brave, adventurous and even slightly romantic may be useful later on, but they won't be enough to get you on your way.

If you've made the decision to go blue water cruising but have to accept that it will not be for some years yet, there may be a problem in keeping commitment to the project at a sufficiently high level to prevent other interests taking over. It seems perfectly reasonable for 'preparing for the cruise' to be priority number one for six months or a year, but trying to sustain the necessary impetus over five or ten years is another matter, and too many people in this situation end up among the ranks of the armchair sailors. Use an enforced delay to read, to learn, to pick the brains of those who do go cruising, and perhaps to gain experience by crewing on the occasional long passage — but never forget this is all a means to an end.

Building from scratch

At first glance it would seem that building from scratch should almost guarantee ending up with the ideal cruising boat for a fraction of the normal cost, plus the unique opportunity either to design a yacht to your own requirements or adapt one of the hull designs commercially available in steel or ferro-cement. Those thinking along these lines usually accept that building is likely to take at least five years, depending on the time and money available and on the size of the yacht.

Unfortunately the majority of those who build from scratch with the serious intention of actually sailing the finished boat are disappointed. Times almost always overrun, often to double what was originally envisaged, during which time people's lives, requirements and even dreams may change — relationships form or break up, children are born, teenagers grow up and leave home, health may deteriorate, and we all get older. If seriously considering a first-time building project ask yourself not 'What boat would I like to be out there sailing now?' but 'What boat would I like to be out there sailing in ten years time?' If you can't answer with a fair degree of certainty, don't gamble on guessing right because the chances are you won't.

Those who are happy with the results of long-term building projects almost always fall into one of two categories. There are those for whom the building is an end in itself and the finished vessel almost an anticlimax; and there are those who, probably after years of experience with a variety of other boats, really do know exactly what they want (often unconventional), build her, and sail her with complete satisfaction for the rest of their lives. Of course, there are also the plain lucky.

The majority of first-time builders get carried away on size, probably because the cost of the hull itself, which is only the tip of the iceberg, does not increase too visibly with the addition of an extra few feet overall and perhaps an extra foot on the beam. Volume and displacement are much better indicators of final cost — the larger yacht will not only need larger, heavier and much more expensive equipment than her smaller sister, she will also need items that the small yacht can do without entirely, since whatever factors are fed into the equation, human strength is a constant which even the carrying of extra crew will never entirely balance. Some equipment may be acquired second hand, but even there the smaller yacht has an advantage since much of the better used equipment which comes on the market does so because of larger yachts upgrading gear which is in perfect working order but simply not powerful enough. Winches are a typical case, and I have also heard of good used roller furling systems being acquired this way.

The ultimate test of the long-term building project is how long the yacht is kept after launching. After ten years of effort one might reasonably expect ten years of satisfied ownership, but this is seldom the case and many home builders know the boat is the wrong one for them before she is even launched. The sheer learning process inherent in the project itself is enough to change most people's idea of the boat they actually want.

The final and perhaps unkindest aspect is that while any yacht represents a considerable capital investment, home-built boats are notoriously difficult to sell and seldom reflect anything like their true value in terms of the money and time poured into them. This is particularly sad in the case of boats which are beautifully constructed and finished, and which will probably make superb ocean cruising yachts though not necessarily for their builders. However, in such a situation the buyer has absolutely no guarantee. Few home builders can resist the temptation to personalize the interior and so further narrow the potential market, and this is naturally reflected in second-hand value. Basically, if you simply want the satisfaction of building your own boat go ahead, but if you seriously plan to go ocean cruising, whether on a budget or not, my advice is to opt for a boat whose advantages and drawbacks you can actually see.

One compromise is to fit out the interior of a professionally built fibreglass or steel hull. Test sailing a sistership should tell you enough to make a sensible judgement about its suitability for you, and the time period will be much, much shorter. By no means all companies will supply bare hulls — too many have found that badly completed interiors do nothing for the reputation of the original builder — but those that do will often give a choice of stages from bare hull and deck mouldings, through structural bulkheads and engine beds glassed in, to a basic sailaway version. *From a Bare Hull* by Ferenc Maté, published by W.W. Norton, is one of several practical books on the subject.

D. CREWING FOR OTHERS

The classic way of sailing on a budget is to do it at someone else's expense. This isn't quite the cynical approach that it sounds, since good crew are in great demand, and for a single person with little money but some free time and a certain amount of knowledge this is an excellent way of gaining experience. One possibility is to travel at your own expense to a place where crew are often taken on at short notice, such as the East Coast in November, but a much safer approach is to organize a berth in advance on a known yacht, with enough time to have second thoughts about either yacht or skipper if necessary. Clubs such as the Cruising Club of America and local yacht clubs may be able to put you in touch with members looking for crew, or you could try one of the crew position directories listed in the classified ads of *Cruising World* magazine. Particular skills such as cooking or mechanical experience will give an advantage, but a yacht at sea is a very small place and most skippers are more concerned about personality than ability.

Financial arrangements vary from the paying guest through various stages of cost splitting to the paid hand, and it is essential to establish in advance exactly what both sides have in mind. Casual crew are not normally expected to help with bills such as fuel and berthing, and though most skippers will expect a contribution towards keep, some may be willing to feed a good crew while they're on board. Few private owners are able to pay even minimal wages. Charter boats are in a different league, but the good ones seldom need to take on casual crew and the others are to be avoided.

It's worth starting out with a few written references — perhaps one from the secretary of your local sailing club — to say that you know one end of a boat from the other, and from an ex-employer to say you can be trusted. Formal qualifications such as U.S. Power Squadron courses may also carry some weight, but are by no means necessary. If you plan to make a habit of crewing, ask each skipper for a reference at the end of a passage and thus pave the way for the next berth. A great deal of advice on the whole subject is given in *The Hitchhiker's Guide to the Oceans: Crewing Around the World* by Alison Muir Bennett and Clare Davis, published by Seven Seas/International Marine.

The skipper's side of the crew question is examined in Section 6A.

2 A BOAT FOR THE OCEAN: CHOOSING FOR SAFETY, SANITY AND ECONOMY

A. WHERE DO I START?

> The perfect boat is not the one you dream
> about. It is the boat that takes you cruising.
>
> (Don Casey and Lew Hackler, *Sensible Cruising*)

The quotation may overstate the case perhaps but it's a very practical outlook. In the best of all possible worlds, after hundreds of hours of agonizing over hull material, keel shape, rig and interior layout, one would probably go out and commission a vessel to be designed and built to one's own requirements or at least have a proven design completed by a good boatyard. Unfortunately this course is simply not open to most of us, leaving us with the choice of cruising in the boat we already own, building from scratch or buying second-hand. The building option has already been covered in Section 1C, but do not dismiss your current boat out of hand if there is any possibility at all of upgrading her for an ocean cruise.

Selecting a suitable second-hand boat for blue water cruising is not always the result of a logical series of conscious decisions. More than one person has confided to me that 'I knew the right boat was out there somewhere and it was just a case of finding her — and I have.' In fact, this outlook is not nearly as random as it might seem, and is usually based on a very firm personal idea of what is essential, what is desirable, what is unimportant and what should be actively avoided.

At this stage you should concentrate only on those aspects which are impossible to change: construction material, dimensions, basic shape of hull (or hulls) and deck structure, interior capacity, rig and engine. The more specific you can be about what you want the better, provided it is based on logic rather than whim. The preferences of crew who will be spending long periods aboard must also be taken into account, as should the intended length of your cruise and the areas you propose to visit. A circumnavigation ideally requires a larger boat than an Atlantic circuit, for psychological as well as practical reasons, while it is obvious that tropical and arctic climates make different demands in terms of ventilation or heating.

The tighter your budget the more difficult it will be to find a boat which meets all your requirements, and the more you may have to compromise. Boats lying outside popular areas are generally cheaper than those near major sailing centres, but genuine bargains do come up from time to time — often when a replacement has been bought before the previous boat is sold — and the longer and further afield you are prepared to look, the greater your chances of finding one. Don't be put off an otherwise suitable boat by anything that you will be able to alter or improve, and ignore or even welcome superficial scruffiness — it may be a sign that the previous owner has lost interest in the boat and will accept an offer well below the original asking price.

Construction material

Steel
The toughest material for a yacht which may have to pound her way through gales, cruise for years without hauling, and survive occasional close encounters with a rocky bottom is undoubtedly steel. A few years ago there were a great many French home-built steel yachts sailing the Atlantic circuit, nearly all of them slab-sided, boxy, slow and incredibly ugly. The other side of the coin was the pretty Dutch-built motorsailer in which I made my second Atlantic crossing, with her classic round-bilge hull form and easy motion. The one thing nearly all these have in common is size. Even with a heavy displacement design it is difficult to build a small steel hull of adequate strength without too much weight going into the hull and not enough into the ballast, so producing a very tender boat. Thus it is unusual to find a good steel yacht much below the 38ft (11.6m) mark, and those there are will be way beyond the price range of the budget sailor.

Ferro-cement
The above remarks regarding hull size are generally true of ferro-cement also. For some reason only the New Zealanders seem to have cracked the problem of producing smaller ferro hulls which are attractive, tough and not overly heavy. I have seen some pretty examples of the Colin Archer type built in ferro, but friends who spent seven years building one to sail to the Caribbean sold her shortly after arrival because she was so depressingly slow. Neither is ferrocement as strong as one might imagine, due to the differing properties of its two components. The cement side of the partnership is relatively brittle whereas the steel mesh is much more flexible, and it is not unknown for the two to separate. However, the main reason to avoid ferro yachts is that they are almost all amateur-built. Many are soundly constructed and painstakingly finished, but only the original builder can really know how much care was taken in setting up and tying off the mesh and bars, and in working the cement through to avoid air pockets. If you are tempted by a ferro yacht — and it can be a means of purchasing volume cheaply — do not expect to sell her easily. The few production classes built in ferro, such as the well-travelled Endurance, start at nearly 40ft (12.2m) and cannot remotely be considered budget yachts.

Wood

Until quite recently the vast majority of vessels, yachts included, were built of wood and I have no doubt there will always be a body of enthusiasts who will consider nothing else. It is true that few things can match a carefully built and lovingly maintained wooden yacht for looks, charm and character, but for a boat which is to be sailed actively wood has several disadvantages. The greatest of these is the amount of time that must be devoted to its care, a task which will be more than doubled in a tropical climate. Exposure to the elements is never kind to paint or varnish, and the strong ultraviolet of an overhead sun will soon cause it to crack and blister. Laid decks dry out and start to leak (though a few buckets of salt water after sundown may help to keep them moist), as do topsides, particularly in trade wind areas where the same side will always be exposed to the sun.

Older wooden boats occasionally hit the headlines by sinking with little warning, due either to springing a plank in bad weather or losing quantities of caulking from inaccessible places, and for some unexplained reason nearly all the yachts sunk by collision with whales have been built of wood. Far more relevant is the fact that few wooden yachts are truly dry. The nature of their construction − numerous different pieces of a relatively flexible material − will inevitably lead to working, as evinced by the gentle creaks and groans of a wooden hull at sea. Not only is it aggravating to be woken by cold water dripping into your ear, but although salt water below decks may not cause rot in woodwork it will damage almost everything else with which it comes into contact, and an accumulation of salt crystals will cause permanent damp on return to a cooler climate. Fresh water, while less damaging to equipment, may set off rot in deck or cabin trunking.

The final threat to a wooden yacht in tropical waters is from ship-worm. The Caribbean teredo grew fat on the oak of Nelson's navy, and their descendants still love to nibble on a juicy mahogany or pitch-pine yacht. I once put my hand right through the hull of a dinghy which had been attacked by teredo − the previous day the stern had fallen off, complete with outboard, and the whole thing had the consistency of soft cheese. Unless you are willing to undertake the task of copper sheathing, do not even consider taking a yacht built of softwood to the tropics. If you must sail a wooden yacht, start looking for a suitable design planked in a teak or iroko, but be prepared to pay much more for her than you would for a similar yacht built of fiberglass.

Fiberglass, or glass reinforced plastic (GRP)

Both my sister and I had already crossed the Atlantic in yachts built of wood, steel and GRP before we were in a position to buy a boat of our own, but when we were we unhesitatingly opted for GRP construction. We had no illusions about it being maintenance-free, particularly in the case of an older boat, but its many advantages made it the only sensible decision.

There are far more second-hand GRP yachts on the market at any one time than those built of all the other materials combined, thus widening the choice at the buying stage and improving the chances of selling easily and quickly should the need arise. Many come from yards with excellent reputations, while larger classes and greater uniformity within them enable one to bypass much of the theory relating to seaworthiness by opting for a design which is already proven at sea, sisterships having made similar passages and survived bad weather without undue difficulty.

Few people still claim that GRP is the perfect material it was once hailed to be, but it is certainly the most familiar to the newer generation of yachtsmen. For those intent on saving money nearly all maintenance can be done by the owner, including the detection and treatment of osmosis. To digress slightly, we spent several months in 1989 drying *Wrestler*'s hull by means of dehumidifiers and a heat-lamp inside a polythene skirt, before painting her hull with three coats of International Gelshield. We have no guarantee of its long-term success, but then to my knowledge no boatyards will guarantee their osmosis treatments for more than three years either. Our work cost approximately $900, plus considerable time and effort, whereas a professional job would have cost in the region of $6,500. Equally important to the skipper cruising away from home is the ease with which amateur repairs can be made in epoxy resin, compared to the skill and tools needed to make the equivalent repair in steel or wood.

An older yacht of any material will be improved by freshly painted topsides, and the idea that GRP is a difficult surface to paint by hand is a total fallacy. True, ordinary gloss paint applied by brush will not give either the protection or the perfect finish of sprayed-on two-part polyurethane, but while the latter type of paint *can* be applied by brush or pad it is difficult to get a good result (I speak from experience!). Either way, the general impression from a few feet away is likely to be quite as good as that of the freshly-painted wooden boat next door, while preparation (no more than a good scrub with detergent and then light sanding to form a key) is much simpler than the priming and numerous undercoats required to get a lasting paint or varnish seal on timber.

Finally, a word on composite yachts — those with GRP hull and wooden deck and cabin trunk. I have no first-hand knowledge of maintaining a composite boat, but many owners mention rot starting where the wood and GRP meet. If considering such a hybrid make sure you get a surveyor who is expert in both materials and knows where to look for potential problems.

Mono vs. multi

Like many monohull sailors I admit to being prejudiced against multihulls for offshore sailing. I neither have nor would wish to cross an ocean in one, and though I am aware that many hundreds of multihulls have made long passages, including several circumnavigations, the knowledge that if a catamaran or trimaran should turn over she is going to stay that way seems to me of overriding importance. (The evidence that a growing number of monohulls may exhibit the same characteristic makes it no less horrific.) Certainly there is as wide a gulf between the cruising multi and her racing sister as between cruising and racing monohulls — some might say wider — and I would not deny that, probably because racing multis tend to be at the forefront of yacht development and, as such, have a high failure rate, cruising multihulls have often been tarred with the same brush. Even so, the most enthusiastic multihull sailors agree that in bad conditions the boat cannot simply be dogged down and left to get on with it as one would a heavy displacement mono; she will always have to be nursed through the difficult patches, imposing severe strains on the short-handed crew.

The most obvious advantage of the cruising multihull is that she does not heel, making life aboard easier and more comfortable. However many catamarans, particularly those with solid bridge-decks, pound horribly when going to windward, which is itself not a point of sailing on which multihulls generally excel. There is usually more living and stowage space in a catamaran than in a monohull of similar length, though all too often this is broken into tiny cabins and compartments. The much lighter displacement of the multihull also makes her very sensitive to extra weight, so unless your bulk stores consist entirely of kitchen towels or a year's supply of babies' nappies, extra stowage space may prove more of a temptation than a bonus.

Another oft-cited advantage of the multihull is speed. In practice cruising multis often seem little faster than modern monohulls, possibly because short-handed crews are reluctant to risk them becoming over canvassed in sudden squalls and so limit sail area, particularly at night. They are invariably difficult to maneuver in confined spaces, an increasing problem in the more popular cruising areas, and most marinas will gleefully double the normal berthing charge.

On the financial side, multis have never been built in anything like the quantity and variety of monohulls, and good examples are unlikely to be cheap. Home-built multis vary from the excellent to the appalling, with prices to match, but amateur designs should be avoided like the plague for long distance cruising, however well constructed. The relatively short history of multihull development — something like 35 years compared to several thousand for the conventional mono — would also make me suspicious of a very early design even from a known stable.

Ten years ago every tropical harbour seemed to sport at least one of the unmistakable designs of James Wharram, unashamedly based on Polynesian originals and consisting of little more than two canoes attached by stout crossbars. In theory these home-built craft, usually plywood and often spartan, provided an excellent stepping stone to cheap cruising. Many made long passages, relatively few came to grief at sea (though they did seem to drag their anchors and land up on the beach rather often) and some of the larger sizes made comfortable cruising homes. However, they were generally difficult to sell, and many owners found they had spent far more on a building project than they could ever hope to recoup. In my opinion Wharram cats are best suited to the young, and even then are something of an acquired taste.

One of the few people I know who has extensive blue water cruising experience in both mono and multihulls (including a Wharram) is Geoff Pack, which makes the section entitled 'The Multi-hulled Ocean Cruiser' in his *Ocean Cruising Countdown* (David & Charles) of particular value to anyone seriously considering a multi for distant voyaging. *Multihulls for Cruising and Racing* by Derek Harvey, recently published by International Marine, covers their design, performance and handling. *The Cruising Multihull* by Chris White (International Marine) is a good review of the subject that includes a catalog of production boats.

Size

Size has much more influence on comfort than on safety, but I would strongly advise against long-term cruising in any boat of less than 25ft (7.6m) LOA. Although many smaller yachts have successfully crossed oceans, few of their skippers would not cheerfully trade them in for something larger — one friend described the motion as her Hurley 22 coped with large seas as 'like being inside a washing machine', and went on to mention the problems of carrying sufficient food and water for long passages, let alone the spares, tools, books and personal gear likely to be needed along the way.

The temptations of a larger boat are more obvious, and many of the classics of ocean cruising have been written from the standpoint of 45ft (13.7m) or more. The consensus amongst experienced cruising people seems to be that between 36ft (11m) and 40ft (12.2m) LOA is probably the ideal size for two people, particularly for a circumnavigation or other cruise of several years' dura-

Photo 1 The author's Rustler 31 *Wrestler of Leigh* sports the full keel characteristic of older cruising yachts. Amongst the many advantages are good directional stability and a protected propeller, together with a reduced likelihood of damage during an accidental grounding (*Photo:* Liz Hammick)

tion, but unless your idea of a budget is radically different from mine, while 38ft may be ideal it is also quite impossible financially. Prices tend to increase in proportion with internal volume and displacement, or roughly the *cube* of the length. The brief survey which concludes this section, of possible ocean cruising yachts advertised nationally during a six month period at under $35,000, demonstrates conclusively that within this sort of budget one cannot expect to find a yacht of much more than 32ft (9.8m) LOA. Fortunately this is a perfectly adequate size for two or possibly three people (though not all designs will have three good sea-berths), capable of carrying the necessary stores and safety equipment with room still left for some of the comforts one would rather not leave at home.

Length overall is only one statistic as far as size is concerned. Maximum beam, shape fore and aft (whether she sports the bluff rounded bow and stern of the Colin Archer type or the fine ends and long overhangs of the pre-war racing yacht), length of waterline and depth of hull (not to be confused with depth of keel) all help to determine internal volume or capacity. Together with displacement tonnage (the actual weight of the vessel and nothing to do with net, gross, or registered tonnage) they are also closely related to the seaworthiness of the design and her ability to cope with bad weather.

Seaworthiness and design

> In spite of all their friends could say,
> On a winter's morn, on a stormy day,
> In a Sieve they went to sea!
> (Edward Lear, The *Jumblies*)

Seaworthiness is a broad concept. At its most basic it implies the ability of a vessel to remain afloat during bad weather, and to continue on her way after it has passed. This is partly a function of design (a strong hull, probably of medium to heavy displacement, combined with a generous ballast ratio to ensure stability), with sound construction and careful maintenance also essential. Any hole through which water could enter the hull is a potential threat to the boat staying on the surface, with unsecured locker lids, low bridge decks and inaccessible seacocks being the most likely offenders. Deck hatches and ports or windows are seldom the cause of dangerous leaks (though often of minor trickles), windows set in metal frames being superior to the type in which screws or bolts bear directly onto the window surface. The variety held in only by rubber seals, sometimes to be seen on early Nicholson 32s, is potentially suicidal and *must* be replaced before sailing offshore.

To continue sailing after the weather moderates requires both rig and rudder to be still in place. I view all unsupported spade rudders with suspicion — not only do they sometimes fail at sea, when more than one rudder stock has sheered without warning, but they are also extremely vulnerable to damage should the boat run aground, particularly if she is subsequently hauled off

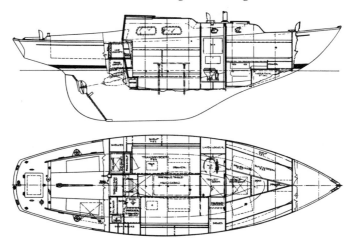

Photo 2 The Alberg 30, designed by Carl A. Alberg in 1962, shows a classic cruiser/racer profile. The well-supported rudder on this full-keel design is not likely to fail.

backwards. Much the same might be said of the type of transom-hung rudder which is unsupported below waterlevel. Least likely to fail is the rudder of the full-keeled yacht, sitting in a shoe at its base and attached by three or four sets of pintles up its length (see Photo 1), while skeg-mounted rudders are something of a half measure (see Photo 2). Few yachts can be steered with the rudder missing entirely, such is its importance to the balance of the hull, though most are steerable by other means should the tiller or rudder stock break or control cables part, allowing the rudder blade to trail. This has happened to me on three different occasions, and each time we were able to balance the boat via her sails while repairs were carried out. I have yet to be dismasted in anything larger than a dinghy, and indeed it seems increasingly rare amongst cruising boats. There is a great deal to be said for the somewhat old-fashioned combination of short mast and long boom as being more likely to survive a knockdown in one piece, while those who have had to do it tell me that it is considerably easier to build a jury rig than a jury rudder.

Also implied by the word 'seaworthy' are other more nebulous concepts. These include an easy motion which is kind to her crew in bad weather and assists them in performing the daily tasks necessary for mutual survival — essentially no more than watchkeeping, sail handling, navigation, eating and sleeping. She must also provide a safe working platform for crew on deck, with a sheltered cockpit, wide and uncluttered sidedecks and a foredeck large enough to tame reluctant headsails, all surrounded by a toerail at least 2in (50mm) in height. Another important attribute of a blue water cruising boat which will spend much of her time under self-steering is good directional stability, plus a reasonably light helm which will not strain the gear as it operates. Finally, for really enjoyable cruising she must have what I can only describe as a 'cooperative' attitude. Other adjectives used to describe this attribute might be 'purposeful', 'forgiving' or 'seakindly' — you get the general drift.

Not surprisingly yachts designed, built and advertised for ocean cruising are more expensive than yachts of similar size intended for less exacting sailing — the Hans Christian and Kaiser Gale Force are prime examples — and are well out of the price range of the budget sailor. Certainly many of the yachts sold today as suitable for offshore cruising would be unable to stand up to a full gale at sea, and consequently must rely on reaching shelter before the onset of bad weather. To be fair, builders are only reacting to market demand, with the priorities of the majority of the buying public inevitably being at odds with the design requirements of a truly seaworthy small cruising yacht.

Fortunately this divide was much less marked during the 1960s and early '70s, as was the line between cruising and racing yachts. Thus many older offshore cruisers and cruiser/racers make excellent blue water boats, an example being the Alberg 30. A yacht of this era may not have the interior volume of a modern design of similar length overall — which is likely to be at least one foot (0.3m) wider and 18in (0.5m) longer on the waterline — but there is no doubt of their seaworthiness in the broadest sense of the word.

It has already been remarked that one need not understand the theory of yacht design to choose a seaworthy boat, and that solid reputation based on the achievements of sisterships is a perfectly adequate substitute for the non-mathematical and those whose minds go blank when faced with graphs and diagrams. If looking for a detailed and technical discussion of the subject, study C.A. Marchaj's *Seaworthiness: The Forgotten Factor,* published by International Marine.

The rig

Unless you are already a devotee of what, without wishing to cause offense, might be called a non-standard rig, there is little point in considering anything other than the basic marconi sloop — in any case, if buying a smaller yacht second hand there's unlikely to be much else available. If you already own a gaff, junk or cat-rigged vessel and are happy with her go ahead — they've all made successful ocean passages and are in their element off the wind, though the light headwinds often encountered on the west/east crossing may prove a different story — but I would be dubious about embarking on one of these rigs for the first time when choosing a boat for ocean passage-making. Enough will be new and difficult without taking on an unfamiliar rig as well.

One disadvantage of a non-standard rig is that if it is to perform acceptably it will not be cheap. People *have* built junk rigs out of telegraph poles and battened their sails with runner bean sticks, but they can't then complain at having all the windward ability of the *Kon Tiki* and probably rather less speed. Gaff, while looking lovely and having a long and distinguished history, is undeniably complicated, and while this in itself may not be a problem it does imply additional cost — extra halyards, extra blocks (though often a saving on winches) and greater likelihood of chafe to both spars and sails. In addition many lighter crew members find a heavy gaff too much for them physically. The cat rig has long been popular in New England, and as epitomized in the Freedom and Nonesuch designs is very easy to handle by one or two people. However, the tall unstayed mast is considerably more expensive than its stayed counterpart, and neither can the special mainsails, whether two-ply, sleeved or fully battened, begin to compare for economy with a conventional suit.

All in all it's not entirely chance that the vast majority of blue water cruising yachts are marconi sloops, often with the addition of a removable inner forestay on which to set a storm jib. Designers and builders realized long ago that simpler means cheaper, and while this sometimes produces problems aboard larger cruising boats where a split rig and smaller individual sails would make good sense, there's little doubt that the marconi sloop is the most efficient rig yet invented (nearly all racing yachts sport it) and is admirably suited to the needs of the smaller yacht. The split headsails of the cutter don't really come into their own below 36ft (11m) or so: the 32-footer's genoa will not be unmanageably large, a permanent staysail stay will be in the way every time she tacks, and performance to windward will almost certainly suffer. (A second stay on which to set a windward running sail is something else entirely, and is discussed in Section 3C.)

Although ketch rig undoubtedly has its advantages — not least the option of furling the mainsail in a blow and pressing on under jib and mizzen — the duplication of masts and rigging makes it expensive, and aboard a yacht of less than 35ft (10.7m) or so there is likely to be the additional drawback of the mizzen mast cluttering up the cockpit. It does provide a handy perch for a radar antenna and allows the crew to experiment with a mizzen staysail (try a jib the wrong way up in lieu of the real thing) but the mizzen itself seldom provides any real drive going to windward, and unless the sheet is eased right off may add significantly to weather helm.

As mentioned above, there's unlikely to be much variation on the standard marconi rig available if you're buying second-hand, and certainly none of the designs discussed at the end of this section were built with anything else. As far as one has a choice, there's a lot to be said for a relatively short mast and low aspect rig to keep the centre of effort low and decrease rolling, though the boat should still be able to set plenty of canvas in the light winds frequently encountered outside the various wind belts. A GRP hull almost certainly means an aluminum mast, and while older alloy masts tend to be heavy in both wall thickness and overall diameter they can suffer corrosion if the anodizing has been damaged (gold appears to withstand wear better than silver or black) or if stainless steel fittings are added without suitable insulation to prevent galvanic corrosion. There is no reason why an aluminum spar should not be painted both for protection and improve appearance, though in practice this is seldom seen. Unlike stainless steel rigging, which has a working life of around ten years, aluminum spars have no established 'replacement date' and plenty made in the early 1960s are still going strong.

Running rigging is covered in Section 3C.

The engine

I once worked for a year aboard a 45ft (13.7m) yacht with no engine, an experience which made me fully appreciate the value of a reliable auxiliary if only for maneuvering inside small harbours and crowded anchorages. While few yachts these days are offered for sale with no engine at all, there are plenty of older boats around still fitted with their original gasoline auxiliaries. Apart from the inevitable problems of an electric ignition system in a marine environment, few people these days will accept the risk of explosion that gasoline entails, and neither will many insurance companies. The options here are to forget the boat altogether or to negotiate a reduction in price which will allow you to have a modern diesel fitted — up to $6,500.

The auxiliary engine need not be particularly powerful, around three horsepower for every ton of displacement being adequate for a cruising boat. Inspection of machinery is not normally covered in the survey, and if the yacht is laid up ashore getting the engine test-run can be a problem. With the agreement of both owner and boatyard you could try detaching the cooling water inlet hose from the seacock so that it can draw water from a bucket (which can itself be topped up by a slow-running hose), but do check that the boat is very securely shored up before turning the key.

If the engine should give trouble during your cruise the chances of finding a local mechanic to work on it are fairly good, even though he may be more accustomed to fishing boats, tractors or even generators than yachts. However he is unlikely to have the correct replacement parts available, so contact the manufacturer or an approved local dealer before departure for a list of recommended spares to take with you (remembering of course that they are in the business of selling parts . . .). As well as routine replacements such as oil and fuel filters, water pump impellers and internal zinc anodes, we carry a pair of injector pipes complete with seat washers, spare thermostat, water pump and fuel lift pump, plus correct gaskets all round. Difficulty in obtaining spares would be one reason to view any older engine which is no longer in production with distinct suspicion. The best small diesels are probably made by Volvo, Yanmar, Westerbeke, and Perkins. Perkins is distributed in the U.S. by Detroit Diesel. Volvo in particular seems to have a good network of engineers and dealers abroad.

Unless you are familiar with diesel engines, a handbook such as *Marine Diesel Engines* by Nigel Calder (International Marine), or *The Care and Repair of Small Marine Diesels* by Chris Thompson (International Marine), will be useful both at the buying stage and if the engine misbehaves later on. The full workshop manual will probably be expensive, but could make all the difference if your engine throws a major wobbly far from home and the local mechanic grows pale and crosses himself as you take the lid off.

All too often fuel tanks on older yachts — and on some more modern ones — are pitifully small, sometimes holding no more than 24 hours' supply. Without going to the expense of fitting supplementary tanks there is little one can do about this other than check that the filler is sited for ease of topping up while at sea. This will be further simplified by carrying extra fuel in small containers: 5 or 10 litre (1–2 gallons) rather than 20 or 25 litre (4–5 gallons) have the advantages of being lighter to manhandle both aboard and ashore, easier to stow, and that should one split less fuel will be lost or end up in the bilges. (Friends sailing a handsome 36-footer with teak decks once had a 5-gallon diesel can burst on the afterdeck. The results were so unpleasant and potentially danger-ous they had to return to harbour to clear up the mess.)

Some thoughts on freshwater tankage will be found in Section 7B.

The yacht as a packhorse

For months before leaving on a long cruise one goes aboard almost daily with armsful of gear and returns home empty-handed. It becomes a challenge to find a home for everything, which is why the amount and location of stowage, par-ticularly for heavy items, is so important aboard the long-distance cruiser. With food and other stores in many cruising areas considerably more expensive than at home it makes economic sense to carry as much as possible with you, but the tighter your budget the smaller your boat is likely to be − a real catch 22 situation. However careful one is to limit excess weight (and few cruising yachtsmen give it much thought) there is no possible way to prevent a cruising yacht sitting down on her marks. Raising the boot-top by 3in (76mm) or so all round − more at the stern if adding heavy self-steering gear − will go some way towards disguising it, and will also discourage the growth of weed in choppy anchorages where the lower topsides are permanently wet.

Generous cockpit lockers are both a blessing and a temptation, as *Wrestler's* enormous caverns prove − spare ground tackle, water and fuel cans, the de-flated Avon − you name it and it's probably there. We try to counteract the extra weight aft by keeping some of the heavier food stores, as well as an anchor and 30 fathoms of 5/16th chain, as far forward as possible, but probably pay for it with more pitching. Ideally weight should be kept as central as possible, but aboard a cruising yacht this prime area is generally devoted to living space and most people would begrudge sharing it with a dozen 5-litre water containers or a spare anchor.

If the weight of cruising stores is viewed in relation to displacement, it is obvious that the greater the weight of the boat herself, the less difficulty she should experience in carrying a given extra weight and the less her performance should be affected. However this is something of a two-edged sword, since ex-cessively heavy displacement in relation to other dimensions probably means poor sailing performance in the first place. The following list of typical weights covers much of the equipment which might find its way on board when upgrad-ing the coastal cruising inventory for a longer cruise. Although individually most of the items are quite light, when totalled up they reach the startling figure of 1720lb (780kg). Taking an average adult as weighing perhaps 145lb (66kg), this is the equivalent of nearly *twelve* people all coming aboard at once! It should be obvious why the ability to carry weight is so important in the blue water cruising yacht.

	lb	kg
35lb anchor, 40ft 5/16th chain & 150ft 5/8in nylon	82	37
Two spare 120ft 1/2in nylon lines	18	8
Aries self-steering gear	75	34
Avon Redcrest dinghy	43	19.5
4-person liferaft in fiberglass (GRP) canister	70	32
2hp outboard engine	32	14.5
Two Propane Gas bottles	44	20
25 gallons diesel	225	102
Comprehensive tool kit	20	9
Two additional headsails (totalling 770 sq ft)	44	20
Two complete sets oilskins, boots and harnesses	22	10
12 large hardback reference books	24	11
36 average paperbacks	18	8
40 charts	10	4.5
Nautical almanac and 3 volumes tables	12	5.4
40 gallons fresh water (in tank)	400	181
10 gallons fresh water (reserve, in containers)	100	45
Food for four weeks at sea (two people)	160	72.5
Reserve food for three months (two people)	240	109
12 2-gal/ cartons fruit juice	26	12
56 cans beer (14 × 4 packs)	34	15.4
10 1/2 gal/ bottles wine or spirits	7	3.2
2 1/2 gal/ wine boxes	14	6.4
Total	1720	779.4

Interior features: requirements for sanity

> No man will be a sailor who has contrivance
> enough to get himself into a jail . . . A man in a
> jail has more room, better food, and commonly
> better company.
>
> (Boswell's *Life of Johnson*)

After deciding your minimum criteria for the yacht as a seagoing vessel you must decide on your 'sanity' criteria — and few things are as subjective. It is essential that all the crew have their say and a balance is achieved between, for instance, the size of galley and chart table, or the amount of stowage available to each berth. What seems a relatively minor annoyance at first can become the flashpoint of a major argument after months of living aboard, especially if one person feels hard done by. It's also worth remembering that although one tends to think in terms of being at sea, most cruising yachts spend the majority of their time in harbour, when there can be different problems. Rolly anchorages and lack of privacy in marinas are perhaps the worst of these.

Photo 3 At first sight *Wrestler's* aft-facing chart table may appear cluttered, but in fact everything is readily to hand. Charts stow flat under the lifting tabletop; chronometer, instruments and switch-board face the navigator; while VHF and receiving radios are on the left together with a starfinder and Aqua Signal chart light. Note the white collision flare and EPIRB within reach of the companionway

Only you and your crew can decide where your own particular 'sanity' level is drawn. Bill and Laurel Cooper in *Sell Up and Sail* (published by Stanford Maritime) cite amongst their requirements: separate sleeping/daytime accommodation, sufficient fresh water (over 200 gallons), and at least 20ft of bookshelves — presumably why they sail a 55-footer (16.8m). Personally, I would be less than keen to cruise long-term on a boat which did not have standing headroom, a flushing sea-water head, permanent fore or aft-facing chart table with seat (see Photo 3), piped fresh water to galley and head (handpumped, of course), gimballed stove with oven and grill, electric interior lighting, and decent windows at the right height to look out of. Large cockpit lockers, so that a minimum of salty gear need be brought into the cabin, would also be high on the list. Minimizing leaks from below comes in the 'necessary for survival' category, but I would certainly include tight decks amongst my essentials for sanity.

Many of the inessentials which nevertheless improve the quality of cruising life can be added to a second-hand boat relatively easily; these might include an icebox if visiting the tropics or permanent heater if heading north, and a saltwater galley pump. Others, such as a spray dodger, a good awning (almost a necessity in the tropics) and a car-type stereo system fall squarely into the equipment category, but are definite pluses on the inventory list of a second-hand craft. I should stress that these are only suggestions. I've met numerous small yachts without some or all of the above whose crews seemed perfectly happy. Age has something to do with it, so has the degree of comfort you are used to ashore, and so has the length of time you intend to live aboard.

The simple life was being taken to extremes by a couple we met aboard a little wooden Vertue in the Caribbean a few years ago. The skipper had left England singlehanded, but met and married an Australian girl in the Mediterranean. First they ripped out the head so as to enlarge the forecabin to take a double bunk, then they solved the twin problems of paying for and stowing cruising stores by the simple expedient of selling the engine — funds and space in one fell swoop. We wondered how much of the boat would be left by the time they reached Australia.

Buying — privately or through a broker?

The most obvious ways to track down a boat which will fulfil your main criteria are to comb the classified sections of the yachting press — *Soundings* carries the lion's share of private advertisements for cruising yachts — and to scan the photos and listings in the brokerage section, contacting individual brokers to check what other craft may also be on their books. When we were looking for a suitable boat in 1982, in addition to combing the small ads I wrote to thirty-two brokers all over the country outlining exactly what we wanted — a 30/32ft (9.3/9.8m) GRP monohull with either full keel or long fin and skeg, at least four berths, full standing headroom, marconi sloop or cutter rig, diesel auxiliary engine: funds available $25,000. The response was interesting. Eight never answered at all, fifteen sent us their standard listings, sometimes with a few boats underlined, and five wrote to say they had nothing suitable on their books just then but would let us know if and when they had. Only four sent us details of boats which fulfilled our criteria, and *Wrestler* was among them — twice. Her specs? 31ft 5in (9.6m) LOA, GRP, long keel, five berths, standing headroom, sloop rig, asking price $24,200. The only way in which she did not measure up to our requirements was in still having her original 1968 gasoline engine, almost certainly the reason she had hung on the market for eighteen months. This, combined with her generally scruffy and neglected appearance, enabled our broker to negotiate a large enough reduction in the price to go a long way towards a new diesel.

So far as cost is concerned it generally makes little difference to the buyer whether the sale is private or through a broker, since it is the vendor who pays the commission (usually 10%). In anything other than the most amicable sale the services of a middleman can be valuable, and even then many people find it easier to discuss money through a third party. A good broker should provide accurate and comprehensive details of suitable boats without wasting your time with non-starters, check there is no possibility of disputed ownership or financial liabilities affecting the vessel, and list the inventory so you know exactly what is included in the sale. (It is not unknown for private sellers virtually to strip a boat before handing her over to new owners, having shown them over with a full inventory aboard.) Probably the broker's most important task is to negotiate a price acceptable to both parties, usually subject to survey, and then draw up a contract and hold the deposit while the survey is carried out. If this proves less than perfect he or she may negotiate a revised offer, and will finally see that both sides fulfill their parts of the bargain, that payment is made and title handed over, and if the boat is registered will advise on the necessary transfer steps.

The survey

Having found a boat within your price range which fulfills your essential requirements and the more important of your 'desirable' criteria, the last step before actually parting with your money should be to get her surveyed. Unless you have a knowledge of yacht construction bordering on the professional, *never* take the risk of buying without expert advice. Apart from the possibly dangerous and almost certainly expensive consequences if you miss something important, any fault found by a professional surveyor should provide leverage to negotiate a drop in purchase price roughly equivalent to the cost of having the problem put right. A survey report will also be necessary for insurance purposes. Amazingly, there is no formal qualification for the job, but on receipt of a business-size stamped addressed envelope the National Association of Marine Surveyors will forward a copy of their list of approved surveyors, who have to satisfy their own exacting standards of experience and expertise.

Do tell your surveyor of your plans for the boat — advising you on the wisdom of your choice is not technically part of the job, but he or she may well have some relevant suggestions. Inspecting machinery, electrics, electronics and additional equipment is normally part of a survey. It's in your interest to ensure the surveyor has access to as much of the boat as possible, which will almost certainly mean arranging to have her hauled out if she is not ashore already. You will need the owner's consent for this, and it would do no harm to get written permission for the entire survey, as it may include scraping off patches of antifouling to check for osmosis, removing lining to look for rot and other work which, though not actually destructive, could leave visible traces.

Like most expert advice a survey does not come cheap. Expect to pay $8 to $10 per foot of on-deck length, perhaps less if the boat is familiar to the surveyor and in good condition, and more if her nooks and crannies and gear are inaccessible or in bad condition. This would mean that a survey on a 32-footer would cost perhaps $300 plus expenses such as travel and possibly meals if the surveyor is not local. Boatyard costs such as hauling out are also the responsibility of the prospective purchaser, possibly adding $175 or more to the total bill whether or not the sale goes through.

Quite obviously, you will not want to go to this expense more than once if it can be avoided, so try to eliminate any boat which is suspect before getting to this stage. Enlist the advice of knowledgeable friends — the owner of a sister-ship would be ideal — and do your own homework by reading up on the subject of GRP yacht construction. *What Shape Is She In? A Guide to the Survey of Boats* by Allan Vaitses, International Marine, should give you a pretty good idea of where to look for problems.

What's on the market (that I might conceivably afford)?

> When a man got his own boat, he free. His
> onliest prison the horizon.
>
> (James A. Michener, *Chesapeake*)

It seemed logical to round off this section with a brief survey of yachts actually listed for sale over a recent six month period, taking the classified and broker-age sections of *Soundings* as the source. In order to narrow down the choice I was forced to make a few broad assumptions as to requirements, based on the views expressed over the previous pages, and apologize to anyone who feels their own particular case has not been met. These assumptions are:

1. While you must decide your minimum essential criteria for both safety and sanity, everything else is open to compromise.
2. You are not, at this stage, looking for a boat in which to circumnavigate by way of the Great Capes, explore the North West Passage, or do anything else beyond the bounds of 'normal' cruising.
3. The hull at least must be GRP.
4. The bulk of your sailing will be with two or three adults aboard, though you might occasionally want to sleep four.
5. You will probably need to sell the boat one day.

And the most arbitrary:

6. You can beg, borrow but preferably not steal up to $35,000 with which to buy and equip her (though it *can* be done for less).

So what did I come up with?

At the small end of the scale, a couple of 25-foot Pacific Seacraft sloops were listed. This is a very well-built little boat suitable for offshore work. Though she will sleep four overnight, for a long cruise she'd be as cramped as most people want to be with two on board. The 1977 boat was $20,500; the 1978, $21,800.

A half-dozen Tritons were on the market. This is a wholesome 28-foot sloop designed by Carl Alberg. Vintages ranged from 1960 to 1965; prices from $11,800 to $19,500.

There were ten Alberg 30s, a larger version of the Triton. Three were of un-known year. The others were built between 1964 and 1979. Prices varied from $19,500 to $29,950. Two boats were at the low end; one was a 1968 with a gasoline engine; the building year of the other was not given, but she had a new diesel.

And there were three Alberg 35s, all built in 1966, one with a gasoline engine at $27,900; one with unknown engine at $30,000; and one with a gasoline en-gine and side galley opposite dinette (no place to sit to leeward on one tack) at $32,900.

Thomas Gillmer's Southern Cross design is a good offshore boat. For sale were four 28-footers, 1979 or 1980, from $27,500 to $33,000; and a 31-footer built in 1978 at $34,500.

Another good boat is the Sea Sprite 28, of which there were three available, 1981 or 1982, from $25,000 to $33,000.

The Sea Wind ketch, a 30-footer built by Allied, has a good reputation as a seaworthy boat. One of them was the first GRP boat to circumnavigate. There were seven listed, built from 1963 to 1969 and all within the narrow price range of $27,500 to $30,000.

There was an intriguing Sparkman and Stephens 30-foot sloop of unknown vintage at $22,500.

The Mariner ketch, 32 feet long, is the heaviest boat here mentioned. Three were advertised, one 1977 and the other two of unknown year. Prices: $32,000 to $35,000.

And finally, to gladden the heart of an English sailor, there appeared a Camper Nicholson 32, as British a boat as there is, advertised in New Jersey. Her year of build was not stated, she came complete with Aries self-steerer, and she just made my $35,000 cut-off.

Hundreds, if not thousands, of different classes have been built since the 1960s and the omission of any particular design is not meant to imply that it would be unsuitable as a long distance cruiser — more probably none came up for sale in the six months I examined. Neither does the survey take inventory into account, even though this can alter the effective value of the boat (in terms of what you might otherwise have to spend) by at least $5,000 — see Section 3E. Lastly, these are asking prices — in some cases the boats may actually have changed hands for considerably less. Obviously they are only the tip of the iceberg as far as numbers are concerned, and individual yachts might prove to be non-starters for any one of a dozen reasons. However as designs, all have stood the test of time, all have proved themselves capable of crossing oceans, and all have held their value well and look set to continue that way.

The most obvious fact to emerge is that on this sort of budget one might as well forget anything above 35ft (10.7m) LOA. There was not a single good yacht larger than 35ft LOA priced under the $35,000 mark in the six issues I consulted. Also, she will inevitably be somewhat long in the tooth. This is actually no bad thing, as the earlier GRP yachts (and particularly those built before the oil price rises of 1974) are often more solidly built than their modern sisters. She will certainly have lost that new boat gloss and will probably have acquired a few scrapes and scratches along the way, but if you plan to take her cruising outside the world of fender-sox and marinas, trying to maintain a perfect cosmetic finish is only one more thing to fret about.

I am convinced that anyone looking for a reasonably priced GRP cruising boat during the current decade is fortunate in their timing. There are more yachts on the market than ever before, and although those moulded during the first ten years of production may have been on the heavy side (I call it the Norman Cathedral principle — if you're not certain about the long-term strength of your material add a bit extra) those from reputable builders still have many years of active life ahead of them. I would be willing to bet that a far smaller percentage of the yachts in production today will still be sailing by the year 2015, though of course some of today's older classics may be celebrating their first half century.

There's no denying that there are plenty of suitable boats around, and even though next year's crop will not be identical the overall picture will not change radically. They may not sound the most exciting or original of designs, but some of the reasons for limiting my choices — and recommending you do too — should have already become clear. A hard chine aluminum boat with tripod mast may suit you down to the ground, but she'd be a brute to sell. A varnished mahogany masterpiece might warm your heart and feed your soul, but it would also be feeding the teredo while you attempted to keep up with the brightwork. If owning your dream yacht is an end in itself then start saving for her, but if your boat is basically the means which enables you to fulfill the dream of going ocean cruising, stick to the proven, the realistic and the practical.

B. PROTECTING YOUR INVESTMENT

> It is ports that rot both ships and men. Get to
> sea as soon as possible.
>
> (Admiral Lord Nelson)

Leaving aside looks and the fact that it will probably catch up with you when you least appreciate it, *neglect costs money* in the form of large repair bills, replacement of damaged gear, and lower resale value. Fortunately boats (and in particular diesel engines) thrive on careful use provided any normal wear and tear is made good before it can deteriorate. These two sides of keeping a yacht in good order — passive conservation and active maintenance — go hand in hand, not least because neglect of the former leads directly to an increase in the latter.

One might reasonably expect the smaller boat with simpler fittings, owned by the man or woman whose pocket will be hardest hit by extra bills, to be better kept than her larger sister. Not always so, as ten minutes spent wandering around any marina will confirm. Owners permanently living aboard have least excuse for neglecting their boats but are sometimes amongst the worst offenders.

Neglect is generally the result of ignorance, laziness or both. First one needs to know where problems are most likely to occur, then one needs to know what to do about them, and finally one has to get up and actually do it.

Conservation of boat and gear

Conservation has a strong element of protection in it, whether one is thinking of boats or rain forests, and is sometimes termed 'preventative maintenance'. With an ocean-going GRP yacht vulnerable in varying degrees to rot, rust, galvanic or other corrosion, friction, ultraviolet, osmosis and possibly ice, as well as the occasional knocks and scratches inevitable in active use, passive protection alone will obviously not be sufficient and some 'making good' is inevitable, but the active side can be drastically reduced by nipping as many potential troublemakers as possible in the bud.

Rot

Not confined to wooden-hulled boats and nearly always caused by fresh water rather than salt, rot is most likely to start where end-grain is exposed. Deck leaks, seeping hose connections and condensation are all possible culprits, and I heard of one yacht with softening in the cabin sole where water had become trapped under carpeting. Rot is less likely to be a problem in a warm climate where ventilation is generally good and condensation does not normally occur, but if you have a refrigerator or icebox condensation will form around and behind it, so make sure this area is well ventilated.

Rust

Again, not confined to steel-hulled boats. The largest chunk of mild steel aboard most yachts will be the engine, so it's important to keep the protective paint film in good repair (touch up with a type able to withstand high temperatures). Other likely rust spots are bolt-on iron keels, and equipment such as cookers, gas cylinders and tools. Chisels and other infrequently used tools are best smeared lightly with vaseline and kept in self-seal bags. Salt deposits attract damp, making it imperative to rinse mild steel surfaces should they come into contact with salt water.

Corrosion

This can attack any metal, including stainless steel (I recently replaced a nut on one of *Wrestler's* rudder pintles which had cavities large enough to give a dentist nightmares) though it is most often seen on aluminum, particularly where the protective anodizing has been damaged. Failures in the electrical system are often due to corrosion at connectors and terminals (see Section 3C).

Galvanic corrosion or electrolysis occurs where dissimilar metals create a weak electric current (salt water is an excellent conductor). We learned this the hard way when *Wrestler's* boom snapped — on close inspection it turned out that the stainless steel kicking strap fitting had been riveted directly onto the aluminum spar with no insulation, and over seventeen years had eaten away most of its host. Other metals may not waste away so visibly, but can nevertheless lose much of their strength through galvanic corrosion. Brass will turn into spongy copper as the zinc is lost (one reason why bronze is so superior to brass) while an apparently sound zinc anode will shatter if tapped gently with a hammer. Check your exterior hull anode in this way from time to time — if nothing seems to be happening make certain the straps to engine and prop shaft are still in place; if it's melting in front of your eyes suspect a leak from the electrical system.

Friction

The most obvious manifestation of friction is as chafe of running rigging and sails, but most of this can be eliminated quite easily. Use headsails downwind (see Section 3C) to avoid wearing the mainsail out against the shrouds, adjust every block so the lead is fair and the line cannot touch the cheek (a swivel or a couple of extra shackles in the system may help), and ease or tighten sheets and halyards by an inch or two from time to time to move the wear around. It's also worth soaking jib sheets and other running gear overnight in fresh water at every opportunity. In warm areas repeated splashes of salt dry into lines and accumulate until they're almost rigid, not only making them difficult to handle but also shortening their working lives — salt crystals are surprisingly sharp. Mooring and shore lines can also be vulnerable to abrasion, particularly if you need to tie up to a stone quay higher than the boat's decks. A suggestion for simple chafing gear is outlined in Appendix 1.

Friction also occurs pretty well everywhere that there are moving parts — winches, blocks, seacocks, self-steering gears, gas cylinder taps, hinges, even the sprung hook on a lifeharness. To paraphrase the old army saying: 'If it moves, grease it; if it doesn't move, spray it with freeing oil and then grease it.' I have occasionally felt pleasantly smug when shackles (like the big galvanized one on the secondary anchor) or fastenings which may not have been disturbed for several years move easily, leaving a slight trace of grease between the threads. Not only is much less effort called for, but the metal will escape damage from forcing with tools or from dried grit scoring inside the works.

Ultraviolet

This is not such a serious problem in northern climates but it can be a killer in the tropics. It's particularly hard on some types of synthetic materials but will turn almost anything, including human skin, dry and brittle. Sails are most at risk and should always be protected by heavy acrylic covers when not in use; if you have to keep bagged sails on deck make up extra thick sacks for them before leaving home. Synthetic line is also vulnerable, though nylon does not appear to be affected as badly as polypropylene. From observation I strongly suspect ultraviolet of accelerating the ageing process of GRP, and its effect on varnish can almost make one cry. Some brands do claim to incorporate an ultraviolet filtering agent, but if taking a yacht with a lot of exterior brightwork to the tropics it might be worth overcoating the lot with white paint. This will protect and cool the underlying wood, and it can easily be removed on arrival home. Otherwise there's nothing for it but touching up the varnish as it begins to peel, plus *shade*. Awnings are discussed in Section 6D, and if tempted to take the subject lightly remember that your boat will benefit as much as you will.

Osmosis

There's not too much one can do about this while actually cruising, except to keep an eye on the hull. Warmer water is known to increase the chances of osmosis developing, but few people are going to cruise Greenland for this reason alone. If you find an older boat which has no trace of blisters I would strongly advise drying her out thoroughly and then applying several coats of solventless epoxy before you go. This will not be cheap, but will be far less expensive than dealing with the after-effects of osmosis, as described in Section 2A.

Ice

Ice is unlikely to be a problem when cruising unless you are a devotee of high latitudes, but it is certainly a possibility if laying up in the Northeast during winter. We all know from school science lessons that water expands when it freezes, lifting deck coverings and shattering engine blocks and water tanks. The best protection is to try to keep things dry — or go south!

Conservation is mostly a mixture of common sense and observation. Keep your eyes open, get to know your boat so well that you will notice the least change in the look or feel of anything and, like Batman, be ready to swing into action whenever necessary.

Ongoing maintenance

Maintenance starts where conservation either fails or is not enough. Too often it becomes a last ditch affair — a winch will not get stripped down and greased until it virtually seizes up, varnish will be neglected until a light sanding will not suffice and it's back to the bare wood, and fittings will be allowed to corrode until something gives.

Try to carry the instruction manual for every piece of equipment aboard, though this may be easier said than done if you buy an older yacht with older fittings, some of them long out of production or made by firms no longer trading. This is one time when a class association may be able to help — equipment installed from new will probably be identical to that aboard others of the same class and age. Spares kits usually come complete with fitting instructions, which are worth keeping even after the contents are used, but if you do have to take a totally unfamiliar piece of equipment apart make a note of the order in which you remove the bits *as you do so*. I once knew someone who stripped down an entire car on this principle, using hundreds of luggage labels in the process, and furthermore claimed to have reassembled it with not a single stray piece left over.

Many yachtsmen planning to ocean cruise will have learned their maintenance skills during years of coastal sailing, but if this field is new to you then invest in one of the many good books on the subject. *Shipshape: The Art of Sailboat Maintenance* by Ferenc Maté (W.W. Norton) is one of the more expensive. It is also comprehensive, entertaining and well illustrated, and you could well recoup its cost in one afternoon. Additional worthwhile titles are:

Boatowner's Mechanical and Electrical Manual by Nigel Calder, International Marine; *Fire Boat Finishes* by Paul and Marya Butler, International Marine; *Upgrading and Refurbishing the Older Fiberglass Sailboat* by W.D. Booth, Cornell Maritime Press; *Fiberglass Boat Repair Manual* by Allan Vaitses, International Marine and *This Old Boat* by Don Casey, International Marine.

3 EQUIPMENT: NECESSARY Vs. LUXURY

A. DECIDING ON PRIORITIES

> The first list we made had to be discarded. It
> was clear that the upper reaches of the Thames
> would not allow of the navigation of a boat
> sufficiently large to take the things we had set
> down as indispensable; so we tore the list up,
> and looked at one another.
>
> George said: 'You know we are on the wrong
> track altogether. We must not think of the
> things we could do with, but only of the things
> that we can't do without.'
>
> (Jerome K. Jerome, *Three Men in a Boat*)

Jerome's characters were setting off for a week in a rowing skiff rather than months aboard a cruising yacht, but the principle is the same, both from the cost and the stowage points of view. When the budget is limited it becomes more important than ever to get the priorities right, and to start off by setting money aside for the things one cannot safely do without. Avoid leaving this stage of the preparations until the last moment to allow time for any serious mistakes or omissions to be rectified even if this is at the expense of something further down the list. You may find a good mail-order chandlery catalogue useful at this stage (see Appendix 3), if slightly intimidating in its variety. To make the planning easier, head up the pages of a notebook with the following scale of priorities, and then devote some careful thought to exactly where on the scale each piece of equipment lies:

1. Essential for safety
2. Necessary to all but masochists
3. Necessary only to the short-handed crew
4. Not really necessary, but makes life more comfortable and/or less effort
5. Unnecessary if the crew know their job, and no substitute for good seamanship
6. Unnecessary by any stretch of the imagination

The first couple of categories are relatively easy to define, with options more of the order of 'Which type/make?' than 'Do we really need this?', but further down the list the decisions become more difficult, based on individual preference and available funds. As with the boat herself, each member of the crew should have some say, particularly when decisions affect the area of responsibility, or part of the yacht herself, in which they have a particular interest. If fields of responsibility have not yet been allocated or evolved on their own, now may be the time to give this some thought.

B. EMERGENCY OR SAFETY?

> *Protèges-moi, mon Seigneur, ma barque est si*
> *petite, votre mer est si grande.*
> (Old Breton fishermen's prayer)

There is a fine but distinct line between emergency equipment and safety equipment, and it is as well to understand the difference.

Emergency equipment (liferaft, distress beacon, fire extinguishers, first-aid kit, flares and the like) is by way of rearguard action, and as such one hopes will never be needed. In some 25,000 miles of ocean cruising we have never had to use any of *Wrestler's* emergency equipment in anger, though of course bilge pumps, Band Aids and the like see fairly regular non-emergency use, and it can go against the grain to spend hard-earned cash on something like a pair of rigging shears which seem almost an admission of defeat — cut away and jettison a mast worth hundreds? Nevertheless you cannot economize on this category without putting both your own and the lives of your crew at risk, since if you ever do need to break out the emergency gear it may well be the only thing left between you and your Maker.

Safety equipment (serious ground tackle, harnesses, radar reflector and fittings such as seacocks and gas shutoffs) is intended to prevent the emergencies ever happening. Certainly some items could be placed in either grouping, with lifejackets a case in point. Few adults routinely wear lifejackets aboard cruising yachts and I cannot imagine donning one unless events had become pretty hairy, but for a small child or non-swimming novice, wearing a lifejacket should be as automatic as fastening the seat belt in a car. Equally, there is a hazy line between safe and merely sensible — shoes with no grip could send you overboard, whereas leaking oilskins will not kill you. However living in damp clothes for days or even weeks is not going to improve health, morale or judgement, and could conceivably lead to a dangerous decision such as entering an unfamiliar harbour in darkness and a rising gale to hasten the end of an unpleasant passage.

Emergency and safety equipment — checklist and prices

Emergency equipment carried on Wrestler's *1987/8 Atlantic Cruise*

	Current list price	Remarks
Beaufort 4-person canister liferaft with Ocean pack	$2063.52	a
Locat LDT 25 radio distress beacon (EPIRB)	$194.80	b
Emergency VHF aerial	$30.32	c
Flares: 12 parachute, 4 red handheld,		
2 orange smoke, 2 dye markers	$402.51	d
Two horseshoe lifebelts with lights and drogues	$202.40	e
Man-overboard buoy attached to one of the above	$102.86	f
Two 3lb Firemaster fire extinguishers	$61.66	
Fire blanket	$21.54	
Comprehensive first-aid kit + prescription drugs	$81.60	g
Two Henderson bilge pumps	$112.90	
Heavy-duty wire cutters	$71.89	h
Assorted softwood plugs	$16.37	i
Cockpit knife in sheath by companionway	$5.60	k
Tire for use as drogue	—	m
Total	$3,367.97	

Safety equipment carried on Wrestler's *1987/8 Atlantic Cruise*

	Current list price	Remarks
Flares: 4 white handheld	$122.37	
Firdell Blipper radar reflector	$136.00	
Fog horn and spare canister	$17.33	
Two sets lifejackets and harnesses	$279.84	n
Three buckets on lanyards	$9.60	p
Total	$565.14	

Remarks

With the possible exception of the emergency VHF aerial I consider all this equipment necessary and would not cruise long distance without it — but that doesn't mean it must all be brand new. For example:

(a) came with *Wrestler*
(b) bought second-hand from competitor in OSTAR
(c) received as gift
(d) far more than standard, but some were nearing the end of their three-year lifespan and others were bought at a discount when already a year old —

the two years for which they were still valid more than covered the length of the cruise

(e) one came with *Wrestler*, the other was bought second-hand

(f) homemade for virtually nothing from a broken fishing rod, polystyrene foam and lead sheet

(g) our first-aid kit was actually assembled much more cheaply than this from scratch. List price does not include the prescription drugs — perhaps an extra $35

(h) an end-of-boatshow bargain from one of the larger chandlers

(j) not yet needed in anger, but very useful for blocking seacocks to take them apart for cleaning. With the right tools you could make your own

(k) swift action with a cockpit knife once saved the skipper of a yacht I was crewing from serious injury

(m) alas poor Mini! It could also double as emergency fendering

(n) will you be joined by others during your cruise? If so you should carry enough lifejackets for everybody

(p) all from ordinary hardware stores — chandlers' buckets cost much more!

NB: For those who wonder why I do not mention a sea anchor, the simple answer is that we have never carried one and I cannot therefore in all conscience recommend it as essential.

Equipment for abandoning ship

While I personally know at least three people who owe their lives to their liferafts, the 1979 Fastnet Race tragically demonstrated the dangers of abandoning the yacht too soon. If you already own, or buy a yacht equipped with a liferaft that is due for inspection, ask to watch it being inflated. (Do not, by the way, pull the ripcord in your living room and watch it mushroom — the canister or valise will probably be damaged beyond repair. At the testing station the sealing gasket is first removed and the liferaft then inflated by air pump.) If you need to buy a new liferaft, spend some time at a boat show examining one fully inflated. I suspect most people will be surprised by the apparent thinness of the fabric and further deterred from abandoning ship too soon.

It's difficult to become familiar with something you hope never to see, but at least display launching instructions where everyone aboard will see them (I favour the back of the head door). A valise packed raft will have to be stowed below, where it is protected from the elements but difficult to reach if the yacht is filling quickly or on fire, whereas a canister raft is normally kept either on deck or in the cockpit, the best option if space allows. A raft which lives in an exposed position on the cabin top must be very well secured in a fitted cradle, with webbing straps anchored via through bolts and penny washers to the yacht herself rather than to the cradle which could be carried away.

A conventional liferaft is an expensive piece of equipment — probably second only to the self-steering gear in terms of cost. For long distance cruising the full 'E' pack will be needed, bringing the price of an Avon four-man valise raft to $3450 for single floor and $3725 for double floor, with the canister model at $3650 single floor and $3925 double floor. The good thing is these have a 12-year guarantee; the bad news: they are seldom sold at much discount. Inspection at an approved center will add another $75 or so annually even if no repairs or replacements are necessary. One possible saving would be to rent a raft for your cruise — sometimes dealers will rent out an overstock raft, but their perfectly reasonable requirement that it should be covered by insurance may prove a stumbling block (see Section 5A). Do not be tempted to get a larger model than necessary, as an underweighted raft will be far more prone to capsize in high winds.

One obvious disadvantage of the 'dinghy as liferaft' option is that it contains no emergency equipment at all, whereas the 'E' pack as fitted by Avon provides: survival instructions; basic first-aid kit; 36 anti-seasickness pills; six pints of drinking water in cans plus tin opener, two lids and graduated drinking cup; inflation bellow repair kit; bailer; two sponges; torch; knife; sea anchor; rescue quoit with 100ft line; two paddles; two parachute flares; three hand flares; fishing kit and six plastic bags. Even so a panic bag should be put together, and this will obviously need to be that much more comprehensive if the liferaft itself is lacking the basics. Some of the items will have to be varied with your cruising area — warm clothing and foil survival blankets or even a couple of giant plastic sacks up north, sun block and a folding umbrella for shade further south — while food supplies and other perishables such as torch batteries should be inspected and replaced from time to time. Foods high in sugar take less water to digest than the protein-rich variety, making canned fruit, condensed milk, biscuits and boiled sweets particularly suitable. Even more important is drinking water, a good reason to always carry part of your supply in plastic cans (see Section 7A) with enough air left in each so it will float.

Other important 'grabables' not solely dedicated to liferaft use are navigation equipment including a small-scale chart (a spare plastic sextant and chart permanently in the panic bag would be the ideal), notebooks and pencils in self-seal bags, first-aid kit, oilskins, clothing, cushions, extra line, flares and Emergency Position Indication Radio Beacon (EPIRB). These last come in various shapes and forms, normally transmitting automatically on 121.5 and 243MHz when activated, and give an incredibly accurate position — witness the one tracked down to somebody's spare bedroom in Edinburgh a few years ago! An article in a recent issue of *Practical Sailor* describes the advantages (and higher prices) of the new 406 MHz EPIRBs. While you might expect to pay $200 for the older type, the new type will cost more like $1,500. What you get for the extra money is improved watertightness, shock resistance, and transmitter output, as well as greater accuracy and even a coding system that will identify your boat! It's a question of how important it is to you to be able to call for help. The final item I would attempt to take along if forced to abandon ship would be the inflatable dinghy, plus pump of course, but I sincerely hope never to have to put my choices to the test.

C. EQUIPMENT FOR SURVIVAL AND SUBSISTENCE: ECONOMY V. SAFETY

Ground tackle

> . . . about midnight the shipmen deemed that
> they drew near to some country; and sounded,
> and found it twenty fathoms: and when they
> had gone a little further, they sounded again,
> and found it sixteen fathoms. Then fearing lest
> we should have fallen upon rocks, they cast four
> anchors out of the stern, and wished for the day.
>
> *(The Acts of the Apostles 27.28–29)*

Fortunately modern anchors are more efficient than in St Paul's day, but equally home waters studded with marinas and mooring buoys seldom encourage their regular use and many inexperienced yachtsmen view an anchor as a challenge rather than a friend. However in many of the great cruising grounds of the world there is no alternative, and even where a marina exists it may well be beyond the price range of budget sailors. I would estimate that on both our long cruises *Wrestler* spent three quarters of the total time away lying to her anchor while we explored, swam, socialized or slept, bringing the relatively high initial cost of anchors and rodes into perspective.

A second-hand yacht will almost certainly have at least one anchor in her inventory, probably a CQR or Danforth type, and provided this is of suitable size it may well serve as the main anchor in most conditions. However unless she has been cruised seriously under previous ownership you will probably need to add a second anchor, which should be the largest you can handle. It won't be used often, but when it is you will bless every extra pound. The old rule of thumb of 1lb per 1ft LOA (1.5 kg to 1m) still provides a sound guideline for the main anchor of a smaller yacht, with the reserve somewhat heavier. If the boat comes equipped with a lightweight kedge or 'lunch-hook', either consider it as a dinghy anchor or trade it in for something useful.

Plenty of tests have been carried out on the efficiency of different anchor types and their derivatives, and it is particularly claimed that the nontrademark 'plow' versions of the Simpson-Lawrence CQR are not always manufactured to the same high standards as the original. While this may sometimes be true, over the last six years we have used the 25lb plow which came with *Wrestler* so many times that I now have complete confidence in it, though when looking for a second-hand reserve anchor we were still prejudiced in favour of a genuine CQR. Ideally the two anchors should be of different patterns to allow for different types of holding, but knowing that our reserve would have to be stowed aft and carried forward for use we deliberately avoided the finger-amputating tendencies of the Danforth type.

Some might consider *Wrestler* slightly under-anchored with a 25lb (11.3kg) plow on the foredeck as main anchor, a 35lb (16kg) CQR in a cockpit locker as reserve or second, and, for distant cruising only, another 25lb plow which was once the reserve on a smaller yacht. A 25lb CQR currently sells for around $325, with a 35lb version at $400, though others of the general plow type may be significantly cheaper. A 22lb Danforth, by contrast, should sell at discount for about $60. If I were considering high latitude sailing or planning to remain in the Caribbean during the hurricane season I would probably carry an even larger fourth anchor. As it is we have yet to use all three anchors at once, and after successfully riding out 70-knot winds in Bayona on two anchors set in a 'V', hope we never need to. However there's always the possibility of fouling or losing an anchor in a deep anchorage, and in many areas a replacement, if available at all, would be prohibitively expensive.

Anchor cable, bow rollers and windlasses

> We ought neither to fasten our ship to one small
> anchor or our life to a single hope.
>
> (Epictetus)

Anchor rodes are at least as important as the anchors themselves. Standard British practice is to have the main anchor on all chain, and we have found *Wrestler's* 180ft 5/16th (55m of 8mm) perfectly adequate. U.S. practice, especially on smaller yachts, is to use a chain leader next to the anchor with most of the rode being nylon or Dacron rope. This combination requires more scope, so when American and European yachts anchor next to each other, you get interesting differences in the way they swing! The larger reserve anchor should be on a combination of chain and rope, as 50ft (15m) of chain will add considerable weight (5/16th chain weighs approximately 1lb per foot, or 1.5kg per metre) and will hold the anchor at a proper working angle as well as keeping the rope from chafing on rocks or coral, while 150ft (45m) of 16mm 3-strand nylon allows it to be laid and recovered from the dingy, an operation which is next to impossible with all chain. Fig. 1 gives more data on measurements, weight, breaking strains and current prices. The difference in price for high-test chain (say $300 for 200 feet of 3/8 in) seems worth it if you think of it as a one-time insurance premium. It hardly needs saying that a larger, heavier yacht merits heavier chain and thicker nylon. Unfortunately many of the more popular anchorages even in distant parts are becoming crowded, and whereas space for an all-chain scope of three times the depth can generally be found, swinging room for the scope of seven times depth necessary for short chain plus rope is not always available.

No anchor can be expected to hold unless laid out correctly — fed slowly over the bow as the yacht reverses down the path where she is expected to lie, and then carefully tugged in and checked — and it is ironic that nearly all our major dramas while at anchor have been caused by other, usually larger yachts, either poorly anchored or on insufficient scope. On one occasion we had the cable of our reserve anchor snagged by another yacht which was motoring through the anchorage with her own second anchor trailing below the surface, one reason

Fig 1 Anchor Cables

Chain

| Diameter | | Working load | | Weight per | | Typical cost/foot | |
in	mm	Proof coil	High test	10ft/3m		Proof coil	High test
5/16	8	1900	3900	7.9lb	4.4kg	$1.70	$3.10
3/8	9.5	2650	5400	15.7lb	7.1kg	$2.40	$3.90

Rope (3-strand nylon)

| Diameter | | Circ* | Breaking strain | | Weight per | | Typical |
in	mm	in	lb	kg	10ft/3m		cost per foot
5/8	16	2	9500	4300	1lb	0.5kg	0.80
3/4	18	2.25	11700	5300	1.2lb	0.6kg	$1.10

*Rope is now measured in millimeters diameter in the UK, formerly in inches circumference. In the USA it is measured in inches diameter.

why I never attach both main anchors to one cable as is sometimes recommended. If the weather is bad enough to merit a second anchor I like it to be totally separate, including being attached to a different strong point on the foredeck.

Bow rollers on older yachts are often more solid than on their modern counterparts, possibly because the majority of boats built before the mushrooming of marinas in the early '70s were expected to spend their lives on moorings. A good bow roller should have high cheeks, slight flare and no sharp edges, but to avoid any possibility of chafe carry an offcut of plastic pipe large enough for

Photo 4 Lying to two anchors in St George's, Bermuda, in about 45 knots of wind. The nylon second anchor cable is protected by a length of plastic pipe, and both pipe and chain are lashed down into their bow rollers (Photo: Liz Hammick)

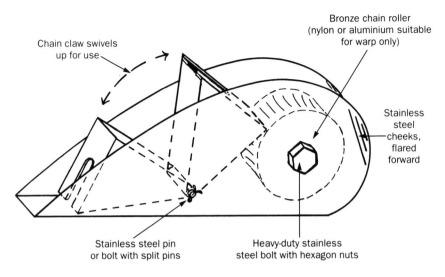

Fig 2a   Chain claw

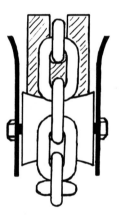

Fig 2b   Chain claw in use (looking aft)

your thickest rode, with one end drilled for a retaining lashing — see Fig 13 (page 160). Many bow rollers can be modified to take a chain claw — Fig 2 (a) and (b) — invaluable on those occasions when the anchor can only be raised a little at a time, and a potential lifesaver should it ever take control.

Provided the foredeck is properly reinforced, adding a manual windlass is quite simple if not always necessary. Most people can raise a 25lb anchor on 5/16th chain by hand without too much difficulty, particularly if the weight of the yacht herself is held on the engine, and many men can manage 35lb on 3/8th. However the help of a windlass is really appreciated when breaking out a stubborn anchor or lifting the length of chain necessary when anchoring in more than 50ft (15m) or so. When adding a windlass or buying chain if one is already fitted, be sure the two are compatible.

New anchors and chain are expensive, but they can often be acquired second hand — a little rust need not put one off, but check very carefully that the chain links are not wasted or the anchor itself distorted. If the chain is in a bag or sack be sure to inspect the whole length as it may well have been turned end for end, an option worth considering if not already done, and provided the metal is sound look into getting both anchor and chain regalvanized. It's amazing how much good second-hand chain seems to be available, reinforcing the idea that many yacht anchors are hardly ever used, but remember that your boat and perhaps your life may depend on it one day and if in any doubt about a particular length don't take the risk.

For an entertaining and thorough study of this very important subject invest in a copy of *Anchoring and Mooring Techniques Illustrated* by Alain Grée, published by Sheridan House. Another good book is *Anchoring* by Brian M. Fagan, from International Marine.

Self-steering and autopilots

> Behold also the ships, which though they be so
> great, and are driven of fierce winds, yet they are
> turned about with a very small helm,
> whithersoever the governor listeth.
>
> *(James 3:4–5)*

Geoff Pack in his excellent *Ocean Cruising Countdown* devotes an entire chapter to 'Ground Tackle and Self Steering' because, as he very succinctly puts it, 'One or the other should be looking after you all the time.' For a two or three person crew, spending your watches steering by hand is not only intensely boring but also encroaches on time which could be used for navigation, cooking, reading or otherwise enjoying yourself. I made my first Atlantic passage as crew aboard a 45ft yacht with no self-steering of any kind, and even with five of us aboard hanging onto the tiller soon became a chore. My second transatlantic was in a 40ft motorsailer with insensitive wheel steering. The electronic autopilot packed up half way across, leaving the three adults aboard to steer three hours on and six off for the next two thousand miles. It put me off hand-steering for life.

What about the possibility of getting the boat to steer herself by use of the sails alone? Many yachts will self-steer with the wind forward of the beam, but remember that twin running sails were developed largely because of the problem of balancing the boat downwind. Slocum managed it and so did other early singlehanders, but give a thought to the type of boat they were sailing — heavy, very long keeled and often a ketch or yawl. By present day standards their passage times were often slow and their courses sometimes erratic, and I have no doubt whatsoever that had self-steering gears been available before the early 1960s they would have been among the first to make use of them.

A word on the difference between self-steering gears and autopilots. The former are entirely mechanical, need no power supply, and steer a course relative to the wind angle. The latter are electronic and generally steer a compass course, though a small wind direction sensor can often be added. Each has its own strengths and weaknesses and ideally one would carry both, but as in all choices between the mechanical and the electronic on board, if you can afford only one it *must* be the former.

Mechanical self-steering gears

Self-steering gears (sometimes referred to as wind-vane steering gears) come in various shapes and forms, but nearly all use the speed of the boat through the water to generate the power to steer. Briefly, the yacht is settled on course and the horizontally or vertically pivoted wind-vane is then feathered in line with the wind and locked into position. When she wanders off course the vane either tilts or swings in order to maintain its angle to the wind, this movement being transmitted via gearing to a blade in the water which twists accordingly (often described as a 'servo-pendulum'). This twisting movement, combined with the boat's forward speed, forces the blade to one side, applying pressure either to a larger steering blade or to the yacht's own rudder to bring her back on course.

All wind-vane gears have the disadvantage that if the wind direction changes so will the boat's course, and for this reason cannot safely be left unattended with land or other vessels nearby. They are also sensitive to weather helm, and if the wind increases may allow the boat to luff. Some makes perform poorly in light winds, and of course all are useless when motoring in calm conditions, though the Hasler and possibly others can steer quite reliably under engine in a cross wind or when motor-sailing.

By far the most frequently seen self-steering gear on blue water cruising yachts is the Aries, long built by Marine Vane Gears* in Cowes. It belongs to the horizontally pivoted blade, servo-pendulum rudder type, steering the boat by means of control lines to the tiller or wheel, and is constructed of hard anodized aluminum. Unfortunately the company has recently ceased building new gears, though spares are likely to be available for some time to come. Their last model, the circumnavigator, weighed around 75lb (34.5kg), and cost ranges from $2750 to $3050 according to the extras is included, though it may still be possible to find one of the earlier models for sale priced at under $1600.

A good servo-pendulum vane gear from California is the Monitor. It costs about $2300, plus about $100 for a spare parts kit. Made of stainless steel, the Monitor weighs 50 lbs. *Practical Sailor* had this to say: "We think the Monitor should be at the top of anyone's list of well-designed, reliable servo-pendulum gears. It is ruggedly built, has been proven in all wind and weather conditions, and according to owners, the manufacturer is great on service if you have a problem."

A much lighter and cheaper option is the Navik, which retails at around $1100. lt works on the same principles as the Aries, and is suitable for smaller and lighter yachts which would have difficulty supporting the weight of an Aries or Monitor on the transom. The Monitor and Navik are both available from Scanmar Marine Products.*

So far as I am aware no manufacturer currently builds different models to suit a range of boats, as Hasler Vane Gears once did. Their SP was intended for boats up to about 30ft (9.2m), the MP (as fitted to *Wrestler*) could handle up to 50ft (15.2m), with the virtually custom-built BP taking over for the largest yachts.

The Hasler was the first wind-vane steering gear to be produced commercially some thirty years ago, and is of the servo-pendulum type but with the large plywood wind-vane pivoting vertically rather than horizontally. Another early model was the Gunning. Dame Naomi James used a Swedish-built Sailormat during her circumnavigation: aboard the 55ft *Express Crusader*, a very powerful and expensive system which uses a narrow servo-pendulum steering oar to drive its own much larger rudder, with the helm lashed amidships.

So much for the different makes of self-steering gear and how they operate. This is one piece of equipment the short-handed yacht really cannot do without, but unfortunately all makes share the major disadvantage of being extremely expensive if bought new. By far the cheapest way to acquire one is to buy it on the stern of the boat, another reason why a boat which has already cruised long-distance is often such a good bargain. They also come up with surprising frequency on the second-hand market, both in the small ads of national magazines and in used equipment stores, while I've seen at least one person leaving the Beaulieu Boat Jumble with an Aries on his shoulders. Being purely mechanical, older gears and even those which have seized completely due to lack of maintenance can generally be given a new lease of life with freeing oil and, if necessary, a few replacement parts.

The final option is to build your own self-steering gear, and if you have both engineering skills and the equipment to fabricate aluminum or stainless steel this may be the answer. The most successful home-built gears are generally those based on established designs — some are almost direct copies of production models — but be sure to allow yourself plenty of time to test, modify and improve your initial efforts. All the commercial gears went through several prototypes before achieving their final forms, and there's no reason to assume you'll get it right first time either.

Lastly, whatever wind-vane you fit and of whatever vintage, give yourself time to learn to use it before leaving. At first it's hard to believe how well a mechanical system can cope in bad conditions, but confidence will increase with use until you are able to relax as it steers you under full sail, storm canvas or even bare poles, conserving crew energy for the many tasks a machine cannot do.

Electronic autopilots

An autopilot is no substitute for a mechanical self-steering gear. Not only is it dependent on a continuing power supply, with an average daily current drain at 12 volts of between 7 and 9 ampere hours, but is susceptible to a whole range of mechanical and electrical failures which may well require factory repair. Add to this the fact that smaller models may not be able to cope in heavy weather — the very time it's needed most — and one can see why an autopilot should not be relied on as the primary means of automatic steering by a short-handed crew. The time an autopilot comes into its own on a blue water passage is exactly when it would at home — under engine. Even a few hours' progress each day through an ocean calm helps to preserve crew sanity, but my experience of ocean calms is that they are usually extremely hot and that the last thing one wants is an enforced dose of sunshine while hand-steering, particularly if water for washing and even drinking is in short supply. An electronic brain will keep a far more accurate course than any mere mortal in these conditions, though in hot sunshine even George will appreciate the shade of an upturned box.

One of the main attractions of the autopilot is its cost, which may be less than a quarter of that of a mechanical system. Best known on the British market are the various models of Autohelm manufactured by Nautech. The 1000, recommended for boats up to 34ft (10.4m), sells at about $475 and the 2000, for boats up to 45ft (13.7m), at about $575. The 3000, for wheel-steered yachts, should be around $690. All can take input from a small wind sensor, an additional $175 or so. The Navico* Tillerpilot 5500, intended for boats up to 33ft (10m), sells for about $500 with a wind-vane bringing the total to around $625. Many more second-hand boats will come with an autopilot than with a wind-vane self-steering gear and it's certainly a useful thing to have, but if I were equipping a boat for a two-handed cruise it would have to rank among the 'nice but non-essential' items.

Sails and downwind rig

> The sail bends gently to the breeze, as swell
> some generous impulse of the heart, and anon
> flutters and flaps with a kind of human
> suspense. I could watch the motions of a sail
> forever, they are so rich and full of meaning.
> (Henry David Thoreau, *Walden*)

Many of the classic books on ocean cruising imply that sails for the job must be purpose-built, and if planning a circumnavigation this is probably true. However ordinary cruising sails which have already seen several seasons' local use should be perfectly adequate for a year or two around the Atlantic circuit or in the Mediterranean. There is little doubt that the newer and more extensive your sail wardrobe the faster you are likely to go, but speed is a luxury and often an expensive one. The absolute minimum would be mainsail and three or four headsails (whether or not the genoa is fitted with roller furling), plus a trysail aboard larger yachts.

Mainsails
Most boats will have a mainsail already, but even if in apparently good condition it will repay some attention. Check it over carefully and get a quote for repairs, reinforcement and a third row of stitching and compare this with the cost of a new sail — it could be a case of new wine into old bottles. A mainsail which relies on a luff-rope groove will quickly drive you crazy if sailing short-handed, but can easily be adapted by the addition of nylon slugs — be careful to place the lower ones so that they do not need to be removed for reefing. If the boom is fitted with roller rather than slab reefing consider having both it and the sail adapted, as getting this type of reef to set decently at sea is often next to impossible and, more importantly, is really a two-person operation and all too

often delayed longer than it should be. (A very experienced yachtsman once told me 'The time to reef is when you first think about it', and though I don't think he realized quite how early that might be in my case the principle is sound.)

A new mainsail is an expensive item — at least $1200 for a 31-footer (9.5m) — and worth careful thought. One possibility is to dispense with battens, since area is not of great importance and they are often a source of trouble. Not only do the battens themselves become lost or broken, but the majority of tears start at a batten pocket. A battenless main looks slightly odd, with a straight or concave leech rather than the familiar convex roach, but has the advantage that you can hoist it or shake out reefs off the wind without the battens catching in the lower rigging, there are fewer hard spots to trigger off tears, and it carries a considerably lower price tag. It may even be built with the panels running vertically rather than horizontally to further minimize the chance of long splits. The latest innovations in cruising mainsails include fully battened sails and those which furl into the mast, but both are expensive and way outside the pocket of the budget sailor.

Trysails

At risk of flying in the face of accepted thought, experience has convinced me that unless the mast is fitted with a second track and the bagged trysail kept permanently in place, by the time conditions are such that it would be useful, getting the trysail attached and hoisted will be quite impossible. The smaller cruising yacht is probably better off with a really serious deep reef in the mainsail, or with the mainsail furled and a small headsail doing the work. If you do opt for a trysail keep it very small indeed — one-third of mainsail area should be about right — and work out a way to set and sheet it independently of the boom.

Headsails

The idea that one needs special matched headsails for downwind sailing is taking a long time to die, irrespective of the fact that their *raison d'etre*, keeping the yacht balanced without the need for hand steering, disappeared with the advent of wind-vane steering gears. Actually the traditional 'twins' set on identical poles had several major disadvantages: in an effort to avoid dipping the pole ends into the water with every roll the clews were cut high, so raising the center of effort and actually increasing the tendency to roll; they were generally too small in area for all but the strongest winds; they needed two complete sets of gear (halyards, poles, pole halyards, foreguys, sheets, etc); and in addition were expensive, took up valuable space aboard, and were useless for anything else. Using the mainsail for downwind sailing is equally unsatisfactory: ocean swells are often irregular, and an unexpected jibe could bring the mast down or worse (worse in this case being injury to the crew); few self-steering gears and no electronic autopilots are totally reliable when running under main and headsail; and chafe against the shrouds is a constant problem. Assuming you carry only one mainsail, for which there's no real substitute, it should be preserved for when it must take the boat to windward. (The optimistic idea that cruising boats seldom go to windward is unfortunately not entirely true.)

The budget-conscious will be reassured to know that any yacht equipped for offshore cruising is already carrying nearly all the equipment necessary to set up an efficient downwind rig, using a single pole and standard headsails, and this is particularly true of the older design with her characteristically long boom. When writing up our 1984/5 cruise for a log competition I described *Wrestler*'s downwind rig thus: 'The No.1 genoa was poled out using a block at the end of the main boom, and the No.2 set on a removable inner forestay which was tensioned via the anchor windlass. It was poled out using one of the spinnaker poles, though this would have been better if slightly longer.'

For more detail about how this is actually achieved, and with reference to Fig 3, the No.1 genoa as usual and sheeted in, and the weather sheet brought round to the lee side as a 'lazy' sheet. The mainsail is then furled (and should really be covered) and the lazy sheet led through a snatch block at its after end, through a second snatch block attached to the base of a stanchion, and into the cockpit. Next the boom, supported by the topping lift, is taken forward using a two-part preventer hooked to the upper shroud chainplates and tensioned via the main-sheet to lie an inch or so aft of the lower shrouds. A little careful juggling on the leeward winch transfers the workload from working sheet to lazy sheet and the No. 1 is in business. Removal is the exact reverse of setting.

The next stage is to set up the inner forestay. On *Wrestler* the head is at-tached to a plate rivetted about three feet below the masthead with the rope tail tensioned using the anchor windlass, keeping the stay about 18in (0.5m) aft of the forestay proper. My experience of conventional twin headstays is that they can never be set up tightly enough to prevent crossing in normal use, when the hanks will either unhitch themselves entirely or attach themselves firmly around both wires, which are usually too far apart at the base to allow unhank-ing much below eye level. When not in use *Wrestler*'s inner forestay is tied off to the base of the port capshroud, where at first it proceeded to attack the forward side of the aluminum crosstree. Before our second long cruise we had a stain-less steel sleeve made for the crosstree, which is now slowly avenging itself on the forestay. However, this type of inner forestay will *not* be strong enough to carry a heavy weather headsail when going to windward — see remarks on roller headsails below.

A spinnaker pole is then prepared with its own lift and guy (a downhaul is unnecessary), with the sheet from the No.2 led through its outer end, and posi-tioned at a suitable height against the windward lower shroud. Once the self-steering is balanced with the wind about 10° off dead astern the No.2 can be hoisted and sheeted in, and lastly the spinnaker boom guy slackened and the boom eased forward to avoid chafe against the shroud. Any tendency to lift can be controlled by temporarily running the boom guy down through a snatch-block attached to a convenient stanchion or shroud base. Again, dropping both sail and gear is the reverse of setting.

It should be possible to steer within an arc of about 60°, with the wind any-where from 20° on the windward quarter (ie the No. 1 side) to 40° on the lee-ward quarter, though with large swells running an arc of about 40° allows greater margin for safety. Jibing is something of a chore as everything needs to

Fig 3   Downwind rig

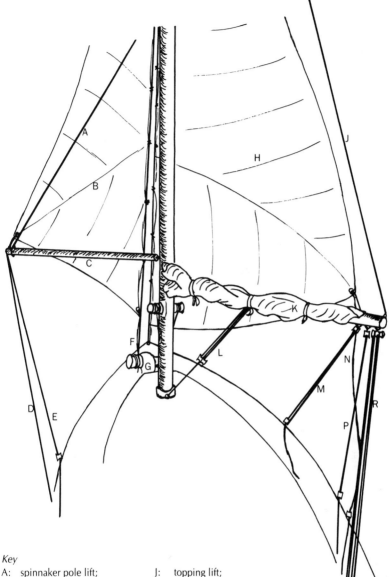

Key

A: spinnaker pole lift;
B: smaller headsail;
C: spinnaker pole;
D: pole guy (for control when hoisting or lowering sail);
E: working sheet led via pole end and deck block to sheet winch;
F: removeable inner forestay;
G: anchor windlass used for tensioning inner forestay;
H: larger headsail;

J: topping lift;
K: furled mainsail on boom;
L: kicking strap;
M: preventer or vang (attached to cap shroud chainplate);
N: lazy sheet led via usual traveller to cockpit;
P: working sheet led via boom and deck blocks to sheet winch;
R: mainsheet used to hold boom off lower shrouds

come in and be swopped over, but when Trade Wind sailing we have found we seldom needed to jibe. The far more frequent task of reducing sail area is comparatively quick and easy as both main and spinnaker booms can be left in place. The routine is to drop the No.2 and hoist the No.3 in its place, then drop the No.1 and rehoist the No.2 on the main forestay, adjusting topping lifts if necessary. In dire conditions the whole system works equally well with No.3 and storm jib (see Photo 5). For a temporary change of course or quick reduction in sail area, bringing the boat on the wind until the smaller sail backs and then releasing the sheet so it collapses against the large one has proved to work well on more than one occasion.

I make no claim to have invented the system of 'economy twins', but cannot sing the praises of this excellent hybrid too highly. Although it spreads a good area of canvas (see Photo 6) it is easily handled by a crew of two and needs no great strength to set up, while comprehensive lifts and guys keep both booms under control at all times. The mainsail is preserved from chafe and ultraviolet until you really need it, and strain on the self-steering gear is eased. Best of all it costs so little; the masthead plate is the major item at perhaps $30, spare snatch blocks should be a part of every cruising boat's armory, and if you don't have a windlass a good heave would substitute, as it doesn't matter if the inner forestay sags slightly. You will probably have to tinker for a while to get the system just right for your own boat, but it will repay the effort.

Roller furling headsails
There's no reason why the system described above should not work using a roller headsail, and I have heard of several yachts with twin luff-grooves using two headsails as running sails, rolling them up together. However, by their very nature roller headsails tend not only to do more work than any single conven-

Photo 5 Wrestler's downwind rig seen from on board, the heavy weather pair comprising No.3 and storm jibs, a total area of only 168 sq ft. Note the dry decks and open forehatch

Photo 6 Wrestler's downwind rig, seen from another yacht. With Nos 1 and 2 genoas in use it spreads an area of 540 sq ft (Photo: Tim Bridgen)

tional headsail but are also more difficult to check for wear, allowing damage to the cloth or stitching to go unnoticed until something parts. If you rely on a roller headsail be sure to lower it for inspection and repairs before each long passage.

Most yachts fitted with roller furling from new carry an inner forestay (often removable) on which a conventional hanked storm jib can be set, but if the roller furling was fitted retrospectively this may be missing. A small yacht often relies on her headsails in bad weather, so if you are installing the system yourself or are in any doubt about what's already there it may be worth getting a surveyor to check that the attachment points will be equal to the considerable strains they could be asked to bear. Additional backstays may be required unless the mast attachment point is near the crosstrees, and the deck should be supported by means of a bar or wire led down to a plate on the hull. Like the trysail a storm jib should be tiny — *Wrestler's* is 57 sq ft (5.3 sq m) — exactly one-sixth of the area of her largest headsail, itself not enormous.

Care of sails
Like all items on board, sails repay the attention given them both before and during the cruise, and tend to reward neglect with sudden and sometimes expensive dramas. The seams are nearly always the first place to go, so inspect them carefully stitch for stitch before each longer passage. Small repairs can be

hand-stitched, though larger ones are best done by machine; unless the material is very heavy an ordinary domestic machine with swing-stitch should be able to cope. (If you have no room to stow a machine remember that many larger yachts carry them and may be persuaded to lend.) It's amazing the distances one can cover by hand-stitching at sea if there's no alternative, but much better to minimize this chore by getting all working sails triple-stitched professionally before departure, with reinforcements at any points which show signs of wear. Most sailmakers can produce offcuts of various cloth weights for the bosun's bag in case you need to patch sails along the way, and may also sell basics such as triangular sail needles and waxed thread. Be sure to carry a sailmakers' palm to fit every adult on board — few women find a man-sized palm comfortable, and vice versa.

The biggest hazard of a tropical climate to modern sails is undoubtedly ultraviolet, making a good acrylic mainsail cover an absolute necessity. A custom-made cover will not be cheap (I was recently quoted $115 for a 13ft 6in boom), and as it is the material which is expensive a home-made cover is only slightly less costly. However it is a definite bargain basement possibility — I found one at the Beaulieu Boat Jumble which had apparently been made to the wrong measurements, but fits *Wrestler* perfectly and cost $40. There should be an iron rule that as soon as the mooring lines are secured or the anchor set the sail cover goes on.

If you have a roller headsail it's essential that the (usually coloured) protective strip along the luff and foot is equal to the job. A friend of mine recently discovered that the strip which she had assumed to be protective was actually part of the sail, and was in any case of too thin a nylon to give any real protection from ultraviolet; she has since had to buy a new headsail. If you're off to the tropics it may be worth stitching additional strips of acrylic along the luff and foot.

Chafe need not be a major problem unless you use the mainsail for downwind sailing, when protective strips where it wears on the after lower shrouds (reefed as well as fully hoisted) will be far more efficient than the traditional baggywrinkle. Larger headsails tend to chafe against the pulpit or lifelines and again a protective panel will pay dividends, but smaller sails can be lifted off the deck with strops. By far the best way to minimize chafe is to catch it before the damage is done, so get everyone aboard into the habit of glancing over the sails and running rigging regularly (after checking that they know what to look for) and be sure to make a thorough inspection yourself at least twice each day.

Replacing sails
Before ordering new sails it's worth investigating the second-hand market, particularly for conventional hanked-on headsails. Conversion to roller furling usually necessitates a new genoa, and many owners are keen to recoup some of the expense by selling their old headsails, often with years of life still in them. Bacon and Associates usually have an assortment of several hundred, and most of the second-hand chandleries have a few tucked away. It's also well worth contacting your boat's class association, if there is one, and keeping an eye on the classified columns of the sailing magazines.

Finding a suitable mainsail second-hand is more difficult, since there's no obvious reason for selling one in good condition. Not only must the luff and foot lengths be correct but so must the means of attachment to mast and boom, and it's also the one sail on board for which there's unlikely to be a substitute. When *Wrestler's* mainsail needed replacement we ordered a new one.

The next decision is of sailmaker. A company whose reputation is based on racing sails is likely to have prices to match, but though the very best long distance cruising probably come from the old-established companies who emphasize high quality and a great deal of hand finishing, these also tend to be expensive. For a yacht which will only be blue water cruising for a limited period a smaller local sailmaker may well be the best choice. You can go in and discuss exactly what you want, your order will be large enough to be valued, and should anything be wrong with the finished sail you can ask a member of the firm to come and see it *in situ*.

It pays to do your homework before placing an order. Even if you have a copy of the original designer's sail plan you should bear in mind that the builder or a previous owner may have fitted non-standard spars, and always measure the actual spars or forestay on which the sail will set. A sailmaker who is asked for a new mainsail will need to know details of the boom, such as the dimensions of the footrope groove and how far aft of the mast the tack is attached, and will probably want a slide from the luff of the old sail in order to match it correctly. He should then provide a copy of the dimensions and other details for confirmation before starting work on the sail, and it is worth getting the tape measure out again and checking these against the spars themselves to be doubly certain that no errors have crept it. Always allow plenty of time in case of late completion or some unforeseen problem, and don't be afraid to suggest the unusual.

The definitive book on the entire subject has long been *Sails* by Jeremy Howard-Williams, published by John de Graff. First written over twenty years ago and now in its sixth edition, it is still fully up-to-date and will answer all the questions one may have and hundreds one would never dream of. Alternatively *A Sailor's Guide to Sails* by Sven Donaldson, published by Putnam's is a more budget option.

Running rigging

There's a great deal to be said for all running rigging being of rope, and unless wire to rope spliced halyards are almost new it will be worth pre-empting trouble by replacing them before leaving — buy a long spool of line, splice or sew in the eyes yourself and costs can be kept to a minimum. The old problems of baggy luffs barely exist with modern pre-stretched polyester (Kevlar, at three times the price, has no place on the budget boat) and there are several major advantages: the wire to rope splice generally gives trouble sooner or later and is outside the skills of most amateurs to replace, provided the halyard is overlong it can be either trimmed or end-for-ended should one section become chafed or worn, and internal rope halyards are a great deal quieter than wire if the boat is rolling at anchor. At the same time the spinnaker halyard and topping lift should be beefed up to serve as emergency jib and main halyards in case the originals get damaged or — much more likely — lost during a sail change (a wrist loop attached to the jib halyard snap shackle may help avert disaster here). If replacing wire halyards with rope, check that the mast sheaves have not become worn and sharp. A few minutes with a file and some fine sandpaper may be required.

There is a further possible advantage of all-rope halyards, though it may sound a little drastic. In an emergency you have two more long lines available (four, if spinnaker/emergency jib halyard and topping lift/emergency main halyard are of the weights they should be) each at least twice the length of the boat. Trebling up shore lines, kedging off, towing — no yacht can have too many lines. Of course something will need to be left in place if one is ever going to get up the mast to re-reeve the others, but anyway, it's a thought.

I am always horrified by the number of skippers who cheerfully run downwind without a preventer rigged to hold the boom forward. Although a backed mainsail can produce all kinds of problems, a strong preventer will buy a couple of seconds' grace during which a quick change of course may avert a jibe entirely, or at the very least allow the crew to leap for cover. (It must be remembered that the mainsheet as well as the boom can inflict serious injury during an accidental jibe, as can the sheet car as it slams across.) Aboard *Wrestler* we use a simple two-part purchase run from the base of the capshroud to the boom end and back, where it is secured by a jamming cleat (see Photo 5). A preventer should never be run to the middle of the boom, or backwinding will almost certainly break the spar. Rigging a preventer is only one of the many uses of spare snatch blocks, a supply of which will be needed to set up a downwind rig and to improve the lead of any line which might otherwise chafe, including lines ashore where this will lift them clear of rough quaysides. Blocks come in so many different shapes and sizes that it is meaningless to quote prices, but while the majority can be ordinary single blocks, a few becket blocks and preferably one or two of the side opening variety should also be carried.

A final use of light running rigging seen on relatively few yachts is a system of lazyjacks (see Fig 4) though they are very cheap and simple to install. Various patterns exist, but for the one shown you will need a length of 1/4-in. line about 18 times the distance from gooseneck to crosstrees, four tiny nylon thimbles, four plastic bullseyes and a miniature cleat. They are assembled as in the drawing, with the standing parts tied around the crosstrees about six inches away from the mast, and the running part attached three-quarters of the way along the boom, run up through a nylon eye, back down through a bullseye, along under the boom, back up, down, under and finally secured to the cleat in a continuous loop — I can see why they say one picture is worth a thousand words! Not only are lazyjacks useful when hoisting or lowering sail, particularly short-handed, but they will also tame the sausage of sail produced by slab reefing without the need for acrobatics on deck. Make sure the loop is slack when the sail is hoisted and chafe will be kept to a minimum.

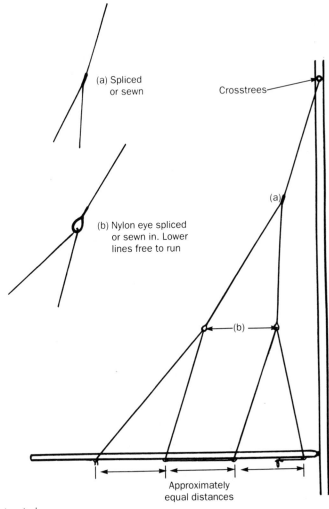

(a) Spliced
or sewn

Crosstrees

(b) Nylon eye spliced
or sewn in. Lower
lines free to run

(a)

—(b)—

Approximately
equal distances

Fig 4 Lazyjacks

Getting up the mast

I don't know why so many skippers new to ocean sailing think they will have to climb the mast at sea. Perhaps it's something to do with those tales of derring do aboard Whitbread racers around Cape Horn, because in fifteen years I have met very few cruising yachtsmen who have ever attempted, or needed, to get up a mast at sea. In any case the movement at the masthead of a small yacht at sea will render any kind of work next to impossible, and the more practical approach is to make sure it's never necessary. Synthetic halyards in good condition seldom break unless subject to chafe and should in any case be backed up by spares, and though tricolour masthead lightbulbs do blow occasionally, one must in any case carry navigation lights at deck level for use under power so the failure of a tricolour light is hardly an emergency. All in all I would forget about going up the mast at sea — far better to make a general inspection from time to time in a nice flat anchorage and before leaving for a long passage.

The other popular idea is that in coral waters one cons the vessel into every anchorage from a perch on the crosstrees. While this may give a good view for the person aloft, who is in the ideal position for reading water depths, aboard a two-handed yacht it leaves only one person on deck and no effective lookout while the other is descending. In this situation my preference is for the crew to hang over the bow, where they can continue their commentary on what is passing underneath until they see the anchor hit bottom.

There are three accepted ways to climb a mast; permanent steps, a bosun's chair, or one of the hoistable ladders currently advertised, though at around $325 for a 40ft (12.2m) length these are hardly a budget option. I have also heard of people using rock-climbing equipment with some success. If you buy a boat with mast steps already in place that's fine, but I have never considered the expense of fitting them justified — fixed steps retail for around $10 each, with the folding type nearer $12, making the total for a 40ft mast between $240 and $288. Incidentally, if your mast does have fixed steps, a lanyard from each one out to the shroud is absolutely essential if you don't want to spend your time disentangling halyards.

For harbour use a bosun's chair is perfectly adequate, and if the two-person crew have difficulty in hoisting each other up there are nearly always other yachtsmen around to help — indeed, I like to have two people on deck whenever I go up the mast, just in case. Alternatively most people can hoist themselves up unaided by using a four-part purchase, something the gaff fraternity have known for years. The very long line needed — 150ft (46m) for a 40ft (12.2m) mast — could also be pressed into use as an occasional mooring line or for other purposes. The bosun's chair itself need not be of the shaped canvas variety, though having recently acquired one of these after years with a wooden 'swing seat' I must admit that it's a great improvement, and probably worth the $40 to $50 price tag. Many people who dislike heights will also feel happier wearing a harness and clipping it to something nice and solid wherever they need to work.

Decks and cockpits

For the yacht sailed by a couple, one person going overboard in more than very light weather will almost certainly mean tragedy, and anything which helps to prevent this is money well spent.

The safe deck
One can safely assume that any yacht built since the mid-1960s will be fitted with a pulpit and lifelines, and very often a pushpit. The ORC Special Regula-

tions stipulate that lifelines should be of multi-strand steel wire, the upper one at least 2ft (0.6m) above the deck and supported at intervals of not more than 7ft (2.1m). The after ends should be secured by a lashing — if you ever do need to recover a person or any other large, heavy object, that cockpit knife mentioned in the previous section will justify itself within seconds. Pulpits should be designed so that there's no chance of going under the rail while handling the anchor (*Wrestler*'s has a removable wire about halfway up, which is excellent) and if buying a yacht with a potentially dangerous pulpit it would be worth having lugs welded on to take a safety wire or lashing — much simpler than replacing the entire pulpit. Neither lifelines nor pulpit will be much use if they come adrift as soon as any force is applied, so stanchion and pulpit bases will need to be bolted firmly through the deck onto plywood backing pads or large washers.

Most older GRP boats sport a solid toerail protected by a teak or occasionally plastic capping, though the more modern pierced aluminum rail does allow greater choice when positioning snatch blocks. My experience has been that aluminum rails are far more likely to allow hull/deck joint leaks than a solid capping rail, and are certainly less comfortable to sit on. Either way, 2in (50mm) is the absolute minimum. An efficient non-skid deck covering is also essential. Of the three most commonly found on fiberglass yachts — sanded paint, a small embossed diamond pattern either moulded into the deck itself or stuck on afterwards, and a synthetic rubber sheeting with raised diamond or circular studs — I have found the last to be by far the most effective in all conditions. Produced in the UK by James Walker & Co under the tradename 'Treadmaster M', it is available from Defender Industries.* It is somewhat expensive at around $40 for a 3ft by 4ft (0.9m by 1.2m) sheet, but if selective about where you put it a little goes quite a long way. 'Treadmaster SP' is similar but has a flatter surface intended for cockpits and seating — sit too long in a swimsuit on the diamond variety and you get up looking like a lattice pie crust. A significant advantage of both types is that they are kind to skin, deckshoes and oilskins. While the first of these is self-renewing the latter two unfortunately are not, and replacing two sets of good quality oilskin trousers will cost nearly as much as stripping a sanded surface and laying synthetic. This, by the way, is an easy DIY job which if done carefully should improve the appearance and add to the resale value of the boat, but don't fall into the trap of making a template for one side and assuming the other will be the same — very few yachts are truly symmetrical.

The secure cockpit

The cockpit is an area where older designs tend to win over the more modern, generally being deeper and therefore much better protected, though the deeper cockpit will of course hold more water should it ever fill, weighing down the stern and making it even more vulnerable to the next sea. Thus there must be at least two drains of minimum 1 1/2 in (38mm) interior diameter and preferably four, though in practice on the two occasions I have seen a cockpit filled the motion was so violent that most of the water was thrown straight out again.

A high bridgedeck is also a necessary safety feature, and if this is simply a continuation of the cockpit seating one has the added benefits of a comfortable companionway perch in bad weather and the likelihood of convenient stowage space below. If your chosen boat has an inadequate bridgedeck, 3/4 in (19mm) teak slats bolted into place will provide an adequate substitute. The entire companionway must be capable of secure closure, and I would strongly recommend replacing those picturesque center-opening doors with solid washboards. Hinged doors didn't keep the baddies out of Diamond Lil's saloon and they won't keep serious water out of your boat. Lastly, cockpit seats must have a means of securing shut (no bad thing to be padlockable either, in some areas) and be reasonably watertight. Strips of self-adhesive foam gasketing may do the trick here.

Being distinctly non-macho I would not sail long distances without a sprayhood, though there's much to be said for keeping this low and fairly small. I have seen a few really fancy models with zip-sided windows that could be rolled up for improved visibility and ventilation, but the cheap option is to keep the hinges greased and drop it entirely. I also like side dodgers, both for the protection they give at sea and the privacy they give in harbour, but there must be a wide gap at the bottom to allow any water that may inadvertently be scooped up to escape. Some people brail them to the upper guardrail in bad weather — others allow them to become rotten and self-destruct!

A final requirement is plenty of cushions, not only for comfort — and you do an awful lot of sitting down on an ocean passage — but also to enable shorter crew-members to steer without permanently strained necks. The plastic-coated variety look smart 'but are unpleasant against bare skin in a hot climate, cloth covered cushions get grubby, and both are relatively expensive. The answer is squares of unadorned foam rubber, at least 4in (100mm) thick and of a good dense grade that doesn't compress to nothing. We refer to the cockpit as the 'porch', using the American meaning of sunroom or terrace, and use it for much the same things — eating, drinking, partying, even working. In a warm climate the cockpit is an important part of your living area, and it should be as comfortable as you can make it.

Harnesses

> A man who is not afraid of the sea will soon
> be drowned.
>
> (J.M. Synge, *The Aran Islands*)

Safety harnesses must not only be strong enough to hold an adult falling or being thrown with considerable momentum, but should be chosen by and for each person with as much care as a new pair of shoes. If a harness is not comfortable and easy to don it's much more likely to still be in the locker when it's needed. The usual reason for not wearing a harness is sheer laziness. Early in our most recent cruise my sister was woken by me stamping around on deck putting the third reef in, and was justifiably furious to find I was not hooked on. Allowing the other person on board to wake up and find themselves alone, faced with the almost impossible task of searching for someone who may have been overboard for hours, is one of the cruellest things one could ever do, not to speak of possibly endangering their own life if they are unable to cope single-handed.

Harnesses should be made to a high standard. This also applies to the line, which should be about 6ft long and have a carabina or asymmetric hook at each end. Apart from the remote possibility of needing to unclip yourself quickly from a sinking or burning vessel, in bad weather it can be left with one end ready clipped on in the cockpit and the other trailing below, to attach to the harness at a moment's notice should there be a sudden call from on deck.

A harness which is not attached to anything is useless, and if your boat is not already fitted with jackstays to allow free movement along the deck they must be added. Although these are usually made of stainless steel wire I find this tends to roll underfoot, and prefer either three-strand nylon of generous diameter or better still webbing, which can be made up on board. There must also be a strong point in the cockpit reachable from inside the companionway, and preferably a second further aft for the helmsman. Again this is a simple DIY job, but bear in mind the possible loadings and through-bolt them to sizeable plywood or aluminum backing pads.

Practical Sailor has back issues that discuss and rate safety harnesses. For what goes into them harnesses are expensive, costing at least $65 including safety line for one suitable for offshore use. In theory it would be possible to make one's own, but this is not something I'd care to recommend and if looked after properly (in other words rinsed out occasionally and the spring clips greased) a good harness should last a lifetime.

Oilskins and footwear

Good quality oilskins and boots can seem an unnecessary expense when heading for warm climates, and indeed they may spend much of the cruise in a locker. However at the beginning and end of an Atlantic circuit you will certainly need them, and it's worth remembering that after a winter in the tropics even northern summer weather can seem extremely cold. We were surprised to find ourselves wearing thermal jackets and full oilskins at night on our return in July/August of 1985, but had them ready in 1988. Unfortunately good quality foulweather gear is pretty expensive, though it can sometimes be found at considerable discounts in end of season sales. Prices range from nearly $700 for a top of the range suit with integral harness from Henri-Lloyd down to just over $85 for a basic jacket and trousers from Achilles. Certainly cheaper oilskins do exist, but I wouldn't care to wear them beyond the Serpentine.

For oilskins to last it's essential to store them properly — salt-free, dry and reasonably clean — when not in regular use. As you near the tropics look out for a harbour where water is abundant, soak all the oilskins aboard in several

changes of fresh water scrubbing gently around the collar and cuffs with detergent if they look grubby, rinse well (try using the dinghy as a basin if they won't
fit in a bucket), dry thoroughly inside and out including pockets and collars,
lightly grease zips and press-studs, and store in a dry locker or hanging space.

It will do your sailing boots no harm to be rinsed inside and out in fresh water
at the same time, though they should not be dried in the sun. Unfortunately
my experience is that rubber boots generally perish during a season in the tropics and there is very little one can do about it, but they should hold together
long enough to see you home. I was told years ago that leather sailing shoes
benefit from being soaked overnight in fresh water from time to time, not
merely to rid them of salt but also to remove sweat and other nasties from the
stitching, and with the price of a typical pair now approaching $50 anything to
prolong their life makes good sense.

Pumps, plumbing and heads

Bilge pumps
It has been said that the most efficient bilge pump of all is a frightened man
with a bucket. This has the added advantage of being extremely cheap, and
both halves of the partnership have many other uses aboard. Even so, every
yacht that goes offshore should have two completely separate mechanical bilge
pumps fitted, one operable from below and one from the cockpit, with locker
lids shut. If she is already fitted with an automatic electric pump consider this
a bonus but do not rely on it — they are often small bore and so clog easily
(which may burn out the motor), while the float switch which activates this
type of pump is prone to failure and usually difficult to reach for replacement.

The most efficient bilge pump I have ever encountered was a massive American affair, operated by a lever which reached above my waist. Aboard *Wrestler*
we put our faith in a Henderson Mk V as the interior pump, with an older
Henderson Mk III in the cockpit. This situation is less than ideal as the spares
are not interchangeable, but both are powerful — the Mk V claims to handle up
to 20 gallons (91 litres) per minute, more than 3 cubic feet or nearly 0.1 cubic
metre — but this will be reduced drastically if the pump is difficult to reach
and operate. *Practical Sailor* tested the Henderson Mk V at 12 to 14 gallons per
minute. Their comment: "Price plus performance makes this a best bet." The
standard Henderson Mk V retails for around $75.

I break with convention in disliking strum or strainer boxes on hose inlets
when these are deep in the bilge and quite inaccessible, on the theory that a
modern, large-capacity diaphragm pump will cope with the matchsticks, soggy
paper labels and other detritus that would have clogged the older piston type of
pump and will gradually block a strainer. If there should be a blockage it's usually much easier to get at the pump than it would be to get at the strum box.

Plumbing
I mentioned 'piped fresh water to galley and heads' among my personal requirements for sanity, not least because of having spent six months living aboard a

small boat without this basic amenity. Very few yachts of ocean cruising size will not have such a system already installed, but pumps do wear out and need replacement from time to time. You may also want to install a saltwater pump in the galley — the saltwater version of the Whale V pump costs $40, to the freshwater version's $25. Some cooks like a foot pump in the galley, and they have an obvious advantage for rinsing hands in the heads when drawing a whole basinful would be far too extravagant. Foot pumps range between $25 and $50 including spout, the larger ones suitable for saltwater as well as fresh. Unless you have a fitted shower there is little point in a pressurized system — they eat electricity, fail at inconvenient times, increase the amount of water used, and wake the entire crew whenever someone wants to fill the kettle at 0300!

A few lengths of clear hose of assorted diameters can be a useful item to have tucked away, though in my experience hoses seldom split in use and leaks nearly always occur at the joints. Wherever a hose goes onto a seacock it must be secured by two stainless steel Jubilee clips (often called hose clamps ashore) which should be inspected regularly. Seacocks not in regular use — typically those on cockpit drains — need to be turned occasionally lest they freeze into position, and will need stripping down and greasing while the boat is ashore. In warmer waters a swimmer can hammer an appropriate soft-wood plug into the aperture from the outside so that the seacock can be removed for maintenance, but this won't work for the engine cooling water inlet which is normally covered by a protective filter.

Heads

> And yet anon repairs his drooping head, . . .
>
> (John Milton, *Lycidas*)

The head may be flushed well over 3000 times during the course of a one-year cruise, and repeated blockages, leaks or a basic inability to do its job will drive you up the wall. Admittedly you do have a back-up system — one of those buckets — but quite honestly this is a poor alternative, particularly for female members of the crew. Therefore it *must* be robust, and if the head already fitted is old and suspect, and particularly if spares are no longer available, you should think in terms of a replacement. If this seems extravagant, try dividing the initial cost by 3000.

The Baby Blake with its vitreous china bowl and Edwardian chromed handles has long been considered the Rolls Royce amongst marine toilets, and similarly appears to last pretty well for ever. Its main disadvantages are weight — 44lb (20kg) — and price — currently $700, plus $50 for the comprehensive spares kit. Thus unless you seriously expect to own your vessel for at least twenty years it may not be justified. The only other proprietary marine head to which I would give house-room is the Lavac Zenith, also available from Blake.* This is the latest in a succession of suction-operated Lavacs, weighs 33lb (15kg) and retails at around $225 plus $35 for the spares kit. As good seat and lid seals are vital to its operation a second set of these at $15 or so would be a wise investment. The Zenith has a china bowl, but beware some of the older models with plastic-covered aluminum bowls which were prone to corrosion.

Otherwise, Wilcox-Crittenden* has a range of Sealco heads from their Mate at $125 to their Skipper at $500.

I can see no conceivable reason for being tempted by an electric toilet, which is just increasing the number of ways in which the thing can go wrong. Neither would I touch any of the heads which are operated by a single straight-up-and-down handle — they are flimsy, clog easily and I have yet to meet one which didn't leak.

When we bought *Wrestler* she had an ancient contraption called, believe it or not, a 'Headmaster'. It might have worked had we been able to get a replacement gasket, but the makers were long gone and nothing else would fit, so that was that. We were left with a handsome pale blue china bowl which it seemed a pity to chuck, so I built a pumping system to go with it. The inlet is a small Whale Gusher Urchin (the Henderson Chimp is similar) costing about $40 including spares kit, and the outlet — you've guessed it! — a Henderson Mk V. We were fortunate that the base of the bowl fitted neatly onto a Lavac pedestal as otherwise I'm not sure how we would have fitted outlet hose to toilet bowl. The result may not be fancy, particularly as I deliberately left both pumps and seacocks exposed for maintenance, but it was cheap to assemble and is certainly efficient.

PS: Need I repeat the old saw about putting nothing (except toilet paper) down the head unless you've eaten it first? And for the ecology conscious, I'm told that white toilet roll biodegrades more quickly than coloured. A handy plastic bag should be hung in prominent view for all those cotton wool balls, Q-tips and hair combings that might otherwise find their way into the valves, to be evicted only by a red faced skipper using a bent screwdriver and blue language.

The electrical system

There are two attitudes towards the whole subject of electricity on board — to avoid dependence and minimize its use as far as possible, relying on the yacht's auxiliary for the small amount of charging necessary, or to consider it an essential and treat it accordingly, complete with back-up equipment and charging systems.

I belong firmly to the first school, partly because it's so much cheaper but mostly because of an experience on my first ocean passage as skipper, sailing a brand new yacht two-handed across the North Atlantic in 1981. Among her equipment she had two heavy duty batteries, also brand new, so we decided to run off one and reserve the other for engine starting. All was fine until the domestic battery got low and we wanted to charge. We then discovered that the reserve battery had followed the dodo into extinction (it transpired later that one of the cells had failed completely) and the engine had been installed so that the starting handle could only be swung about half a turn — though I doubt whether we could have started the 23hp engine by hand in any case. All this with some 2000 miles to go.

What we did have were a powerful wind-vane self-steering gear, a spare log of the towed variety, an RDF with an internal battery which was fully charged, and plenty of dry batteries to power depth sounder and torches, leaving as the only real casualties the running lights and VHF. I won't deny that we were relieved when the engine was finally persuaded to start a week or so later (at last the solar panels had seen enough sun to do their job), but we'd never had serious doubts about our ability to reach our intended destination in good order, electricity or no. Had we been relying on autopilot, satnav and electronic log things might have been very different.

Dead batteries are only one of the potential failures which can beset the electrical system. For the light that you switch on to burn: (1) the alternator must be working properly so the batteries will charge, (2) the blocking diodes, isolator or changeover switches must transmit the full current, (3) the batteries must hold their charge, (4) the wiring to the switchboard must be in good order, (5) there must be no short-circuits or overloading which might tip the contact breaker or blow the fuse, (6) the wiring to the appliance (possibly via a junction box) must be in good condition, (7) the switch must make a firm contact, and finally (8) the bulb must work! I have experienced trouble at some time or another with all but the first of these.

In spite of all these potential trouble spots the benefits of electricity are enormous. It's the only practical method of starting a heavy diesel engine, 12v VHF sets are almost universal these days, together with a vast choice of navigation and domestic electrical and electronic equipment, and so far as efficiency and convenience are concerned there is no real substitute for electric navigation and interior lights. Finally, what civilized cruising yacht would be without a stereo system?

Batteries, circuits and trouble-shooting

If your power requirements will not be great neither need your battery capacity. Two batteries are the minimum, but since one must be reserved solely for engine starting the addition of a third effectively doubles the domestic reserve. Capacity is measured in ampere-hours, and in addition to a heavy-duty 50 AH battery dedicated to starting the 20hp engine, I have found a pair of 75 AH deep-cycling batteries to give a perfectly adequate reserve for domestic use. There are several ways to tackle the problem of allowing the alternator to charge the entire bank while preventing the batteries discharging into each other. The most sophisticated is blocking diodes which act as one-way valves, but these are expensive, need good ventilation, and are beyond the amateur to repair. Simpler (and cheaper, being around $30 or around $55, depending on type and maximum loading) is a changeover switch with positions for off, 1, both or 2. Simplest of all is to fit an isolating switch (around $8) on each battery and turn them on and off as required, making sure at least one switch is on *at all times* when the engine is running to avoid possible damage to the alternator.

Switchboards and wiring on older boats are often fairly rudimentary, with extra circuits frequently added by the simple expedient of twisting another wire onto the relevant terminal. Take the trouble to explore the whole installation at your leisure and in daylight (it's amazing how many electrical failures happen after dark) using a test light to trace every single wire from appliance to switchboard, sketching where they run and noting any junction boxes or joins *en route*. This wiring diagram need not be fancy (Fig 5 shows my drawing of the wiring runs in *Wrestler's* heads, looking aft; the original uses colour to indicate the different wires, which is a great deal easier to read) but since wiring very seldom fails in the middle of a run it will give you an immediate lead as to where to look first. A full-scale multimeter with positive and negative terminals is very nice, but the cheap alternative, which I have used for years, is a pre-wired compass bulb with the sheathing stripped back slightly to expose the cable ends.

It has often been said that electricity and the marine environment don't mix, though it might be more accurate to say that copper terminals and salt water mix only too well, to form pretty green copper-sulphate — a very poor conductor though easily removed with warm water, an old tooth brush and fine emery paper. Any permanent joint should be soldered (try your local car shop for a 12v

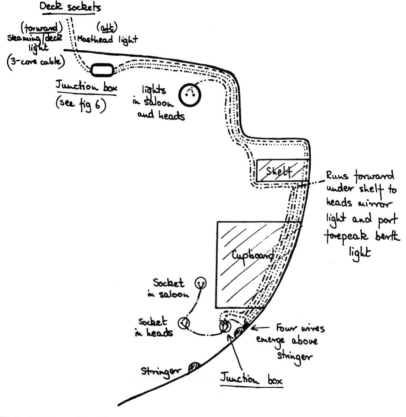

Fig 5   Specimen wiring diagram

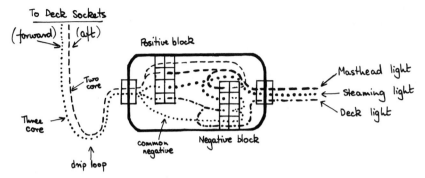

Fig 6   Specimen junction box wiring diagram

soldering iron, and learn to use it properly) and then wrapped in electrical or self-amalgamating tape. In addition the electrical tool box should contain a proper crimping tool, spare terminals, plastic ties to keep wiring in place, and a selection of spare fuses and switches or at least one circuit breaker. Mine also reveals assorted miniature screwdrivers, rubber grommets (to protect wiring as it runs through holes), cable connector strips and screw-in plastic terminal blocks. I would consider these the bare minimum to keep the power circulating.

If electrics are a new field to you a good basic book (Seven Seas/International Marine) is *The 12 Volt Bible for Boats*, by Minor Brotherton. More extensive are *Living on 12 Volts with Ample Power* and *Wiring 12 Volts for Ample Power*, (Rides Publishing Co.), and Nigel Calder's *Boat Owner's Mechanical and Electrical Manual* (International Marine).

High on the list for replacement should be any plug and socket joints on deck — vulnerable to solid salt water and the odd kick, they account for at least three out of four failures of masthead equipment. Much better to run an unbroken cable through a deck gland, with a generous smear of sealing compound and a small interior loop to shed possible drips, to an interior junction box with its own wiring diagram (see Fig 6). When the mast needs to come out it will take a bare thirty seconds to detach each wire and slacken the gland, and perhaps five minutes to reassemble afterwards. However plenty of sockets, running off different circuits, are invaluable dotted around the interior. Possible plug-in bits and pieces include autopilot, soldering iron, anchor light, spotlight, inspection light, reading/chart light, small fan and 12 volt power tools. Slightly more exotic but nevertheless able to run on 12 volts is the computer on which this book was written (though I still have my portable typewriter on board . . .).

Even with all these goodies available electricity must still be regarded as a convenience rather than a necessity, and though we have toyed with the idea of alternative generating systems we have so far managed perfectly well without. However this section would not be complete without a brief look at what is available.

Generating by wind, water and sun

Wind generators are usually the first choice of the cruising yachtsman and certainly produce more amps per dollar than solar panels — provided the wind is blowing. As always you get what you pay for, with low-powered wind generators such as the Aerogen 25 ($400) producing little more than a trickle charge. More expensive models, including the Aerogen 50 ($600) and Ampair 100 ($700) are entirely different animals, able to churn out 7 amps or more in 35 knots of apparent wind — quite enough to fry the batteries if they are not protected by a voltage regulator, costing another $40 or $75 respectively. The Ampair 100 is also available in a water-driven form, powered by a towed rotator, with the dual wind/water model retailing at around $850. Both the Aerogen and Ampair are available from Defender Industries.* Many small yachts are unable to mount a wind generator at sea, and most models come in alternative forms for permanent or temporary mounting.

Solar panels are the logical choice for the yacht which is permanently on the move, and are seen by the acre on short-handed racing yachts. Usually mounted on the cabin top they can be slippery when wet and will lose a good part of their generating ability if in the shadow of the mainsail, though most claim to work in diffused light as well as bright sunshine. Maximum output depends almost entirely on area, which itself depends on price. For example, the Sovonic flexible panel that produces 1.6 amps is 54in by 15 3/4 in and costs $300. The 2 + amp panel is 50in by 25 3/4in and costs $400. A voltage regulator is likely to be required to prevent over-charging in areas of strong sunlight.

If you have a permanent source of power-drain such as a refrigerator, either a wind generator or solar panels will be essential unless you enjoy listening to your engine for a couple of hours each day, which also gets expensive in diesel. However I did some math before our last Atlantic circuit, and worked out that we could buy about 100 gallons of diesel for the price of the cheapest auxiliary generating system. The resulting 350 hours running, used at the rate of one hour twice a week, would keep us going for 175 weeks or well over three years — even if most of our electricity wasn't produced as a by-product of progress through the water.

Tenders and outboards

> The moon was up, the lake was shining clear
> Among the hoary mountains; from the shore
> I pushed, and struck the oars and struck again
> In cadence, and my little boat moved on,
> (William Wordsworth, *The Prelude*)

If your budget is such that marinas, where they exist at all, are seldom visited your dinghy takes on even greater importance, and a quick calculation suggests that *Wrestler*'s tender was used nearly 2000 times during our recent fifteen-month cruise. Thus too much economizing is a mistake — the tender must be a workhorse equal to carrying at least three adults and their bags in safety (you may occasionally want to give lifts), be tough enough to withstand surge and abrasion when secured at a landing, be easily carried ashore by one person in areas where it cannot be left afloat, have the stability to serve as a base for diving or snorkeling expeditions and be readily stowable aboard.

A rigid dinghy large enough to carry three adults in safety is unlikely to fit on the deck of a 32-footer, and even if it does will be a liability in bad weather with its extra resistance and windage. Regretfully, rigid tenders and sailboards are the province of larger yachts which even then risk losing them in heavy seas, often along with the fittings or stanchions to which they are lashed. One compromise would be a folding dinghy such as those manufactured by Porta-Bote which have polypropylene bottom and side panels and fold to a 4in package which could be lashed flat on the cabin top. They come in lengths of 8, 10, and 12 ft, all costing about $830 through Sears Roebuck. The Porta-Bote can be used with a small outboard. A sailing rig is available for about $400. A crew of three or more looking for a second dinghy might well consider one of these.

As a first choice of tender for the smaller yacht nothing can approach the ubiquitous inflatable for sheer practicality, though no one can claim that they are cheap. However, a good quality 'rubber-dubber' should last many years if looked after carefully, and though it is sometimes claimed that their working life in the tropics is only a few seasons I suspect this may have more to do with the way they are often abused than any inbuilt life expectancy. Carrying rather than dragging ashore, not over-inflating in the morning when temperature and pressure will soar later in the day, removing the sand that accumulates between floor and buoyancy chambers or floor boards will all help prolong an inflatable's life.

At present one still sees more Avons in use by British yachtsmen than all other inflatables put together, and even the occasional black Avon dating back to the 1960s. Of the current range the 9ft. dinghy equipped to handle a small outboard of, say, 3hp would sell for about $1300; a similar 10-footer for about $1525. These boats carry a ten-year guarantee. Other options include the Zodiac — their 8ft AX2 can be bought for $640.

In view of their high cost new it is fortunate that inflatables can very often be bought second-hand, either privately or at boat flea markets, though they are a primary target for theft so do check ownership and the reason for sale. A tired inflatable can be smartened up by a coat of flexible paint, which will also help counter any porosity, but whatever the age of your dinghy you should carry a spares kit including patches and glue (which tends to solidify and may need replacing every couple of years).

Inflatables have gained an undeserved reputation for being difficult to row, largely due to a mental block on the part of the manufacturers who invariably supply them with miniature oars. Either buy new oars a foot or so longer than the originals and sell the old ones, or add some extra length to the handles using a simple butt joint reinforced with glassfibre tape. At the same time it's worth adding a protective strip of tape around the ends of the blades, and we also used up some rather old epoxy resin by giving the oars a couple of coats before varnishing, which has saved a lot of effort since. Another tip when rowing an inflatable is to ask your passenger not to sit on the stern, as the floor will turn concave and act as a most efficient drogue. Ask them instead to crouch or sit in the bottom of the dinghy, or if they absolutely must sit on the stern to keep as much weight as possible on their feet, in order to keep the floor convex. The improvement will be dramatic.

It goes without saying that children and non-swimmers should wear buoyancy aids while in the dinghy, but few people carry that other standby, a small anchor on 50ft (15m) or so of line. A 7lb (3.2kg) folding grapnel costs around $20, and will not only be invaluable on snorkeling or diving expeditions but could prevent you drifting out to sea should you lose an oar. A removable row-lock attached to the outboard bracket is also a sensible backup.

Outboards
Rowing through an anchorage is a very sociable activity, but there are undoubtedly times when it would be nice to go a little faster or a little further. At least eight different makes of small outboard are available, 2hp models starting at around $400, with 3hp models from about $500. The British Seagull has long had a reputation amongst cruising yachtsmen for endurance and simplicity, while most of the others are quieter and may take less effort to start. One intriguing possibility is the electric Minn Kota which is claimed to be almost silent. There are two models, the 35 with a maximum of 17lbs thrust at $110 and the 65 with 28lbs at $215. Endurance depends upon the battery. We have never owned an outboard.

Spares and tools checklist

The importance of carrying instruction books, tools and spares has already been stressed, and to demonstrate that I do attempt to preach only what I practise there follows a rundown of the spares and tools routinely carried aboard *Wrestler* in addition to the emergency and safety equipment listed in Section 3B. Although there are doubtless some items missing, it has fulfilled our cruising needs so far.

Handbooks for all equipment

Reference books for electrical and mechanical troubleshooting

Woodworking, mechanical and electrical tool kits

Small portable vise

Spare Hasler wind-vane and blade

Comprehensive Bukh engine spares and special tools

Assorted lengths of rigging wire, spare terminals and 'bulldog' clamps

Sail repair kit including needles, waxed thread, palm etc

Spares kits for all salt and fresh water pumps, plus extra gaskets

Spare bulbs for all exterior and interior lights

Lengths of electrical cable plus a wide range of terminals

Electrical and self-amalgamating tape

Various oils and greases, from WD40 to seacock grease

Avon dinghy repair kit

Various odd warps, in addition to mooring and anchor warps

Sundry lengths of plastic hose for warp protection

Odd lengths of shock cord with end fittings

Fiberglass mat, cloth and resin

Various pieces of plywood and hardwood

Hundreds of assorted stainless fastenings of all sizes

Assorted glues, fillers and sealing compounds

Paint, varnish and brushes plus cleaning materials

Sheet gasketing, hose clamps, etc

D. EQUIPMENT FOR SANITY: ECONOMY V. COMFORT

> Man must choose whether to be rich in things
> or in the freedom to use them.
>
> (Ivan Illich, *Deschooling Society*)

Deciding what extra, non-essential equipment to indulge in is even more difficult than working out your own personal 'sanity' criteria for the yacht herself. However you do have a major advantage — you can change your mind as you go along. In fact this is probably the only sure way to discover what you will need — and what you will miss — during your cruise, making time spent living aboard before departure even more desirable.

'Sanity' equipment falls naturally into two types — that which is purpose bought and can be built into the boat with reasonable ease but once fitted is virtually integral, and those items which jump into the bag every time one packs for a weekend afloat. Many of the latter are totally unrelated to cruising though they may be extremely important to their owners, and I have frequently met people who would no more contemplate leaving their guitar or paintbox at home than they would their oilskins. Ask yourself: is this important to me on land? If yes, fine, but if not then forget it.

A third aspect of preserving sanity has little to do with equipment but a great deal to do with time and trouble. It can be summed up very simply — if something repeatedly irritates you or anyone else aboard, deal with it. I cannot overstress that a cruising boat is a very small place where minor annoyances can mushroom out of all proportion. Anything, be it a locker catch which doesn't, a bunk which causes backache or a leak into someone's clothes locker — if you want to sail a happy ship *get it fixed!*

Possible subjects for inclusion in the sanity criteria are so many and varied that I can only chose a representative from each of the three classes — one which is important to me personally — and leave each person to work out their own priorities in the comfort stakes. If you have the desire, the time and the money to pursue the subject further, *Comfort in the Cruising Yacht* by Ian Nicolson (Sheridan House) and *Cruising in Comfort* by Jim Skoog (International Marine Publishing Co.) should provide plenty of ideas.

Interior lighting

When we bought *Wrestler* in December 1982 it irritated me that we seemed to be living in a world of shadows, a common problem among boats designed for use during the northern summer. Having sailed in the tropics previously I knew how early — and quickly — darkness falls there, and as the evening meal would usually be prepared after dark was particularly keen to have good lighting in the galley area. Additional 12 volt lights are relatively cheap and easily installed, and now there are no less than fourteen dotted around the interior, including one inside the hanging locker. Far from increasing our electrical drain I suspect it has decreased, on the principle that one light in the right place is more efficient and uses less power than two badly placed ones.

Most of these additional lights are of the standard circular or rectangular variety which burn ordinary 5 or 10 watt bulbs and retail from about $12 upwards, but one rather more expensive fitting which I would replace immediately if it were damaged is the Aqua Signal chart light (West Marine*). This has a swivel mount and a blue filter capable of dimming the 5 watt halogen bulb from a bright spot to a barely visible glow, and with the plug-in rather than the permanently installed mounting serves not only as an excellent chart light while at sea but also as my bunk reading light in harbour. The only drawback is that the light costs around $42 initially, with replacement halogen bulbs another $9. These are almost impossible to obtain abroad, but I have found that on average they last between twelve and eighteen months, even when in use almost every evening. Personally I dislike fluorescent strip-lights although they do draw less power, finding them too harsh to live with. They can also be a problem if your batteries are low, when incandescent bulbs will burn dimly, whereas fluorescent tubes will sometimes refuse to light up at all.

Every cruising yacht should carry an oil lamp if only for emergencies, though nothing can beat the lovely warm glow they give off, particularly if fitted with a polished brass reflector. In a cool climate they also produce a welcome amount of heat, but this becomes their major disadvantage in the tropics. Surprisingly, it can be difficult to find good quality paraffin (kerosene) in some places, so it's worth carrying a supply of several gallons which will last a single lamp for months. Although most chandleries stock oil lamps, for a good selection try West Marine Products* or Defender Industries.* A small brass lamp plus bell shade — absolutely essential if you don't want to blister the deckhead — costs around $50 with perhaps $10 for a couple of spare glass chimneys and will give a lifetime's pleasure.

Music

A typical 'removable' luxury unconnected to the sailing or working of the boat is a cassette player, whether of the portable or wired in variety, and many cruising people make do with the former, sometimes with an adaptor so that it can run off the ship's 12 volt supply. I removed the almost new cassette player from a car I was selling and installed it aboard *Wrestler* together with a pair of reasonably good quality speakers, and it has given us thousands of hours of listening over the last five years. Installing a cassette player is surprisingly simple (though it must be remembered that speakers have massive magnets inside, so must be kept well away from the compass!) and though the sound may not be quite what your stereo at home would produce it should be perfectly acceptable. It's also possible to fit a second pair of speakers in a protected corner of the cockpit for use at sea, though these will need either to be waterproof, and therefore expensive, or old enough to be written off if they get wet.

We were fortunate enough to be given a splashproof personal stereo which is marvelous for use at sea, but at first had a problem keeping it supplied with 1.5 volt batteries. This was solved by investing in four rechargeable nickel-cadmium batteries and a 12 volt charger, available from car accessory shops, with the additional advantage that they also fit the echo sounder and smaller torches.

Thoughts on musical instruments suitable for the cruising life will be found in Section 8E.

Stowage and coping with rolling

> Dinner ran a smooth course, but just as coffee
> was being brewed the hull, from pitching regu-
> larly, began to roll, . . . Every loose article in the
> boat became audibly restless. Cans clinked,
> cupboards rattled, lockers uttered hollow groans.
> Small things sidled out of dark hiding-places,
> and danced grotesque drunken figures on the
> floor, like goblins in a haunted glade.
>
> (Erskine Childers, *The Riddle of the Sands*)

Although little can be done to prevent a boat rolling, careful stowage is a classic case of a little extra care and attention avoiding all kinds of unnecessary aggravation. For once the smaller yacht with her crowded lockers should be at an advantage, but often only one thing has to be removed to set the others chattering. Offcuts of foam rubber are the answer here, or even an old wine-box bag (see Appendix 1). For storage boxes on open shelves bungee cord is the best restrainer, while talkative pans in the galley can be muted by interleaving with sheets of kitchen towel (which also helps preserve non-stick surfaces). One problem which may not be so easily solved is unbaffled fuel or water tanks placed directly under: bunks — listening to the contents slopping around is enough to put thoughts of seasickness into the most unimaginative mind.

Efficient stowage also implies being able to find things when they are wanted, a task made easier if the yacht is properly organized and kept reasonably tidy. Self-seal bags in various sizes (see Appendix 1) are indispensable for everything from shell collecting to food storage, and can do a lot towards keeping the contents of each locker under control. After a short time living aboard you will know where all regularly used articles are kept, but for the infrequently used items and particularly safety gear a stowage plan may be helpful. Whoever is responsible for edible stores should draw up a separate stowage diagram for victuals, marking food off as it is eaten, but even so the occasional rummage through the entire boat may bring unexpected rewards. After six months living aboard a Nicholson 31 friends found a bottle of French-bought wine which they knew had to date back to the previous owner! (It survived only a matter of hours after discovery.)

To return to the problem of rolling, its other by-product — things not staying put — is equally aggravating. In the galley this implies fiddles and pan-clamps (see Section 7A) but I cannot miss the chance to give a plug to that marvelous material, Dycem.* Available from chandlers either by the roll or in moulded mats (we have found the former most useful), Dycem is a plastic film which feels slightly tacky to the touch and clings with the tenacity of a baby chimp to its mother. It keeps crockery in place when cooking or eating, navigation instruments and charts on the chart table, and lasts almost for ever with the occasional rinse in fresh water. West Marine Products sells a rubber non-skid shelf liner ($9 for a 1ft by 12ft sheet) which they claim has similar properties, but I have not yet had the chance to test it at sea. Unfortunately Dycem is ineffective when wet and could be damaged by hot pans — revert to the old stand-by of a damp towel.

E. PAYING FOR IT ALL

Evaluating the inventory

> Ships are only hulls, high walls are nothing . . .
> (Sophocles, *Oedipus Rex*)

Had Sophocles been a yachtsman he would have known that the hull is only the tip of the iceberg, and that equipping a yacht from scratch is an extremely expensive business. By far the cheapest way to solve this problem is to let someone else do it for you, and if you can find a suitable second-hand boat complete with dinghy, liferaft and self-steering gear you have already saved yourself up to $3000. If she also has serious ground tackle and full emergency and safety equipment (another $2000 or so if bought new) you are probably looking at a boat which has done it before.

The difficult decisions come when faced with a choice between two yachts, one better equipped but also more expensive than the other. Get to work with your calculator to find out exactly how much the extra inventory is worth in terms of replacement cost, but at this stage include *only* those items which you would actually buy. Alongside the current list price try to estimate what you might reasonably expect to pay: how much time (and energy) do you have for shopping around? Do you have friends or other contacts who might be a source of second-hand gear? How handy are you at repairing and resuscitating older equipment? Allow a small credit against the value of non-essential items — you might at least be able to sell some of them — but largely disregard it.

A pattern should emerge from your deliberations making it obvious which boat, other factors notwithstanding, is the better buy. However don't fall into the trap of buying a second choice boat purely for her inventory, and if there are certain aspects of the design, interior or permanent fittings with which you are less than happy then continue your search. The inventory you can change, the boat you are stuck with.

Equipment sources: new

Unless you are lucky enough to find a boat with a very full inventory it will be worth investing considerable time and effort at the equipping stage. Although some manufacturers' addresses are included in Appendix 3, these are intended mainly as a source of product information, spares, instruction manuals and so on. Direct from the maker is seldom the cheapest way to buy anything in the marine world, and manufacturers' prices are often undercut by anything up to 20% by the large chandleries. However by dealing direct with the manufacturers you do have access to knowledgeable assistance with any problems that might crop up, plus the name of the best person to write to from the Canaries asking for a replacement spring, part number 001341(d), to be sent to Barbados.

As far as the large chandleries are concerned, it's noticeable that they have distinct strengths and weaknesses in different areas with regard to both variety and price, and if needing a fair amount of equipment it's worth writing off for mail-order catalogues from several companies — most are free, and then comparing prices and specifications on each individual item. This is a fascinating though time consuming job, and going through several catalogues item by item may well remind you of necessities which might otherwise be overlooked. Another approach is to decide which company appears to offer the best value across the board and then enquire about an overall discount — more likely to be forthcoming if you expect to spend well into four figures. A few things, such as paint and distress flares, cannot be sent by post and are most convenient bought across the counter, or it may turn out that a local chandler would be sufficiently keen on getting all your custom to order what he does not normally stock and pass on some of the trade discount.

Having tracked down the best prices on new equipment, before committing yourself to an order try to acquire as much as possible from your list from other sources at bargain rates. One excellent hunting ground is the last day of a major boat show, when many chandlers who've been exhibiting either have slightly shop-soiled display models or simply don't want the trouble of repacking all their stock and taking it home. Provided you have a list of exactly what you need, complete with dimensions and list prices, you will know if what you are looking at (a) will actually do the job and (b) is really such a bargain anyway. A surprising amount of brand new equipment also comes up at boat flea markets, covered in more detail in the next section.

Equipment sources: used and reconditioned

> Some day my boat will come in, and with my
> luck I'll be at the airport.
> (Quoted Nigel Rees, *Graffiti 2*)

Chance plays a big part in the search for second-hand equipment, mostly in being in the right place at the right time, but you can give it a helping hand with minimum effort. Put the word around about what you are doing, ask friends to pass on your name and telephone number if they hear of anything you might be interested in, keep a close eye on advertisements in the local press and national sailing magazines, and always try to have enough ready cash to put down an immediate deposit on anything you really want.

Bartering with other owners can be a good source of used equipment. Many older yachts will come with equipment which is in perfectly good condition but too small or flimsy for the cruising life — fenders are a typical case. Instead of ending up on the dump or cluttering up the garage these can be traded, answering the prayer of the owner in the next street trying to equip a 22-footer. Often the right place at the right time for this sort of trading is a boatyard at fitting-out time.

Marine flea markets are held in many areas, mostly in spring and autumn — keep an eye on the yachting and local press for dates and venues. At flea markets even more than usual it is essential to know what you want and what you *don't* want. Most vendors will only take cash, and wandering around knowing that your inner pocket contains $1500 or so in folding money can lead the strongest willed person into temptation.

When buying second-hand there is usually no come-back if your purchase proves defective, and whatever the source I automatically apply the same degree of cynicism I would when buying a used car. What is the history of each item and why is it for sale? Too light for a larger boat is an acceptable reason, as is the owner's recent return from a long cruise without another in prospect.

A final possibility when shopping for major items is to contact the manufacturers or main distributors, to ask if they have any used, reconditioned or 'last year's' models which may be available at considerably less than the catalogue price. These have the advantage over ordinary second-hand items in that they usually have the same guarantee as the equivalent new unit. Possibly the most extreme example I ever heard of this approach resulted in a nice pair of powerful winches, each with a deep scratch on the top. They had been installed aboard a brand new flush-decked racing yacht, which was being delivered across country when the truck driver miscalculated the height of a bridge!

4 THE CONFIDENCE FACTOR

A. OCEAN NAVIGATION: EQUIPMENT AS A SUBSTITUTE FOR EXPERIENCE

> But of his craft to rekene wel his tydes,
> His stremes and his daungers him bisydes.
> His herberwe and his mone, his lodemenage,**
> Ther was noon swich from Hulle to Cartage.
>> (Geoffrey Chaucer, Prologue to *The Canterbury Tales* —
>> The Shipman)
>
> (** His harbours, moon and pilotage)

Anticipated problems with navigation often figure large among the worries of skippers planning a first ocean passage, driving them to part with considerable sums on sophisticated navigation equipment, most often satnav. With a basic satnav retailing at around $1000 (though it's possible to pay $3000 or more) it's plainly worth considering whether this is a piece of equipment you really need. There are certain circumstances in which satnav is invaluable — when racing; when exploring high latitudes; in some parts of the Pacific where low-lying coral reefs abound; or when forced to cross areas of notoriously bad visibility such as the Newfoundland Banks. However if planning to stick to the Mediterranean or the lower latitudes of the Atlantic it is one more expensive extra which you can almost certainly do without. Remember that satnav v. sextant is not an either/or situation; being electronic a satnav is at the end of a chain of so many potential failures that it will always be necessary to carry the traditional backup of sextant, and to know how to use it. Ocean navigation is actually rather simpler than coastal, with far less detail and generally less need for extreme accuracy, but such is its reputation as a black art that few novices are willing to believe this.

The building blocks

The first requirement for blue water navigation is a good working knowledge of coastal pilotage — laying off courses with allowance for current and leeway, dead reckoning, visual and RDF bearings, and plotting on a large-scale chart. Much of the equipment used in ocean navigation will also be familiar, and logbook, pencils, dividers and parallel rule or patent plotter are likely to be on board already. A ruled up exercise book makes a perfectly acceptable logbook at one-tenth the price, square or triangular pencils are worth seeking out, more often available in souvenir than in stationery shops (mine came from the Ffestiniog Light Railway!), dividers should be the singlehanded variety and 7in or 8in long, while the choice between parallel rule or plotter is purely personal. None of these is very expensive — probably $30 to $40 in total.

Although one tends to think of an ocean cruising yacht as being perpetually at sea, actually getting there is only a part of the average cruise. Most yachtsmen spend much of their time within sight of the shore, exploring strange areas and identifying unfamiliar landmarks, often with little help from formal navigation aids such as buoyage or beacons and well outside the areas covered by Decca or its American cousin Loran C. This is the time when one relies on compass, log and depthsounder, the first two also essential for keeping an accurate dead reckoning while ocean passagemaking. Being so vital they deserve more than a cursory glance:

Compass Few GRP boats produce much deviation if the compass has been installed sensibly, but you should confirm this by checking against known transits or a good hand-bearing compass. (Personally I ignore deviation of less than 3°) The occasional yacht will be fitted with an electronic rather than magnetic compass, but being vulnerable to failure and a source of battery drain a magnetic backup will also need to be installed. A good bulkhead compass costs $100 or so, while a binnacle compass suitable for a wheel-steered yacht would be nearer $275. It will be much easier to read if the face is not scratched and crazed, so be meticulous about covering it when not in use. A good hand-bearing compass will be another $75 or so, but you may already have one for coastal navigation.

Depth sounder An essential tool in unfamiliar waters, so it must be reliable. For some reason it is the only electronic instrument commonly available with an option of internal batteries or connection to the 12v supply, and there's a great deal to be said for the former — provided you remember to turn it off. Some of the best-known brands are the Polaris ($170), Standard ($240), Signet ($300), and Datamarine ($370).

Distance log Whatever may be fitted through the hull, I would not cross an ocean without a mechanical towed log as backup. Best known makers are Thomas Walker Ltd of Birmingham, whose Knotmaster KDO, complete with tough wooden case and spare line, rotator and sinker, costs about $240. Modern rotators are made of black plastic, but the older metal ones could catch the light and attract fish or even sharks, a problem that a coat of matt navy paint will solve. Many more rotators are lost to chafe, and the line should be hauled in for inspection every couple of days while on passage, and if necessary the fittings moved. If oiled from time to time and rinsed in fresh water after use a Walker log will probably outlast the boat. Defender Industries* carries Walker logs.

RDF A fourth item many yachts will already have is an RDF set, very useful for landfalls even though not strictly essential. A powerful aerobeacon picked up from 250 miles offshore is most encouraging towards the end of a long passage, and even in areas where marine transmitters are few and far between every airport has its aerobeacon. The Lo-Kata 7 retails at about $325.

If you will be sailing in waters near enough to the coast of North America to be within coverage of Loran C, that electronic position-finder is worth considering. Goldberg's Marine carries a wide selection, from the Micrologic Commander that will pick up weak signals, important in fringe areas, at $2300; to the less powerful Raynav-520 at $325.

The planning stage

Perhaps obviously, the first thing to decide is where you want to go and when you plan to be there. Few people seem to have trouble with the 'where', and the 'when' is often dictated by climatic considerations such as trade winds, hurricanes and winter gales. Some careful research at this stage will pay dividends, perhaps suggesting options you may not have considered, giving a fair idea of likely progress (see Section 8A), and steering you away from possible pitfalls and disappointments.

The classic reference book has long been *Ocean Passages for the World* (NP 136), published by the British Admiralty Hydrographic Department and available from the Armchair Sailor. Naturally enough it is slanted towards the needs of merchant shipping, and Jimmy Cornell's *World Cruising Routes*, published by International Marine is the yachtsman's equivalent. However if you do not intend to venture outside the Mediterranean or Atlantic it is doubtful whether either are justified — both are quite fascinating and will fill you with visions of the South China Seas and beyond, but expensive if only twenty pages are relevant to your actual needs. For thousands of Atlantic sailors this gap is filled by *The Atlantic Crossing Guide*, second edition, compiled by Philip Allen on behalf of the RCC Pilotage Foundation and published by International Marine.

An excellent source of statistical information are the *U.S. Pilot Charts*. Each covers one area for one month, with the North Atlantic and Mediterranean on one sheet, the South Atlantic on another, both covering the Caribbean. Thus if you were planning an Atlantic circuit you would probably want the North Atlantic sheets (No. 16) for December, June and July (or a month or so earlier or later) costing $6 each. Data collected over many years of observations provides averages and extremes of wind strength and direction as well as information on ocean currents, wave and swell heights, visibility, temperature, barometric pressure and iceberg limits. A recent alternative aimed at those cruising the Atlantic circuit, providing much the same information in a more condensed form plus explanatory text, is the *International Marine Atlantic Pilot Atlas* compiled by James Clarke, not cheap at $75. It is likely to be several years before this starts to come up second-hand.

Charts, cruising guides and almanacs will already be familiar from coastal cruising, but both quantity and cost take on an entirely different aspect when considering a long-term cruise. Economies cannot be made beyond a certain point, but there is no reason to spend money unnecessarily. National Ocean Service charts currently cost $13.25 each, and when one considers that on our 1984/5 Atlantic circuit we carried no less than fifty-five charts (though admittedly not all were new and neither were all really necessary) the total bill of $728.75 at current prices would seem ripe for pruning. Nor do cruising guides and pilots come cheap at anything up to $40 each, with a typical Atlantic circuit ideally requiring five or six.

How can one cut down this potential bill of $1200 or more? The first step is to spend several hours at the nearest Chart Agent poring over the appropriate National Ocean Service (domestic) or Defense Mapping Agency (foreign) chart catalogs to decide which you really need. These will mostly be small scale passage charts and larger scale landfall, coastal or island charts. The very large scale harbor plans are generally unnecessary — any harbor which merits a chart to itself will, by definition, be used by shipping and therefore be well buoyed and lit — though there is no doubt they can be reassuring to a tired and doubtful skipper. The Imray-Iolaire series covering the Caribbean, available, for example, at Hub Nautical Supply at $17.35 each, are good value and include harbor plans on smaller scale charts, so killing two birds with one stone. Again, it is preferable to browse through possible cruising guides before making a choice. However, although most chandleries carry shelves of books they may not cover much further than the next river. The Armchair Sailor Bookstore has a very comprehensive catalogue of books, videos, charts and pilots (free on request, and well worth sending for anyway). This is an extensive list from which one can order direct.

When you've decided what you will need it's well worth trying to buy some or all second-hand — though not *too* second-hand. Considering the high proportion of yachts which cruise for a limited period and return home, often to be sold, the numbers of reasonably new, little used charts and pilots around must run into the thousands. Recent pilots and cruising guides sometimes find their way onto the lists of specialist second-hand bookshops (see Appendix 3), and one occasionally sees charts advertised in the classified columns of yachting magazines, otherwise a wanted advertisement in a national magazine or club journal, or simply on a club notice board, might produce results. A straight approach to someone who has just returned home is another possibility — I sold many of our original charts and pilots to a departing yacht in Falmouth Harbour within hours of our return to England in 1985, and later regretted it. On leaving again in 1987 we were fortunate enough to buy a complete set from a friend who had recently swallowed the anchor. *Never* rely on buying charts along the way. You may be lucky, but few chart agents hold large stocks of distant areas, and your success in finding a chart of, say, Antigua while in Barbados will depend almost entirely on how many yachts have passed through already. Your chances of finding a chart of Barbados while in Madeira or the Canaries are virtually nil.

Tracing paper (preferably in large sheets) is definitely part of the long distance cruiser's armoury, and I remember once spending about three hours tracing an entire chart of Bermuda, reefs and all (this was before I knew enough to label the reef areas !!!NO GO!!! in big letters and ignore the detail). The modern equivalent of tracing is photocopying, which is, on occasion, equally invaluable.

Older charts will need updating from either the appropriate edition of *Reed's Nautical Almanac* ($27.95) or the relevant volume/s of the U.S. Coast Guard *Light Lists* priced between $14.75 for Publication No. 110 covering the Caribbean, and $23 and $24 respectively for Volumes 1 and 2 covering the U.S. East Coast. The cost of these is negligible compared to that of new charts, and the work can be spread over the course of the cruise — provided you remain at least one chart ahead! Weekly *Notices to Mariners*, the only way to keep charts totally up-to-date, are available at the larger chart agents, and if your backup is willing to extract and forward the relevant pages you can keep really up to the minute. Recent second-hand cruising guides may in fact be identical to brand new ones on the chandlery shelves, for the simple reason that publishers expect each edition to have a life of four or five years before being updated. Cross-checking with corrected charts or relevant *Coast Pilots* will help, though a degree of inaccuracy is probably inevitable. It is essential to remember in this context that the further from Northwest Europe or the USA you go to less reliable the navigational aids are likely to be, and the longer notification of changes will take to filter through. The cardinal rule is, as always: if in doubt stand off, and wait until daylight to close an unfamiliar coast or island.

Sextants (and satnavs)

> The quality and workmanship in one of these
> machines** is something to behold. Just having
> one in the house will add joy to a rainy day and
> a couple of years to your life; using one is an
> experience in precision.
>
> (John P Budlong, *Sky and Sextant*)
>
> (**ie a traditional brass sextant)

I can't repeat too often that it is dangerous to think in either/or terms where electronic systems and traditional navigation are concerned, and even if you choose to buy a satnav, safety demands that you *must* carry a sextant as well. My advice is to buy a fairly cheap plastic sextant at least a year before you plan to leave (the Davis Mk 15 at about $100 would be suitable) and either sign on for evening classes or buy one of the many books on the subject, preferably both. This sextant will eventually become your reserve, but whether it becomes reserve to a better instrument or to a satnav is up to you. Either way, it is only common sense to know something about the subject before making your decision.

Regarding a sextant for regular use, I have heard good reports of the Davis Mk 25 (about $170) — the top of the range as far as plastic is concerned — but to my mind there is nothing to beat the traditional brass instrument. Unfortunately

Photo 7 The author taking a sextant sight whilst the boat self-steers under running sails (*Photo:* Liz Hammick)

these don't come cheap. The conveniently small and light Zeiss Yacht Sextant (which is actually aluminum) retails for $375, with the full-sized Zeiss Drum Sextant at around $450 in its most basic form. A truly lovely instrument, such as a Tamaya or a Cassens & Plath, would set you back about $850 or $1000 respectively. The good news is that high quality sextants are often available second-hand, one of the best sources being Thomas Foulkes* who generally keep a stock of several dozen and will sell abroad by mail. I well remember buying mine there in 1980 — it cost me $230 complete with Inspection Certificate, lighting, two telescopes and sturdy case, and is amongst my most treasured possessions.

One major problem which bedevilled navigators from the time of Columbus — that of keeping really accurate time — has been solved with the advent of quartz clocks. Not only are most very accurate, but they are also cheap (carry several), whereas the traditional chronometer cost a small fortune. Go for a digital rather than analogue face for ease of reading, and keep a record of losses or gains over the month before you leave to find out if the occasional correction will be necessary. Not having a radio capable of receiving 'time ticks', I swallow my pride before an ocean passage and seek out a yacht with satnav or a short-wave radio in order to check the clocks. You can get a time tick from a recording by phoning the U.S. Naval Observatory at 202-653-1800. During the three or four weeks most yachts spend at sea a quartz clock should not gain or lose more than a couple of seconds, quite accurate enough for navigation.

Having taken and timed your sight you will need a nautical almanac and sight reduction tables. Regarding almanacs, *Reed's* has already been mentioned as a source of chart corrections, and in addition carries tide tables. However the primary use of an almanac when ocean sailing is in working out sights, the exact position of the sun (or other body) from moment to moment being given in tabular form. Although *Reed's* does carry all the necessary information, I personally consider the additional expense of *The Nautical Almanac* ($20) to be justified. Having only the one subject to cover it can do so in greater detail, leaving the navigator significantly less interpolation to cope with. Almanacs are annual publications, and if you'll be away over New Year you will need to arrange for the new one to be sent out.

Hand in hand with a nautical almanac go sight reduction tables. I would strongly recommend Publication No. 249. This comes in three volumes, of which the first covers stars (great fun if you get hooked, but quite unnecessary to yacht navigation!) so only Volumes 2 and 3 covering latitudes (your latitude that is) of 0–39° and 40–89° need be bought — and stowed — at a combined cost of $20. Fortunately nearly all the instructional books and most evening class tutors use Pub. No. 249. Sight reduction tables do not date (other than Vol. 1, the *Selected Stars*, which has a life of about 15 years) and may therefore be another candidate for purchase second-hand.

The electronically minded may be tempted by a navigation calculator which takes the place of sight reduction tables and of an almanac as well. Examples are the Sharp Celestcomp at $280, or the Tamaya NC-77 at $370. However nothing electronic is ever infallible, making the right books an essential part of the ocean cruising inventory.

With the sight taken and reduced it must be plotted, for which I prefer the *Universal Plotting Sheet*, published in the USA by the Defense Mapping Agency. These measure approximately 12 1/2in × 14in (320mm × 350mm) — large enough for about two days' work on a scale suitable for keeping up the dead reckoning between sights — are good for any latitude, and are printed on both sides. A whole pad costs only $3.50. One very experienced navigator I know described a truly budget solution: choose any chart of a suitable scale and the right latitude, replace the given longitude with your own, and you're in business. He claimed to have plotted his way across most of the Sahara, including the Atlas Mountains, in this way.

There are plenty of excellent books on celestial navigation, two of the best also being unusually cheap. These are the classic *Celestial Navigation for Yachtsmen* by Mary Blewitt (published by John de Graff and now in its 9th edition), which has probably taught more people to navigate than most of the other books on the subject put together, and *Celestial Navigation* by Tom Cunliffe (International Marine). The latter seems to me to have a slightly more straightforward and less theoretical approach. A third very useful book is *The Sextant Handbook* by Bruce Bauer (International Marine) which explains the choice, use and adjustment of the instrument itself, so removing some of the mystique which often surrounds the subject. My own particular favourite amongst the many books on celestial navigation is *Sky and Sextant* by John P. Budlong — well worth buying if you can find a copy. A more advanced book that explains several methods of marking sights very clearly is Warren Norville's *Celestial Navigation Step by Step* (International Marine).

I cannot pretend to be an expert on satnavs, never having never sailed with one in working order. Defender Industries* has a good selection from the Furuno Vigil RM at a bit over $1,000 to Ratheon's RaySat 200 at over $2500. Or, if you want to really blow the budget, go out and buy a Global Positioning System electronics package, like a Magellan GPS Nav 1000 for $3000 or maybe a Magnavox MX-4400 for $16,500. If you are really set on spending this sort of money invest some time in talking to a specialist electronics company, but remember that they're in business to sell electronics, so will naturally do their best to persuade you satnav or GPS is essential.

Landfalls

No ocean voyage is complete until you are safely anchored or moored at your destination. During the days and weeks on passage it matters little whether you are exactly where you think you are or five miles further south, but during the last stages it becomes rather critical, and on sighting land there is a natural tendency to celebrate and relax vigilance. This is often coupled with what 1 call the '24-hour syndrome' (a general reluctance to go off watch and risk missing the excitement, while very often underestimating the time it will take to close the coast) with the net result that many crews are more exhausted and therefore error-prone during the last few miles than at any other stage of the entire passage. Remember that *at no time* during an ocean crossing is a seaworthy yacht so vulnerable to human error as when the sharp bits are close by, so don't relax the watch system or be tempted to break out the bubbly until you are safely tied up.

I know of three yachts lost on Atlantic passages in a one-year period, all while making landfalls. Two were wrecked on the windward coast of Barbados, in both cases the crews having sighted the island before dusk only to run onto outlying reefs in the dark. The third yacht went aground on the western tip of Faial in the Azores, her crew (a couple) having seen and identified the island at night and decided to heave-to until daylight. (Why they then turned in rather than standing watches in the proximity of land I was unable to find out.) Through sheer good fortune, in none of these three cases was anybody lost or even seriously injured though all three yachts were matchwood. The first two yachts had satnav, and though in both cases it had packed up days before they went ashore it would probably not have saved them. What 1 suspect it *had* done was accustom the skippers to taking for granted a degree of accuracy which would be the exception rather than the rule with traditional methods, whether sextant sights or dead reckoning. Thus instead of working on the 'My fix says we're there, but allow a five mile circle of error to be on the safe side' basis, they were used to thinking 'The satnav says we're there, so we're there.'

The fact is that yachts have come to grief using both traditional navigation methods and modern ones. Satnav is a lovely shortcut, but until it has a better track-record for reliability the safety-conscious skipper will not rely on it as his sole means of navigation. Whichever method you choose for daily use, be aware of its limitations, always err on the side of caution, and don't give up on the sextant until you've tried.

B. WATCHKEEPING: EQUIPMENT AS AN AID (BUT NEVER A SUBSTITUTE) FOR EYES

> A capital ship for an ocean trip
> Was the Walloping Window Blind —
> No gale that blew dismayed her crew
> Or troubled the captain's mind.
> The man at the wheel was taught to feel
> Contempt for the wildest blow.
> And it often appeared, when the weather had
>   cleared,
> That he'd been in his bunk below.
>
> (Charles Edward Carryl, *A Nautical Ballad*)

The lesson here is do not rely on Big Brother watching you — a good reason for keeping a permanent lookout, day and night, whatever the weather and wherever you may be. This is obviously impossible for singlehanders, but I've been surprised by the number of two-handed crews who do not bother to keep night watches, and suspect that being run down by ships may account for a large proportion of the (admittedly small) number of yachts which disappear without trace each year. It is a fact that more than one ship has arrived at her destination with a yacht's mast and rigging hanging from her anchors, with the crew quite unaware there had been a collision.

When one thinks of the millions of square miles to choose from the chances of you and a ship wanting to occupy the same piece of ocean at exactly the same moment should in theory be vanishingly small, but nearly every experienced ocean sailor could tell of at least one close encounter. I shall never forget the occasion, on my second Atlantic crossing, when we met a Greek freighter approximately half way between Florida and Bermuda. It was one of those hot sunny days with visibility at least thirty miles, but after watching her for some time it gradually became obvious that if we didn't take evasive action we were indeed going to be competing for the same patch of sea. She passed fifty yards away, radar turning, but with no signs of life aboard. Possibly the crew had died from some mysterious plague, perhaps it was the siesta hour, or maybe they were deep in back issues of *Mayfair* — whatever the cause, we saw no one and had no reason to believe they were aware of our presence. (The year was 1978, before VHF was universal aboard yachts, or we might have tried calling her up.) Every time I'm tempted to get lazy about watchkeeping I remember that Greek ship churning straight towards us in broad daylight and perfect weather.

Apart from the collision aspect, keeping a permanent watch also tends to preempt dramas on deck, since deteriorating weather or an approaching squall can be anticipated and appropriate action taken before it arrives. Even if a gear failure should occur without warning there will at least be someone awake and fully dressed to deal with the consequences before they can escalate. Changes in wind direction which affect the self-steering can also be compensated for immediately, rather than after the yacht has been running off course for an unknown period, playing havoc with both progress and the dead reckoning. Finally, considerable savings in electricity can be made by 'running blind' and only turning the navigation lights on when there's someone around to see them. This in turn means a saving in fuel for charging, more than just a financial benefit aboard the small yacht with limited tankage. If you don't keep a watch you *must* burn lights during darkness, but even then there's no guarantee they'll be seen.

Watch systems and sharing the workload

Since the budget boat is unlikely to carry a crew of more than two or three, and will probably be without electronic watchkeeping aids such as radar or a radar detector, working out a system which the crew can live with is of particular importance. Unlike the larger crew, who can usually afford to treat being on watch as a job in itself, the short-handed crew can afford to spend very little time scanning the horizon like something out of a Hollywood B movie, but must use watch periods for all the routine chores necessary to keep the show on the road. The two essentials for short-handed watchkeeping are reliable self-steering (see Section 3C) and enough self-discipline to break off whatever one is doing at sensible intervals to take a careful look round for shipping and to check the sky, the sails and the compass. (In this context a sensible interval might be as much as fifteen minutes in good visibility, or as little as two or three in bad conditions, and should be agreed between skipper and crew at change of watch.)

As watchkeeping dictates the basic structure of the day it must fit in with the general division of labour chosen, and we have found a system of four-hour watches, broken by two-hour periods over lunch and supper when we are both up, works well and alternates the routine from one day to the next — see Fig 7(a). The morning watchkeeper does the day's navigation and puts together a snack lunch, while the other person, on watch during the afternoon, prepares the cooked evening meal. This system would be perfectly feasible with shorter night watches — see Fig 7(b) — if the afternoon watch were broken to compensate, but would be impractical for a crew who did not alternate the routine jobs. For those who prefer to stick to set roles Figs 7(c) and (d) suggest possible watch systems which take into account both navigation and food preparation. Those who like a cooked breakfast could juggle the overlaps to suit.

With three or more aboard the possibilities are more varied, and many yachts only keep formal watches during the hours of darkness. Few things disrupt sleep more efficiently than other people's conversation, and it may well be worth designating an official night during which everyone is expected to be as quiet as possible, divide it equally, and then leave naps during the day to take their chance. Again the system can either be static — see Fig 7(e) — or rotate over a three-day period by alternating who takes the first watch. Watchkeeping with four is even more relaxed, and we have found a ten-hour night giving each person a single 2 1/2 hour watch with 7 1/2 hours in their bunk to be positively luxurious.

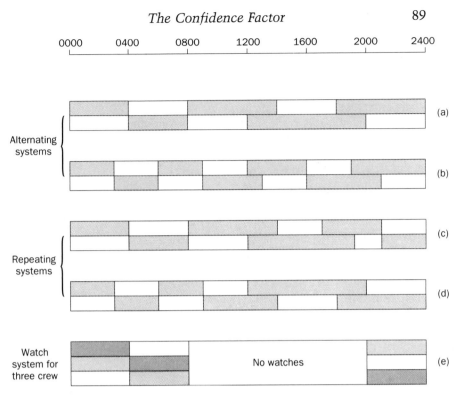

Fig 7 Watch systems

Radar, radar detectors and radar reflectors

Aids to human watchkeeping are often divided into the active and the passive — unfortunately one might also divide them into the very expensive and the fairly expensive.

Radar
To my mind probably the most useful of the high-tech electronics, radar nevertheless has three major drawbacks: it is heavy on electricity and like all electrics is susceptible to a whole range of failures; mounting the scanner can be a problem unless you own a ketch; and even the economy models start at around $2000, effectively taking it out of the scope of the budget sailor.

Radar detectors
These instruments, activated by radar transmissions from other vessels, usually comprise an omni-directional antenna linked to an alarm, with the set itself rotated much in the manner of an RDF antenna to get a bearing. They are deservedly popular with singlehanders, and valuable to any yacht forced to cross large areas of poor visibility and relatively light shipping such as the Newfoundland Banks. (Busy shipping lanes with radars beeping away like flocks of demented seagulls can be difficult to decipher.) For the two-handed crew determined to ignore the section on watchkeeping it would provide a measure of

safety, though nothing like that of a human watchkeeper, but at around $300 for the Lo-Kata Watchman seems an expensive way to buy extra time in one's bunk.

Radar reflectors

Passive radar reflectors come in several types, one might almost say several grades, with the vast majority of ocean-going yachts opting for the Firdell in its distinctive sausage-shaped casing. These are claimed to give a good echo from all directions and be unaffected by the yacht heeling. Ships to whom we have spoken on VHF have always reported a strong signal from our Firdell Blipper hanging at the crosstrees. The Blipper costs about $100.

The standard octahedral reflector is much cheaper at $30 or so, but numerous tests have proved that it returns definite blank sectors where the echo is poor. To be any real use an octahedral must be at least 18in across, making it difficult to mount unless the boat is fitted with twin backstays, and held in the 'catch rain' position, while all types should be hoisted as high as possible for maximum range. Cheapest of all, and totally useless, is the plastic bottle filled with aluminum foil — forget it.

Which of the above you go for, from $2000 radar to $30 reflector, is likely to be dictated almost entirely by your pocket, but never forget that without a human with their eyes open to monitor the situation and take evasive action if necessary they are powerless to protect you.

5 MONEY, ITS CARE AND HANDLING

A. FINANCIAL PLANNING

Realistic running expenses

> Annual income twenty pounds, annual
> expenditure nineteen nineteen six, result
> happiness. Annual income twenty pounds,
> annual expenditure twenty pounds ought and
> six, result misery.
>> (Charles Dickens, *David Copperfield*)

In Section 1B I touched on the difficulty of forecasting likely expenditure during a cruise due to the number of variables. However if relinquishing a regular income to live off savings even a rough estimate will be better than none, and, leaving out unforeseen and emergency expenditures which are discussed separately, one approach is to list the various regular outgoings and decide on a weekly or monthly allowance for each. As the cost of living varies drastically between different areas — it's at least twice as expensive to eat in the Caribbean as it is in the Canaries — at different times and in different areas one's standard of living may alter dramatically, which at least avoids monotony. The tighter your budget the fewer categories you will have to worry about, and aboard *Wrestler* we have frequently had weeks at a stretch when our *only* necessary expenditure was on food. Catering, cooking and storage are covered in Section 7B, but from the cost point of view I have yet to cruise anywhere that one cannot eat a reasonably healthy diet for $30 per week, and often for a great deal less. Aboard *Wrestler* cooking fuel seldom reaches as much as $1.50 per week, and I see from our accounts book that on both our long cruises diesel averaged out at less than $4 per week ($200 over twelve months, and $225 over fourteen months, respectively).

Routine maintenance costs during our 1984/85 cruise totalled all of $15, reaching a staggering $22 three years later. However on both occasions we left with everything in good order, carried a wide variety of tools and spares on board and did all our own running repairs; had this not been the case costs would doubtless have been much higher. Any yacht which is away for more than one season is likely to need as least as much money allocated to annual maintenance as she would at home, plus an allowance for crane or haulage fees in areas where there is insufficient tide to anti-foul by the gumboot method. The only other regular expenses that crop up in *Wrestler*'s accounts book are clearance mooring and marina fees (which I cannot separate because they were so often paid *en bloc*). Through sheer coincidence these totalled $225 for each cruise — comfortably under $5 per week.

This total of under $4000 for a one-year cruise for two adults is pretty close to the minimum. It may mean a monotonous diet for months at a time (we ate enough chicken wings in 1984/5 to put me off them for life!), allows nothing towards the minor civilizations of life, and frankly is not to be recommended. Ocean cruising is supposed to be enjoyable, and after the expense of buying and fitting out the boat herself it seems little short of crazy to jeopardize the success of the cruise by subjecting the crew to a standard of living significantly below that which they would expect at home.

Unfortunately I have much less accurate records of our expenditure on non-necessities, which in any case tended to fluctuate in direct relation to the balance (if any) remaining after the basics of life had been paid for. At various times our cruising luxuries have included meals and drinks ashore, ice, car or taxi hire, and small souvenirs. Hospitality, usually liquid, is one of the last areas on which the economy axe falls, and I don't ever recall the price of a stamp being considered sufficient excuse for not writing letters, which are a great deal cheaper than international phone calls. I justify my own greatest cruising expense, colour photography, as a long-term investment.

To repeat the estimated costing made towards the end of Section 1B, to my mind $5000 per year is about the minimum that two adults with a boat in the 30/32ft (9.2/9.8m) range can reasonably attempt to keep to without foregoing all the pleasures of visiting foreign lands. However it will not stretch to many luxuries and in particular to few meals or drinks ashore in most areas, so if eating ashore is something you are reluctant to forego, either allow for it in your financial planning or ensure your cruise concentrates on areas such as southern Europe where eating ashore is generally cheap.

Try to keep a tally of how much you're spending and on what. It's all too easy to regard foreign currency as Monopoly money (not least because the denominations are often small compared to the pound or dollar) and to lose all sense of its value. We've found that entering all the boat's expenses in an accounts book helps us keep track of where her allowance is going, and have for years run a separate kitty to cover food, drink and other domestic necessities. Although we keep no formal accounts of where this money goes we do periodically keep records of how much we put in, itself sometimes enough to start the alarm bells ringing and usher in a period of tightened belts.

Exchange rates

One of the most difficult aspects to second guess when trying to estimate long-term cruising costs several months in advance is how far your pound sterling, dollar, or whatever will stretch in terms of local currency.

American yachtsmen cruising the Caribbean have an advantage, as most local currencies are tied directly to the US dollar. The Virgin Islands use the US dollar itself (making the British Virgin Islands the only place in the world issuing stamps bearing the Queen's head but priced in American dollars and cents), the Eastern Caribbean dollar used by the English-speaking islands from Anguilla to Grenada has for some years been tied to the US dollar at a rate of US$1:EC$2.60, while the currencies of Barbados and Trinidad & Tobago fluctuate slightly in relation to the EC dollar without ever slipping very far away. Only in the French islands, where ordinary French francs are in use, is the state of the US dollar ignored completely.

Thus it is not until one crosses the Atlantic — either west or east — that exchange rate fluctuations may begin to bite. As remarked in Section 1B, we suffered badly in 1985 when the pound was weak and the dollar strong. All our savings were in sterling and we had based our calculations on an exchange rate of around £1:$1.40, only to see it fall below £1:$1.10. Throughout the Caribbean we thus received some 25% less than we had allowed for each time we exchanged sterling into local currency (other than francs of course), effectively cutting our budget for running expenses to the bone. We were determined not to get caught the same way on our next cruise, watched the upward progress of sterling throughout the summer of 1987, and changed a large proportion of our cruising funds into dollars when the rate reached £1:$1.60. In the event it rose further while we were away and had we hung on we would have done slightly better, but at least we knew where we stood in relation to the Caribbean currencies.

Not being an economist I hesitate to give hard and fast advice on such a complex subject. If (when?) we go blue water cruising again we shall probably hedge our bets with much the same strategy — funds for the European part of the cruise in sterling, US dollars earmarked for those areas where it provides a stable exchange basis. Those with more detailed knowledge of financial markets may prefer to gamble on rates improving while they cruise. However every ocean cruiser who intends to visit areas outside the sphere of their own currency should be aware that a potential problem exists.

The emergency reserve

> Money is like a sixth sense without which you
> cannot make complete use of the other five.
> (W Somerset Maugham, *Of Human Bondage*)

Anyone who spends their entire time worrying 'What if . . .' will probably never really enjoy the cruising lifestyle, but the number of yachtsmen around who sport the ostrich philosophy is positively unnerving. However careful one is and whatever precautions one takes accidents will occasionally happen, and only after making sensible provision does it become reasonable to ignore the possibility. This is where the emergency reserve comes in. This fund should be kept quite separate from the money earmarked for regular expenses, kept strictly to cope with the unforeseen, and *not eaten* towards the end of the cruise! If that sounds a little peculiar just consider: most budget cruisers run short of ready cash before they reach home, by the end of an Atlantic circuit some of the yacht's gear may be nearing the end of its active life, and for, say, a New England yachtsman the stretch of water from Bermuda northwestward is likely to be the nastiest of the whole voyage. Ideally the reserve should remain untouched, other than for emergencies, until you tie up in your home port but for us the rule seems to relax of its own accord in Falmouth.

How big need this reserve fund be? The obvious answer 'as big as possible' is little help and anyway begs the old question of variables. There are some major expenses which will be unavoidable should they crop up — flying an injured crew-member home, paying for repairs to the yacht's structure, spars and engine, and replacing essential gear should it be lost, stolen or written off, are among the most likely. However, caution and common sense, sound gear, careful long-term maintenance and never driving the boat too hard will all decrease the likelihood of equipment failure. Another approach is to minimize the amount of equipment on the essential list — by all means have it on board, but be prepared to shrug your shoulders and say 'too bad' if it packs up. For a typical low-tech yacht crewed by two adults I would recommend a reserve of at least $2500, though more will never go amiss. If you have extensive electronic equipment and are unwilling to cruise without it, up the reserve to $3500 or more.

How is this sizeable reserve best handled? I am in favor of carrying up to a quarter of it in cash, partly because there are still a few places either without banks, or where it (singular) opens Tuesdays and Thursday afternoons only. Hard cash can help avoid delays if one should need to set repairs or other work in motion, make a deposit on replacement gear or even oil a few wheels, but too much cash on board can be a temptation and the balance is probably best left ashore. The simplest and most obvious is a savings account, where it can earn interest and yet is readily available. Those who carry yacht and/or medical insurance can reasonably consider this as part of the reserve, but should not forget that certainly in the former if not the latter there will be a sizeable excess on *each and every claim*. Some fortunate blue water cruisers may settle for a smaller reserve, backed by an undertaking from dependable relatives or friends willing to come to the rescue financially should the need arise.

The final use of the reserve is to pay your mooring fees and keep you fed on your return, during the inevitable gap between arrival home and securing a regular income. It is ironic that the better off the owner the less relevant a reserve fund is likely to be, while those who will have most trouble accumulating extra funds before departure are the very people whose entire cruise might otherwise be wrecked by a single large, unforeseen bill.

Insurance: yacht and medical

Yacht insurance

Over the past few years getting insurance coverage has become a major problem for ocean cruising yachts. Not only is it expensive (at least 2.5% of the total value of the boat, plus the cost of an out-of-water survey if she is more than a few years old) but it has become increasingly difficult for two-person crews to obtain coverage at all. There seem to be a number of reasons for this, some more valid than others:

1. Many two-person crews include one person who is considerably less experienced than the other, and very often only one person who understands navigation (though this is often equally true of larger crews).
2. Some two-person crews (particularly when the skipper is a former singlehander) do not stand regular night watches.
3. There is no doubt that fraudulent insurance claims are occasionally made and (rightly or wrongly) this is considered more likely the further the boat is from home territory and the fewer people there are on board.

More generally:

4. Compared with the hundreds of thousands of home-based yachts which are a good overall bet simply because so many are hardly ever used, a few hundred ocean cruisers are very small beer financially and barely worth the paperwork.
5. Most repairs are much more costly away from home waters, as are replacement parts. If a marine surveyor has to be called in, hours and travel expenses may be many times what they would have been at home.

The net result is that the smaller boat, sailed by a couple who have no wish and possibly no space for extra crew, may be totally unable to get insurance for an Atlantic crossing. If coverage is forthcoming it will almost certainly carry a high excess — ours was $800 for general cruising and $1200 for the Atlantic passages on a total insured value of $30,000, with lower excesses on the dinghy and individually listed personal possessions.

In spite of these problems I have always felt that if most of one's savings and perhaps years of one's life have gone into an ocean cruising boat, it is worth spending considerable time, effort and money to arrange insurance coverage for her, even if one eventually settles for third-party and total loss only. Other people, whose opinion and experience I respect, put forward the view that sailing uninsured makes one more aware of good seamanship and even less likely to take risks, or that the money is better invested in extra ground tackle or more charts. There is certainly an element of truth in this, though cutting corners by economizing on such necessities would be inexcusable whether insured or not, and it's hard to imagine the skipper who bases his or her decisions on 'am I insured?' rather than 'what's the seamanlike thing to do?' It also ignores the possibility of serious damage from another yacht in a crowded anchorage, when knowing that the other person is technically at fault will be little consolation if they have neither insurance, money, nor any intention of paying compensation. Finally, an increasing number of marinas and yacht harbours will only accept yachts covered for third-party risks, and bearing in mind the damage that could be done by a boat catching fire or a heavy yacht ramming others while maneuvering, one can see their point. Always ask for a duplicate set of documents, duly stamped, to carry aboard but leave the originals in safekeeping ashore.

Having made the decision as to whether you want to insure — and no one other than co-owners should be allowed to influence you on this — the obvious first move is to sound out your current insurance company or broker. If you have been with one company for several years, and are planning a limited duration cruise, they may be willing to arrange one-off insurance simply to keep your business on your return — assuming, of course, that they consider you a good risk and wish to keep your business. If you do not have recent insurance, or your present company or broker is politely uninterested, the advertisements sections of the boating magazines usually list marine insurance companies. Any potential insurer will need details of the yacht, the crew and the proposed itinerary, and the more carefully researched your plans the better impression you will make.

The fact must be faced though, that however seaworthy and well-equipped the yacht and however locally experienced the crew, you are unlikely to get insurance coverage unless at least one person on board has previous oceangoing experience, and a crew of three will almost certainly be stipulated for the longer passages. In exceptional circumstances it may be possible for a two-person crew to get coverage, but only if both have extensive ocean sailing experience already under their belts. Even with thirteen crossings between us and an unblemished insurance record our broker had trouble finding underwriters who would accept us in 1987, and such is the hardening attitude that he could give no guarantee of being able to organize two-handed coverage in the future.

Medical insurance
The other insurance coverage carried by many cruising sailors is for personal injury and medical expenses. Always read the small print carefully, as ocean sailing is sometimes classed as a 'dangerous sport' along with sky-diving, mountaineering, pot-holing and the like, while other policies may be invalid outside a specified area. Injury or illness abroad could certainly be expensive, both in terms of hospitalization and flights home.

A familiar yacht is a relatively safe and very healthy environment — both our brushes with hospitals while living aboard have been due to accidents ashore — and we have neither carried medical insurance nor needed it. However the situation changes if children are aboard, when it should also cover the mother's flight costs in case it is necessary to get a sick child home in a hurry. If the adults on board do not carry full medical insurance, then injury and illness must be included among the possible emergencies which make some form of accessible reserve fund essential.

B. PAPER V. PLASTIC

There are several ways to handle your cruising funds — hard cash, travellers' checks, and various types of credit transfer. It is an aspect of long distance cruising which has become much simpler over the past decade with the increasingly wide acceptance of credit cards, but even so there are other alternatives and it may be wise to spread your eggs over several baskets.

Carrying cash on board

> The Owl and the Pussy-Cat went to sea
> In a beautiful pea-green boat.
> They took some honey, and plenty of money,
> Wrapped up in a five-pound note.
>
> (Edward Lear, *The Owl and the Pussy-Cat*)

If you decide to carry a reserve of hard cash beyond your immediate needs give both its acquisition and its stowage serious forethought. In all the areas I have ever cruised nothing can beat an American dollar for acceptability, sometimes in preference to the local currency, and though one might expect Europeans to be happy with sterling or the German mark neither seems to have the same appeal as a greenback. However, one may pay for convenience with a poor exchange rate, and I always try to arrive in each new country with at least $100 in local currency, sometimes to the obvious disappointment of the officials. Your bank may take up to a fortnight to supply the more unusual currencies. Make sure you ask for small denomination notes, as larger bills are often difficult to change in village economies and local markets.

Carrying large quantities of cash aboard is obviously not without its potential problems, an aspect which must be taken very seriously. The simplest way to decrease the risk of theft is to keep totally silent about how much cash you have with you. Tell no one, not friends on other yachts and certainly not casual crew. A few countries demand that foreign currency be declared on arrival, the answer to which must remain between you and your conscience. I take the view that it's not only unwise but tactless in the extreme to tell the customs officer and his three assistants that you have more money aboard than they will earn between them in an entire year.

Your cash reserve will be safest split into at least four parts for stowage around the boat, with one smallish chunk readily accessible in case you need to pay a bill or fee with anyone else aboard. Fortunately nearly all boats are well provided with natural hiding places, and while these might not escape a trained customs officer they ought to be proof against casual theft. Even should an intruder find one cache there is a good chance he would then stop looking. As you work on the interior before departure tracing wiring and checking hose connections, keep an eye open for suitable 'dead' areas where a small self-seal bag could be concealed. If nothing else it's an interesting mental exercise.

Transferring funds as you need them

> The size of sums of money appears to vary in a
> remarkable way according as they are being paid
> in or paid out.
>
> (Julian Huxley, *Essays of a Biologist*)

Unless you choose to carry your entire worldly wealth in cash you will need some method of topping up the kitty as you go along.

Travellers' checks bought before departure for encashment as needed have long been the standard method of carrying non-cash funds while abroad, and though they have largely been superseded by plastic, a few may still be useful, particularly if you dislike carrying large quantities of cash. Their chief advantage is that those issued by the major banks are accepted almost everywhere, but the same cannot always be said of those from smaller banks. They also have several distinct drawbacks: commission will almost certainly be charged at both buying and cashing stages, sometimes totalling nearly 10% of check value; no interest can be earned on the money tied up; and although they are normally covered by insurance if lost or stolen, proving they have gone can be a time consuming business and cost a fortune in international phone calls. Finally, you have to decide in advance how much you will need to spend − one thing for a fortnight on the Costa del Sol but quite another for a year of blue water cruising.

Credit cards have simplified the cruising yachtsman's life enormously. They fall into two major groups (it is probably worth holding one from each) and can be used for purchases and to draw cash abroad just as in the US, though a passport will usually be required for positive identification. It is not generally necessary to have an account at the issuing bank to hold their credit card, but the time to apply is well before you leave, while you still have a permanent income and can pass yourself off as a solvent and reliable member of society. Unless you want to incur interest payments currently approaching 30% you will need a reliable home agent (see Section 8C) to pay the bills on time, though your bank may be willing to handle this directly from a current or deposit account. Some companies make a conversion charge when money is drawn or a purchase made in a foreign currency and the exchange rate used is always that of the day the bill goes through, not the day on which the purchase or cash advance was made, though only if exchange rates are fluctuating wildly is this likely to make much difference to the final bill.

The **Barclaycard/Visa** family is widely accepted in the UK, USA, France and Spain, and is invaluable throughout the smaller islands of the Caribbean − if there's a palm tree there's probably a Barclays International underneath it. As well as payment for goods, up to $100 per day can be drawn in local currency (subject to your own credit limit) at any bank displaying the Visa sign. A commission of 1.5% is charged on cash advances and there may also be a local handling charge, but there is the usual interest-free credit period until the bill comes in. An annual account fee of £8 has recently been introduced. Free *Travellers' Guides* are available which give details on current Barclaycard acceptance in each area, as well as general tourist information.

The most familiar name in the other group is **Mastercard.** It is almost identical in use to Visa. **American Express** is more than just a credit card as their offices will also hold mail and organize major credit transfers. The $55 annual fee may be worthwhile, for American Express operates what they call Global Assist, an emergency service for travellers abroad that can come up with emergency cash, English-speaking doctors, etc.

Should you need to obtain a really large lump sum — perhaps tapping your emergency reserve — it may be necessary to arrange a **Telegraphic Transfer** from your bank at home. By far the best way to do this is through your home agent, who should hold Power of Attorney for you. If you have to contact the bank yourself to ask for funds to be sent abroad there is not only the problem of time differences to contend with, but also proving that the message is genuine (they are unlikely to accept instructions via telephone, telex or fax). Once authenticity is established — and providing the funds exist — most banks are able to make a Telegraphic Transfer to any bank in the world. The process will take a minimum of two working days (again allowing for time differences), though transfers to tiny banks in the back of beyond will naturally take longer. It also saves delay to convert the money at source and send it in the currency of the country to which it is going. Typical charges for the service might be $20 to $40, depending on whether or not your bank is used to such transactions. The whole operation involves a fair bit of work for those concerned and I would regard it only as a last resort, but it does have the advantage that the bulk of your reserve fund can remain on deposit at home and earn worthwhile interest until or unless it is actually required.

C. SECURITY ON BOARD AND ASHORE

Taking your sails out of their wind

Unfortunately there are areas of the world where piracy and other attacks are relatively common — the coast of Colombia, the South China Sea and the Red Sea spring to mind — and by far the best advice I can give is to avoid them like the plague. However, contrary to popular gossip personal safety throughout most of the world's accepted cruising grounds is no worse than at home — probably better if home is a European or North American city.

Obviously no one wishes either to be attacked or to lose possessions, and it is worth making basic security a habit. The best deterrent of all is probably a large dog, but these are notorious for their need to go ashore at regular intervals. Otherwise a yacht at anchor is much less vulnerable than one tied alongside, and the harbours of small towns and villages always safer than those of cities. The pilot book should tell you about conditions in a particular area.

It is worth remembering that however much you may be economizing to eke out your cruising funds, anyone aboard a cruising yacht is unbelievably rich in the eyes of most people outside Europe and North America (incidentally many cruising areas are also areas of very high unemployment) and it is immoral as well as dangerous to flash large amounts of money around. If a large purchase needs to be made, tell the people involved and anyone else who may be listening that you have to go to the bank to collect the money, as you only have enough on your boat for day-to-day living. Then go to the bank and straight back to the shop, preferably in company. If drawing money on cash or credit cards never draw much at one time. Even telling hopeful bum-boat vendors: 'Your limes/fish/jewellery are really tempting, but I only have enough money for tomorrow's food' all helps to reinforce the idea that here is a yacht which really isn't worth their while.

Before our first Caribbean cruise in our own boat in 1984 I rigged up an elaborate security alarm system with pressure mats, trip wires, lights and loud sirens. It was based on a car system and didn't cost very much — about $35 in total — but turned out to be a complete white elephant as we never felt insecure enough to use it, and this is remembering that most of the time we were two girls on board. After that cruise I removed most of the components and used them for other things, and since then if we have ever felt the least bit uneasy have relied on a very powerful 12 volt spotlight (the equivalent of a car headlamp) plugged in and ready to hand. If used at close quarters it would effectively blind anyone caught in the beam and prevent them seeing anything — or anyone — behind it. Again we've never used it, but a couple of times have been quite glad it was there.

Unfortunately thefts by other yachtsmen are not unknown, with inflatable dinghies particularly vulnerable, but a combination of really prominent markings and older equipment is a good deterrent as thefts are generally for resale. This sort of theft is very seldom associated with violence.

Firearms

We have never carried a gun on board and can't imagine doing so, for the following reasons:

1. Almost all customs forms ask whether firearms are carried, and in most areas they will be confiscated while the yacht is in harbour.
2. Unless you're familiar with firearms they're probably as dangerous to you as to any intruder.
3. Producing a gun turns a potentially dangerous situation into a potentially lethal one, whether the intruder is armed or not. An armed intruder is likely to use his own gun on the principle of attack being the best method of defense; an unarmed intruder may be frightened into a physical attack to try to gain possession of it. Basically, there is no point in carrying or producing a gun unless you are prepared to use it first and ask questions afterwards.
4. An unidentified dinghy coming alongside in the dark *could* be full of armed intruders. However it's much more likely to be the (possibly merry) crew from a nearby yacht trying to find their way home, local children who may have petty theft in mind but are certainly no real threat, a local fisherman hopeful of a drink, or even an official earning some overtime.
5. I don't know of any instance where a local has been shot dead by a visiting yachtsman. However, on the few occasions where the reverse has happened the standard procedure in many countries appears to be to take everyone in the vicinity into custody, witnesses and all (including in one case the widow

of the victim), while the police consider the matter. I would not give much for the chances of any yachtsman who killed a local even in proveable self-defense getting off without a long jail sentence or worse.

6 THE PEOPLE PROBLEM

A. THE CREW DILEMMA

Far more blue water cruises fall apart at the seams because of friction amongst the crew than because of problems with the yacht, perhaps because few skippers invest a quarter of the time and effort into selecting crew that they do into preparing their boat. Long term cruising creates strains entirely different in human terms from those of racing, for which a group of people who may have little in common ashore will often unite against a common challenge, and similarly the most disparate of crews will generally pull together when faced with extreme bad weather or similar external threats. We have met various combinations of platonic friends cruising together in everything from seemingly perfect accord to a state of undeclared war, but it cannot be coincidence that the vast majority of ocean cruising yachts are sailed by couples, with or without children aboard, and there is little doubt that a long-term partner makes the best crew.

The single skipper has various other options. Many start off singlehanded, though a remarkable number seem to acquire girlfriends *en route*, while others try to sign on crew for the entire voyage before leaving. The personal column of a magazine such as *Cruising World* is as good a place as any to start, both by answering any suitable offers and placing your own message — I know plenty of people who have done both with considerable success. Another possibility is provision of crew by a service such as The Crew List, Marine Data Services.* Do try to sign up your crew with enough time in hand to get to know them — and they you of course — which will also allow time for second thoughts on both sides if necessary. Whatever exciting places you visit and however luxurious your boat, if those aboard do not get on well nobody will enjoy the cruise.

Other skippers without permanent crew may invite sailing friends to join for part of the cruise, perhaps a month or so at a time, but this too has its potential problems. The expense and organization of frequent crew changes gets steadily more difficult as the yacht puts more miles between herself and home (the crew may find their own air fares and will often contribute towards food and running expenses, but the international phone calls will mount alarmingly) while plans which were firm on the day of departure may have to be called off at short notice due to family commitments, illness, promotion, job changes and a whole range of other perfectly genuine reasons which will nevertheless leave the skipper effectively stuck.

A fourth possibility is to cruise and explore mainly singlehanded, taking on casual crew from the dockside for the longer passages. Some of the possible pitfalls of this option are discussed at the end of this section.

The less experienced couple

Many skippers will not have the luxury – or dilemma – of choice when signing on crew, having married theirs years ago, and couples with established relationships ashore are certainly in the best position to plan voyages of several years' duration. In an ideal situation both may have been sailing for years, either together or independently, and of such people are the strongest and most enduring cruising partnerships formed. More often one person will have been introduced to sailing by the other and the problem here can be finding the time to gain the necessary experience before departure, particularly in the case of younger couples who plan a one-year cruise before settling down to the responsibilities of career and family. If the budget is limited and they decide to sail a smallish yacht two-handed it is essential that both should be reasonably competent, with at least a basic grasp of boat handling and navigation to fall back on should the other person become incapacitated.

In spite of this seemingly obvious fact an amazing number of family-crewed yachts do set off on ocean passages with at least one person on board – very often one out of two – having barely sailed out of sight of land before. Not only is this potentially dangerous, but it also puts considerable extra strain on both parties. The skipper is forced to carry a higher degree of responsibility than if they could be certain of competent back-up in an emergency, while their crew faces all the trauma involved in leaving home, friends and a settled way of life without having any clear idea of what they will be encountering instead.

In an ideal situation any prospective ocean cruising crew should spend several seasons sailing together locally before jumping off for 'the big one'. Unfortunately in many cases this is simply not practical, even when one person is desperately lacking in sailing experience. The best solution is probably some intensive tuition at a sailing school, possibly on a course which concentrates on building skill and confidence in all aspects of boat handling rather than being structured towards a captain's license. Sailing school courses do tend to be expensive, and if the skipper is also aware of gaps or rusty patches it might make better sense to find a qualified instructor willing to teach you aboard your own boat. Some schools keep a list of part-time instructors with whom they may be willing to put you in touch, while other instructors advertise their services in the classified sections of sailing magazines and on club notice boards. Ask to see the instructor's captain's license – which must be updated at five-year intervals – and confirm with your insurance company that they have no objections. Most policies specifically exclude the use of a private yacht for teaching purposes, but any company with sense should make an exception for a course intended to increase the skills of the owner or crew. School is no real substitute for experience, but the less knowledge a person has to start with the more obvious the jump in ability will be, providing a valuable boost in confidence for the nervous or hesitant. For both skipper and crew to be aware of the other's growing expertise can be nothing but positive.

Love me, love my boat

Whereas the inexperienced but enthusiastic partner may take to the cruising life like a duck to water, other people prefer their sailing in small doses (often as a passenger rather than active crew), and a small minority have no affinity whatsoever with the sea, are permanently ill at ease while afloat, very probably scared and usually seasick. The reluctant crew tag, if applicable, invariably attaches itself to the female half of the partnership, something I've always felt to be extremely unfair. I've met plenty of men who like to sail and expect their wives to accompany them, and a few wives who regularly sail either alone or with friends, but have yet to encounter a woman who enjoys sailing and expects a less than enthusiastic husband to tag along — he's more likely to be off playing golf.

Whether this antipathy is based on fear, attachment to home comforts or simply a preference for doing something else is immaterial. It's plainly unreasonable to expect anyone to live for months or even years in an environment where they will not be happy, and though it would be a shame to totally drop the idea of long-term cruising because one person is less keen than the other this is a factor which must be taken into account at the planning stage. One possibility is to stick to short distances and coastal or inland waterways only — exploring the European canal system might be an acceptable compromise — while another is to sign on additional crew for the longer passages so that the less enthusiastic partner can travel by air or ferry, joining the yacht at her destination. This will be expensive, but for the person who enjoys sailing in moderation but neither wishes to tackle ocean passages nor to be left out entirely it could prove the best solution. A third and by no means unknown option is for one partner to take leave of absence from the family home for a limited period while the other holds the fort.

Children aboard

> Nervous breakdowns are hereditary. We get them
> from our children.
>
> (Quoted Nigel Rees, *Graffiti 2*)

The first consideration for parents who contemplate an ocean voyage with their children is obviously the safety aspect. Most older cruising children swim like fish while the very young get used to wearing a miniature lifejacket along with their diaper, and I have only ever heard of one child who drowned off his parents' yacht (ironically, it was alongside a jetty at the time) compared with the frequent fatal road accidents one reads about at home. However the fact remains that if the boat should be wrecked in an isolated spot or sink offshore a small child's chance of survival would inevitably be less than that of an adult. At least three yachts with older children aboard have foundered at sea, in each case the entire family being rescued after surviving for days or weeks in a life-raft with apparently no long-term ill effects, but the smaller the child the more susceptible they will be to everything from shock to sunburn, and particularly to dehydration.

The other consideration is medical — small children can become dangerously ill very quickly, and if the yacht is at sea or in an isolated anchorage there may be no help at hand. It is essential that someone aboard has a thorough knowledge of first aid, since time may be much more of the essence than would be the case with a sick adult. Drugs suitable for children will also need to be added to the first aid kit.

The early years
Having decided that the risks are acceptable, is long-term cruising with the very young — ie under about three — so desirable anyway? Many parents see the period before their children reach school age as their only possible chance to cruise, but sadly the majority of couples I have talked to who set off on a first ocean cruise with one or more children of this age group aboard regretted the decision, or at least felt that neither they nor their children had gained as much from the experience as they had hoped. Although small children are seldom seasick, keeping an active two-year-old entertained and out of mischief can be a full time job, and one experienced skipper cruising with his wife and young son remarked to me that in many ways it was like sailing singlehanded, with the additional disadvantage of seldom remaining undisturbed for very long off watch.

Certain factors can be isolated as having a strong bearing on the success or otherwise of the cruise. Couples who have already cruised extensively together without children are at an obvious advantage — both parents know what to expect and how best to prepare both boat and children for months of close proximity. Those calm, capable mothers with a knack for keeping an eye on three things at once, not only experience but create far fewer problems than those who perpetually fuss — small children, like animals, can sense moods a mile away and nothing will worry or scare them like a worried or scared parent. However, from observation it would seem that the general attitude and involvement of the father is often the deciding factor. Those who really enjoy the chance to spend time with their children not only gain more from the opportunity but also give their wives a mental and physical break; those whose one idea at the first sign of tears or temper is to get ashore to the nearest bar — and I have met several — sooner or later face mutiny. Mothers speak of missing the support network of family and friends, becoming over-tired even in harbour, and feeling guilty because they are unable to do their share of the yacht's chores whilst at sea.

If the yacht is large enough, the most practical solution is to enlist extra help, though this may be much easier said than done. Finding the right person — an experienced sailor liked by both children and adults, with time to spare and not too prone to seasickness — may prove one of the most difficult tasks of the cruise planning stage. Assuming that you cannot pay a serious salary, the best choice might be a responsible school-leaver or student taking a year off between school, further education or career. Either way you should expect to provide food and probably some pocket money, together with fares as appropriate.

Older children

When sailing with older children — the definition of 'older' having much more to do with mental than actual age — an entirely different question arises. One can reasonably expect a two-year-old to do whatever you choose to do yourself, but can the same necessarily be said of a twelve-year-old? A few children hate the sea just as fiercely as do some adults, and it is doubtful whether one can reasonably expect such a child to go ocean cruising. Assuming that yours are keen on the general idea and have some local sailing experience already under their belts, cruising with older children can produce great rewards for all concerned. The major worry will probably be education. Many cruising children are taught by their parents, and those I have met varied from the very well informed, with standards in the three Rs which would have won them prizes in any school ashore, to a few virtual gipsies who were all but illiterate. If the cruise is unhurried it may be feasible to register children with local schools for a term here and a term there, a marvellous opportunity for the outgoing child to meet peers of different race and background, and the possibilities for field geography and language studies are obvious.

Anyone considering long-term cruising with a child aboard should study Gwenda Cornell's excellent *Cruising with Children* (Sheridan House). Although babies and infants are covered briefly, the book concentrates mainly on the older child; the Cornells' own children were five and seven when they left for a six-year circumnavigation. The section on education aboard is particularly informative, as one might expect from a mother who is also a qualified teacher. Another good book is *Babies Aboard* by Lyndsay Green (International Marine).

Casual crew

Taking on casual crew on the dockside is something to be avoided if at all possible, though occasionally it may be inevitable. Organizing in advance to be joined by extra hands for part of the cruise — perhaps the transatlantic passage if insurance stipulates three people — is much less risky. Risky not in terms of an inexperienced crew jibing and bringing the mast down (though I do know someone who did just that), but in terms of turning out to be less pleasant than they seemed ashore, or even bringing drugs or firearms onto your boat without your knowledge. Without being overdramatic and suggesting mutiny or piracy on the high seas, in the eyes of the law skippers are responsible for the actions of their crew, and more than one yacht has been impounded because drugs, of which the owner had no knowledge, had been brought aboard by temporary crew. Other skippers have discovered only when the Canaries were 200 miles to windward that their brand new crew drank (starting at 0800), refused to touch less popular tasks such as the graveyard watch or the washing up, or simply took to the best berth and lay there groaning into a basin for three weeks.

This is not to imply that casual crew are always a problem — far from it. I know several couples who have picked up crew in the Canaries and become fast friends long before reaching the West Indies, and more than one supposedly short-term crew has ended up marrying their skipper. Anyone who has crewed on another yacht regularly and has a letter to confirm it is likely to be a good bet, but the person who has crewed on a dozen different yachts in two years should be invited to explain why.

It's important to remember that the skipper is legally responsible for repatriating crew who leave the vessel abroad, and most immigration authorities take this fairly seriously. In other words, if you *or they* decide it's time to part company but they do not have the money for a ticket home you will have to find it, with no time to shop around for cheap rates. Technically UK and other European nationals need be repatriated no further than the nearest EC territory, of which the French Caribbean islands as Departments of France are legally a part, but I have yet to hear of this being put to the test. Of course crew often leave amicably to join another yacht, but in many places when a crew member transfers from one yacht to another not only must both skippers visit the immigration department to have the papers stamped, possibly paying a documentation fee as well, but the yacht the crew member arrived on will not be allowed to sail until the other has actually departed with the new crew aboard.

Crewing for others as seen from the crew's point of view is covered in Section 1B.

B. LIFE ON A BUDGET . . . AND IN A SMALL SPACE

Acclimatization — living aboard before leaving

> For you dream you are crossing the Channel,
> and tossing about in a steamer from Harwich —
> Which is something between a large bathing
> machine and a very small second class carriage.
>
> (Sir W.S. Gilbert, *Iolanthe*)

There's enough trauma in leaving home and friends to set off across an ocean for the first time without doing it suddenly. To live on board for a while before leaving is a sensible stepping-stone, not only from the practical point of view but also psychologically. Most people on moving into a new house go to some effort to put their own stamp upon it and this is even more important aboard a boat, particularly in the case of anyone who has even the least doubt about the wisdom of the whole project. These personal touches might include new curtains, photographs of family or pets, pictures and, as you travel, a growing number of souvenirs from different ports — in other words, exactly what you would expect ashore. Several long-distance cruising yachts, including *Wrestler*, even carry resident plants in swinging holders.

At least part of your acclimatization should be spent on an anchor or mooring, certainly not permanently alongside a marina pontoon, and preferably not entirely in protected water. If every cruising yacht spent a week at anchor in a somewhat exposed or busy harbor during preparations for a blue water cruise many crews would rethink their domestic arrangements, particularly as regards coping with rolling and its side effects — see section 3D. Living on board will also give you a chance to work out stowage possibilities and discover which lockers are handiest for regular use. This is not always as simple as it sounds, since the nearest locker will not be the most convenient if it means dropping half the table or disturbing an off-watch crew. The mental leap is to think in terms of *living* aboard, rather than the near-camping attitude that many people bring to their annual two- or three-week cruise.

Having to live off the yacht's resources will quickly bring to light any ways in which she is lacking, as well as giving you time to discover and iron out some of those minor irritations which can otherwise become annoying out of all proportion when you're tired, worried and perhaps dispirited. I'm reminded of the petty irritation factor every time I sail, and particularly skipper, someone else's boat. It can range from important things such as the anchor chain being un-

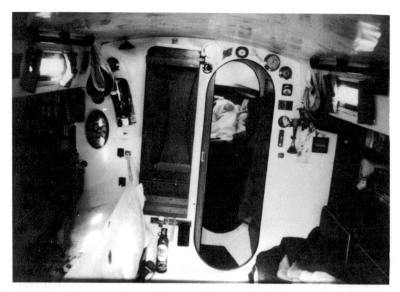

Photo 8 Wrestler's simple interior, looking forward. Bookshelves and small souvenirs cover the main bulkhead with its folding table, while some idea of our angle of heel can be gained from the swinging lamp

marked to blunt cook's knives in the galley or a sharply angled corner which habitually skins your ankles. Make a list of improvements to be made before departure, not forgetting that the irritation factor also applies to your crew, permanent or temporary, so actively invite suggestions. Too many wives and girlfriends have learned never to criticize anything to do with the yacht, but suffering in silence for two or three weeks and doing so for a year or more are totally different things. Ask for feedback, particularly about areas like the galley that may be someone else's province, and don't dismiss any suggestion or complaint as ridiculous until you've given it proper thought.

The practical benefits of having lived on board will be obvious immediately you sail at night. You'll know automatically where to find the best handholds, you'll be much less likely to get bruised on hard corners because you'll know to an inch where they are, you'll know of any slippery areas to be avoided, and you won't have to think about where to find torches and safety gear. Few people sleep well on their first few nights in a strange place, and overcoming this hurdle before setting off on passage also makes good sense.

If you've already lived aboard for years while completing or renovating the boat you may have a different problem, as had friends who spent ten years building a large ferro-cement ketch. Camping inside her bare hull in a field, and then living aboard surrounded by pieces of timber as they fitted out her interior in a marina berth, inevitably led them to view her primarily as a houseboat and cruising as a series of quick dashes between suitable stopping points. It is difficult to see how best to avoid this relatively common pitfall, though deliberately choosing to visit a distant area which necessitates at least one ocean passage *en route* is likely to change one's attitude the hard way.

Budget limitations and the occasional splurge

> Excess on occasion is exhilarating. It prevents
> moderation from acquiring the deadening effect
> of habit.
>
> (W. Somerset Maugham, *The Summing Up*)

There is no doubt that living on a strict budget for long periods can become a strain, and if the cruise happens simultaneously to be going through a bad patch due to area, weather or sheer bad luck the question 'Why are we doing this?' will inevitably crop up. Money may not guarantee happiness, but my own experience is that lack of it is at the root of as many problems afloat as ashore, particularly when one person finds it easier to be careful with the pennies than the other. There are ill-defined lines separating meanness, thrift, generosity and downright wastefulness, and no two people will draw them in quite the same place. My sister and I can both live very cheaply for long periods provided the incentive — usually blue skies and warm seas — is there, but whereas I eventually begin to feel that I've earned a brief relaxation of the rules, she views any change in policy as throwing into question all efforts to live economically over the preceding weeks. We solved this quite simply — I make sure I carry enough money to indulge in the occasional luxury which I neither share nor need to excuse, after which I can go back to austerity without feeling too deprived. Equally Liz feels that the economies practiced from day to day have not been wasted, so we're both happy.

This system may be less appropriate for a crew who know each other less well, such as one put together through an advertisement or from one of the various crew services. It is often agreed at the outset that the weekly budget for food and running expenses will be $XX, to which everyone will contribute equally, but that this will not cover expenditure ashore. The problems crop up when some form of communal luxury — perhaps a meal out in a good restaurant, or hiring a car for the day — is contemplated. If some of the crew have the funds available and some do not there will inevitably be friction and whatever is decided someone will be unhappy — at being deprived of a pleasure they can afford, at being left out because they cannot, or at having to pay for a poorer crew member (who will soon find themselves either volunteering or being volunteered for all the least enjoyable chores to pay off the debt, itself a quick way to create resentment). If putting a crew of individuals together, aim for a measure of financial parity.

Clothes — choice and care

> Even in the dim gaslight he clashed on my
> notions of a yachtsman — no cool white ducks
> or neat blue serge; and where was the snowy-
> crowned yachting cap, that precious charm that
> so easily converts a landsman into a dashing
> mariner?
>
> (Erskine Childers, *The Riddle of the Sands*)

What will you need?
With stowage space inevitably at a premium there can be a temptation to cut down on the clothes you take along. However if this means having to rush out and buy tropical clothing in a tourist trap, with prices three times what they would be at home, you will kick yourself. More common is the tendency to over-pack, and should you become very desperate about stowage space don't forget that surface postage back to the US is quite cheap from most places.

Obviously clothes needed will depend largely on the climate of your route and destination, which I strongly recommend should be southwards — in any case, a resident of Britain or the northern USA knows plenty about cold climates already. If you're intent on going north (or far south), nearly all the larger oilskin manufacturers have polar-wear ranges. Do remember, though, that an ordinary northern climate will seem much colder than usual after a winter in the tropics, and thermal jacket, woolly hat and thick socks will probably be worn on your return, even in July or August. In intermediate climates such as the Azores or Iberia a light sweater or cardigan may be useful, but you're unlikely to need more than one. However, even the Azores can be extremely hot (on Midsummer Day the sun is only 16° from the zenith, much higher than in Barbados at Christmas) so don't be caught without your sun hat and high-factor cream.

For comfort in a hot climate, avoid synthetics and anything tight. How much you wear at sea will depend on choice, situation — whether you are a couple or have casual crew aboard — and your colouring. For the paler amongst us loose cotton shirts and longish shorts are a necessity, topped off by a large sun hat. A cotton hat or visor to shade the eyes will save you from premature frown lines, but must be tied on. Whether or not you wear shoes when sailing is up to the skipper (though the foredeck crew certainly ought to when handling the anchor) but comfortable sandals for shoregoing are essential.

In many cruising areas, including the Caribbean, there is a distinct division between beach and town wear, with men expected to wear shirts and girls to wear cotton skirts or loose shorts. It irks me to hear visiting girls complain of being harassed by local youths, without appearing to realize that their clothing, or lack of it, is taken as a direct invitation. Neither will many bars or restaurants welcome customers who are not wearing shoes. Occasionally one may need a fairly smart outfit — a light suit or jacket and slacks, or a favourite dress — but most invitations are at short notice and spiriting clothes straight from a locker onto one's back without them looking that way can be a problem. The traditional way of pressing trousers is to place them, carefully folded, between bunkboard and cushion and then sleep on them, and when selecting a dress choose one which will drip dry.

New clothes of reasonable quality are expensive in many areas (even if local taste coincides with your own) but material is usually cheap and frequently ethnic and colourful, making dressmaking a popular hobby. This does not necessarily mean carrying a sewing machine — long passages generate spare time on a scale one seldom encounters ashore, and I have made skirts, blouses, shorts and even a dress by hand on different cruises. Knitting, while an excellent way to pass a quiet watch further north, tends to leave one's hands unpleasantly hot in the tropics.

Washing clothes
Most harbours and anchorages sport laundry facilities of some kind, whether it's a local lady who washes by hand, a service laundry using machines, or a bank of the coin-operated variety. However all tend to be expensive, and in the case of the first option be sure to agree a price beforehand. On one, admittedly very dry, West Indian island we met some Americans who had been charged a preposterous US$50 to have a single sackful of clean laundry returned — more a ransom than a bill. Equally, if taking clothes to a service laundry be sure they understand what's required. Swedish friends cruising in Spain went to collect a sailbag full of jeans, heavy sweaters and towels only to find that everything had

been dry cleaned — the bill was enormous and the smell took weeks to wear off. Coin-ops are simplest, but many use coins which don't often come up in change (that's probably why) so it's worth scouting in advance.

All in all, nothing beats the time-honoured bucket — or more accurately buckets — for convenience and economy. An overnight soak in Clorox or equivalent for dirtier garments or those which have had to wait some time before washing, followed by a shorter soak in hand washing detergent or powder plus a quick scrub with a nailbrush produces quite acceptable results. Even when water is short, by dint of a little extra work it's possible to do a surprising amount of laundry in only a couple of gallons. The trick is to squeeze out as much of the soap as possible before rinsing and then divide the available water between at least three buckets. Starting with smaller items, rinse them in each bucket in turn, squeezing out between buckets so as to transfer as little soap as possible onwards. By the end of your efforts the final bucket will still be much cleaner than if you had used only one full one, and the muscles in your hands will ache from the unaccustomed exercise.

You will gather from the above that I consider washing clothes in salt water to be strictly for the mermaids. Even in a warm climate everything feels sticky, whites turn grey and nothing gets really clean. Most people suffer from spots in embarrassing places after a few weeks at sea — probably something to do with all that sitting down — and salty, chafing underclothes are a quick way to turn these minor annoyance into full-blown infections. Carry enough underclothes to last most of the way across the ocean, and when calculating water supplies allow for occasional rinsing along the way.

Drying is of course no problem in a warm climate, and the bleaching effect of strong sunlight works wonders on pillow cases and other whites. However by the same token darker colours will soon fade, and don't make a habit of hanging elasticated garments in the tropical sun or they'll start to sag. If you're wind-rode at anchor and hanging washing on the lifelines, put an extra peg on the forward end of each garment under the wire (see Fig 8). It always amazes me

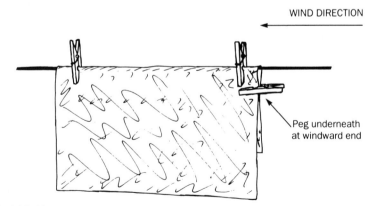

Fig 8 Washing

when people casually hang clothes over the boom or lifelines, apparently trusting to luck and the law of gravity to keep them there. Wet heavy clothes quickly become dry light ones, then one gust of wind and they're gone.

Storing clothes

If you leave a cold climate to visit a warm one the bulk of your clothing will need to be packed away for six or eight months. Clothes stowed in lockers take up much less space if packed in Ziploc plastic bags with most of the air expelled before sealing to keep them compressed as well as clean and dry. However carefully stored, though, garments will inevitably get musty, and it's worth hanging them out to air from time to time, particularly in the last harbour or anchorage before you anticipate needing them. The idea that clothes kept on hangers will chafe as you roll across the Atlantic may be true aboard larger yachts, but the hanging locker of a smaller yacht is usually wedged far too tightly for anything to move anywhere. Zip-up plastic suit or dress bags are a good idea for each person's set of tidy clothes.

Leather shoes, belts, etc have a nasty habit of growing mildew, though there are various spray-on preparations which claim to prevent this and storage in a sealed bag after thorough drying in the sun certainly helps. If mildew does appear, a good brushing followed by a wipe with a damp cloth will usually get rid of it.

C. IN SICKNESS AND IN HEALTH

Seasickness

I wish there was something useful and constructive I could say on this subject, but I fear there isn't except perhaps 'you're not alone'. Of the hundreds of experienced yachtsmen and women I know, fewer than 5% claim to have never even felt remotely queasy. Another 25% or so say they occasionally feel less than brilliant but are seldom actually sick. The vast majority, myself included, accept queasiness at the beginning of a passage as routine and may or may not be actually sick depending on conditions, but are confident of being relatively bomb-proof within a couple of days. The unfortunate remainder are prone to queasiness either continuously or at intervals the whole time the boat is at sea. Anyone lucky enough to belong to the first group who is disparaging about less fortunate crew members deserves to end up singlehanded, and though statistics do indicate that women are more prone to seasickness than men, I strongly suspect this has a lot to do with a greater reluctance on the part of men to admit to such 'weakness'. It may also reflect the typical division of labour — few things are more likely to trigger a bout of queasiness than labouring in the galley, whereas helming is one of the best ways to avoid seasickness or cure its milder forms. The standard advice of not too much alcohol or heavy food the night before sailing, staying warm and dry, keeping your mind occupied and avoiding work below unless absolutely necessary is of course worth heeding, though not always easy to follow.

Unfortunately nearly all seasickness cures and remedies taken internally produce side effects, usually including drowsiness — no problem if you're on the night ferry to Spain, but decidedly hazardous to the 0400 watch. Stugeron seems to offer the best overall results, though people allergic to penicillin may react badly to it. Accupressure wrist bands have the advantage of no side effects but I have yet to meet anyone who finds they really work, while another alternative, which seemingly does work, is not available in the UK! This comes in the form of a small patch, not unlike a sticking plaster, which is placed behind the ear and lasts for about three days. Sold over the counter in the USA and Canada under the name Transderm it drew unstinting praise from everyone I spoke to who had tried it. Like all drugs Transderm can produce side effects, and whatever type of seasickness remedy you use be sure to read the instructions on the packet and test any new product ashore first to find out how you react to it.

Personally I am resigned to spending the first day or two of any rough passage with a bowl handy, which is at least cheap. The old idea of being sick over the side should be firmly discouraged, or at the very least the sufferer helped into a harness, as the sense of balance will be at its worst and grip not much better. It's also a quick way to lose glasses and false teeth . . . They say the only certain cure for seasickness is to sit under a tree, but if a little suffering is the price that must be paid for it to be a palm tree, so be it.

General health care, and medical services abroad

The cruising life is a pretty healthy one, and with basic common sense plus reasonable luck the second part of this section should be redundant. Health care on board differs little from that ashore, though increased exposure to the elements, lack of exercise and limited fresh water can occasionally result in minor problems. Appropriate clothing can do much to combat the first, whether in the form of two pairs of thermal mittens or a large sunhat and Factor 15 sunbloc. Nor are either of the other two common problems likely to kill you, but they can detract much from the enjoyment of a cruise. To get the worst over first, limited exercise combined with a diet of tinned or processed food can quickly lead to constipation, not helped by the lack of privacy aboard the smaller yacht. High fibre cereals are light, compact to stow and keep well, while fresh or dried fruit and raw vegetables should also feature on the menu as often as possible. A practical consideration is to install several firm handholds in the heads compartment (bracing with the legs may be self-defeating . . .). The most common result of washing water being in short supply, particularly in a hot climate, is spots in the seat area — again not a killer but nevertheless very irritating. Poor circulation due to long periods spent sitting down is probably a contributory cause, but a sponge down with fresh water every day and a total ban on plastic cushions unless covered with a folded towel is usually enough to keep them at bay, though a very bad crop which show signs of becoming infected might indicate a course of antibiotics.

It hardly needs to be said that a good dental check-up before leaving is a must — tell your dentist what you are doing and where you are going, explain that you may not see him again for a year, and allow plenty of time for whatever work needs to be done. I don't doubt that excellent dentists exist all over the place but would avoid visiting one except in an emergency. (If you do get toothache in harbour check whether there are any dentists aboard other yachts. A remarkable number seem to be sailors and they invariably carry the tools of their trade).

Eyes also need some protection, and good sunglasses are important in the strong light to be found at sea. Polarized lenses are by far the most effective at cutting down glare and reflections, and particularly valuable when 'reading' the bottom in shallow water. Unfortunately they don't seem to be available in combination with prescription lenses for the short or long sighted, but clip-on additions are available. Your optometrist can prescribe (rather expensive) lenses that will cut out all of the damaging ultraviolet rays from the intense direct and reflected sunlight often experienced in tropical waters. Sun or prescription glasses need to be secured by either a neck-string or a band around the head — they show little inclination to float and are expensive to replace. Opticians are to be found in nearly all larger towns, but unless it's an emergency I would guess that having the optician who holds the original prescription make up replacement glasses or lenses and your home agent send them out to you would be more likely to produce good results at a reasonable price.

Any active way of life is going to result in the odd scrape, cut or bruise, but serious injuries are rare aboard cruising boats and many of those which do occur are due to carelessness, laziness, or both — downwind sailing without a preventer is a case in point. Obviously every cruising boat should carry a comprehensive first aid kit, plus additional prescription drugs such as antibiotics and pain-killers. Most of the contents will be standard over-the-counter items from any druggist, and it should be much cheaper to assemble it piecemeal for stowage in a couple of plastic boxes than to buy a purpose-made yachtsman's kit. I shall not go into detail about what it should contain on the basis that you either (a) have extensive medical knowledge already, or (b) have no medical knowledge and will therefore need a good first aid book, which will not only provide a list but tell you how to use each item. Two worth having are *Advanced First Aid Afloat* by Dr. Perry F. Eastman (Cornell Maritime Press) and *Your Offshore Doctor* by Dr. Michael H. Beilan (Putnam). Most important, both accept that you may be unable to get immediate help. As with dental problems, if you need medical advice while in harbor first canvas the other yachts; VHF can be a great help here. What with doctors, nurses, para-medics and vets (yes, vets — we're animals too) there's a good chance of enlisting professional help.

One practical tip is to split your first aid kit into two, labelled 'basic' and 'serious'. The basic kit should contain the everyday sticking plasters, sunburn lotion, aspirin or paracetamol, etc, with the serious kit packed to keep sterile dressings, distalgesics and prescription drugs clean, dry and safe. Add a few patent cold cures to the basic box; I have yet to see them on any yachtsman's first aid list, but we have several times caught heavy colds while in harbor.

Consider joining the International Association for Medical Assistance to Travellers. Membership is free (donation requested), and you get a world directory of IAMAT doctors in 125 countries who speak English or French, got their training in North America or Europe, and charge fixed, reasonable fees.

A word has to be said in this context about the prevalence of the HIV virus (AIDS) in some parts of the world, with blood transfusions carrying a particularly high risk. Have blood groups checked before you sail, and in the unlikely event of an accident overtaking you in a suspect area it may be possible for one member of the crew to donate blood for immediate use by another. An injury that requires stitching could also pose a threat — grab a packet of sterile needles from the first aid kit before taking the victim into the emergency room, together with a sealed hypodermic syringe in case a tetanus injection is necessary.

Happiness in a hot climate

> At twelve noon the natives swoon
> And no further work is done,
> But mad dogs and Englishmen
> Go out in the noonday sun.
> (Noel Coward, *Mad Dogs and Englishmen*)

Different people react to hot climates in very different ways, with the fair skinned and the overweight suffering about equally. Permanent crew are unlikely to fall serious victim to a change in climate if only because a yacht moves relatively slowly and the body has time to adapt, but anyone who flies out to join a yacht in the tropics should be watched unobtrusively for the first couple of days. Like alcohol, by the time you know you've had enough sun it's usually too much.

Shade
An awning of some kind is a must, for your boat's sake as well as your own, as Geoff Pack stresses in his *Ocean Cruising Countdown* (David & Charles). The awning which he and his wife made for their Rival 34, drawing on knowledge gained during several seasons running charter boats, is near the ultimate — stretchers front and rear, halyard loop in the centre and generous side flaps. *Wrestler*'s much simpler version with only one stretcher and no side flaps (see Fig 9(a), and also visible in several of the photographs) is adequate but leaves room for improvement. If I were redesigning it today it would be larger, with stretchers front and rear as well as in the centre and much deeper side flaps, but still quite simple to construct — see Fig 9(b).

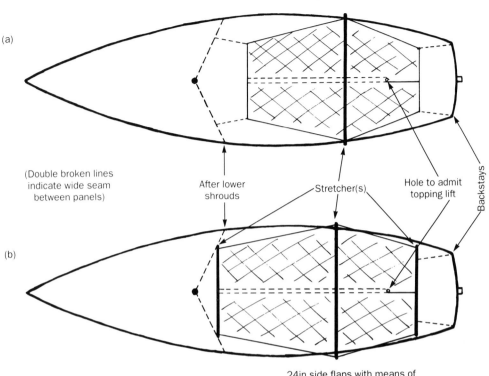

(No side flaps)

(a)

(Double broken lines indicate wide seam between panels)

After lower shrouds

Stretcher(s)

Hole to admit topping lift

Backstays

(b)

24in side flaps with means of brailing up when not required

Fig 9 Awnings

The main requirements of an awning are somewhat at odds with each other. It must be easy and quick to set up and yet be as large as possible — the more deck area that lies in shade the cooler the interior of the boat will remain. It should also be well enough braced and secured to withstand a fair bit of breeze without either tearing or taking off. The best choice of material is a dark coloured acrylic, a synthetic material with the weight and feel of canvas; the worst a pale nylon which will let most of the ultraviolet straight through. Unfortunately acrylic is pretty expensive, and the fact that it apparently lasts for ever is of little relevance to the skipper planning a single winter in the tropics. It may be possible to buy a roll of 'seconds' quality, otherwise any heavy canvas-type fabric may have to suffice. An ordinary domestic sewing machine should be able to sew awning-weight material without trouble but it may need an extra pair of hands to help manoeuvre the bulk while stitching. Every awning should incorporate drains attached to pipes at its lowest sag points (plastic dinghy drain fittings are useful to make the connection), ready to top up the water tanks with every passing shower. Not only does rainwater come for free, but is often cleaner and nearly always tastes better than that from ashore.

Fixed cockpit awnings — known the other side of the Atlantic as 'bimini tops' — are seldom seen aboard northern cruising boats, and unless you plan to remain in the tropics over the summer or one of the crew is very susceptible to sun, are probably not necessary. However a spot of portable shade in the form of a large umbrella can sometimes be very pleasant, and I have long coveted one of those produced by a well known drink manufacturer, which apparently comes complete with white table and chairs and swarthy Italian waiter.

Ventilation

While an awning can be made for any yacht, good or bad ventilation is much more integral and therefore difficult to improve, with deck hatches usually something of a mixed blessing. We have found *Wrestler*'s standard arrangement of forehatch plus two dorade vents reasonably adequate, and though we did consider having a second hatch fitted aft of the mast to improve air flow in the saloon eventually decided against it on the grounds of cost. Another valid consideration is that at least 50% of all hatches leak, either through the flange itself or because of poor fitting, and while most people can live with the idea of a leaky forehatch, perpetual drips from overhead in the saloon are something else entirely.

Some yachts may not have opening portholes except perhaps in the head. Retro-fitting is unlikely to be practical, and even if it were the high price and increased possibility of leaks would dissuade most owners. Having sailed yachts with both opening and fixed ports in the main cabin in hot climates, my

Photo 9 A pause between passages in English Harbour, Antigua. Both awning and wind scoop are in use in this very protected anchorage, and the blade of the self-steering gear has been lifted clear of the water

Photo 10 Wrestler's wind scoop, made by my sister from the clew of a blown out spinnaker

own feeling is that while the former can sometimes be very pleasant they're by
no means essential.

More to the point is to increase the ventilation already available, usually by
means of a wind scoop. Before we visited the tropics in 1984/85 I made a scoop
which turned out to be wrong in almost every respect — it was too small to
produce a decent draught, the nylon material rustled incessantly, and it took a
web of lines across the foredeck to set up. Friends aboard a 36-footer used a
Mirror dinghy spinnaker with much greater success, so in 1987 when another
friend blew out a spinnaker on the Atlantic passage we begged one of the clews
and Liz set to work. Being a clew it's not quite symmetrical, but other than a
light batten for the top, tape to reinforce the edges, a line each side for tension
and four loops around the base with corresponding hooks inside the hatch it

came for free. It's also simplicity itself to rig or drop and extremely efficient. Likely sources for blown spinnakers would be sail repairers or the end of a windy regatta.

Even without a wind scoop rigged, ventilation at anchor will be much improved if the forehatch opens forward, which also makes short-handed sail changes considerably easier. The assumption that one is more likely to ship water through a forward-opening forehatch is only partly true, since in my experience most spray crosses the foredeck at an angle, but while an aft-opening hatch with removable side-screens will keep out most of the spray it will also provide little ventilation. The ultimate is a hatch which can be opened either fore or aft by altering the hinging bolts, but last time I checked they started at the $600 mark which puts them way outside the budget league. It will be noted that, even in the blowy downwind conditions depicted in Photo 5, *Wrestler's* hatch is fully open, and who worries about ventilation when going to windward anyway?

Natural ventilation is only effective if the wind is blowing, so if you plan to cruise areas of consistently light winds or to stay in the Trade Winds areas out of season when the winds are light (check on *Pilot Charts* for average wind strengths) it may be worth investing in one or more 12 volt fans. These vary from the simple plastic type sold mainly for use in cars to the sophisticated, and expensive, oscillating variety. Check how much power it draws before you buy, and if possible go for the plug-in type which can be moved from place to place.

That other tropical life-saver, a fridge or ice-box, is discussed in Section 7A.

D. SOCIAL CONTACTS

Making friends

> No man is an island, entire of itself.
> Every man is a part of the continent — a bit of
> the main.
>
> (John Donne, *Devotions*)

The fear of loneliness can be very real when leaving home and friends, and one of the claims made in favour of organized races and rallies (see Section 8A) is that they are such a good way to meet other long distance sailors. While this is undoubtedly true, it rather overlooks the fact that most cruising yachtsmen are by nature friendly people with plenty of time to stop and chat, and an opening remark such as 'What an attractive boat', 'I do admire your varnishwork', or 'Didn't we see you in so-and-so' is usually enough to get a conversation going. On arrival in a new anchorage I make a point of talking to at least one yacht in passing each time I row ashore — those of us who rely on oars rather than an outboard have a very obvious advantage here — and have made many new friends this way.

It's well worth keeping a visitors' book, whether formal or simply a few pages at the back of the log. Not only is it fun to look back on after the cruise is ended, but a quick glance at signing time will often bring to light mutual friends, enabling one to keep track of people not seen for weeks or months. Of course entry into every new anchorage brings the question 'I wonder who's already here?', and for those on their second or third long cruise there is always the possible bonus of finding a yacht last met with several years before.

It very often happens that yachts of similar size find themselves progressing at much the same speed, and it's only a matter of time before arrangements are made to cruise in company or meet in such-and-such a place for supper. Single-handers in particular often find themselves adopted by a fully crewed yacht, while it is natural for those with children on board to keep company with young friends. By and large one meets a far wider variety of people than one ever would ashore, and far from long distance cruising being a lonely or intro-spective affair we find that the company of people of all ages, all backgrounds and all nationalities is one of the things we miss most on returning home.

Beads and mirrors — presents for local people

There will almost certainly be times during your cruise when you want to give thank-you or parting gifts to local people, and as the most appreciated are those from abroad it is a good idea to lay in a supply before leaving. Alcohol, usually whisky, was once the standby, but while it might be appropriate for a particu-larly helpful man it will be less so for his equally helpful mother or teenage son, and most non-smokers neither carry cigarettes nor would feel it right to hand them out as gifts. However two small items which are always appreciated are disposable lighters and ballpoint pens, and if you can get them with the name of your boat embossed in gold, so much the better.

Many local yacht clubs go out of their way to welcome foreign yachts, and a good coloured photo of your boat for their visitors' book will usual be appreci-ated. Of course in an extreme case the presentation of a burgee is the ultimate thank-you, but new burgees are expensive and it seems a little mean to present a very worn one.

Local children often come and ask for hand outs, frequently in the guise of 'for my collection'. Postcards of typical home scenes — maybe a view of your harbor — are a perennial favourite, and you may even be given a local view in return. Foreign coins are another collectible. We were amused the first time a West Indian child asked for chocolate and pointed out that it would melt long before we could get it on board, but can usually find the odd cookie if asked politely.

I've often wished I had a Polaroid or other instant camera (known as a Now-for-Now camera in the Caribbean) with which to thank local people who have allowed me to photograph their market stalls, animals or homes, and was in-trigued to hear of a friend cruising the Pacific who takes videos of local scenes and then stages impromptu movie evenings under the palm trees, complete with bags of popcorn!

7 FEEDING AND WATERING

A. THE GALLEY

If you buy second-hand and do not contemplate a major interior refit you will have most of the decisions regarding the galley taken out of your hands, but even so the sometimes spartan facilities of older yachts can often be improved. There's generally unused space going begging in which racks for everything from mugs to spices can be fitted, and it may be possible to add false floors or otherwise break up the deep, cavernous lockers (usually placed in totally inaccessible positions right behind sink or stove) so beloved of 1960s yacht designers. It's very important that everyone who will use the galley is able to reach what they need without having to stand on tiptoe or scale the furniture, and it will certainly be worth keeping 'regular use' items such as tea, coffee, sugar, salt, pepper, packet soups and cookies in the most accessible locker available.

Along with poorly designed stowage, a second necessity desperately lacking on many older yachts is a reasonable area of work surface, some but not all of which should be protected by fiddles. It's often possible to increase counter space by means of a folding extension (though hinges or other supports will need to be over-sized to provide total rigidity) and a flat chart table can be pressed into service as a bar on social occasions. We are lucky on *Wrestler* in having an engine step some two feet square and exactly the right height for food preparation forming part of the companionway. Although we always take care to use a chopping board (much more to do with not damaging the teak and holly surface than for hygiene) the unvarnished hardwood can take hot pans straight off the stove without ill effect, while the high companionway cheeks stop anything going astray. The only essential is to warn the person in the cockpit not to step down without looking . . .

Another item which is usually sadly lacking in older boats is any provision for rubbish. Many modern designs incorporate neat swing-topped bins concealed inside locker doors, and with a little ingenuity it may be possible to fit one in an older yacht though probably at the expense of some shelf space. A simpler, and considerably cheaper, alternative is to collect all the shopping bags that come your way for several months before leaving home and install a couple of strong hooks from which to hang them — the handles make handy ties when full. In harbour or on short passages where rubbish can be disposed of ashore everything can go in the same bag, but on longer passages we separate rubbish into 'chuckable' and 'non-chuckable'. I would like to be able to say that the chuckable rubbish consists entirely of biodegradables — vegetable peelings etc — but a small yacht on passage for more than a few days simply cannot store all the empty tins, bottles and other packaging aboard, particularly in a hot climate, without becoming a mobile health hazard. Tins should be liberally punctured and bottles broken — a smart tap with a winch handle over the side or stern is the best bet — but all plastics (including emptied rubbish bags) *must* be saved for disposal ashore.

Safety

The galley is one of the potentially more dangerous areas aboard the cruising yacht. Burns and scalds are by no means unknown, and tend to centre on those less familiar with the action of a yacht at sea. The really experienced sea cook will usually be aware of violent movement a fraction of a second before it happens, gaining enough warning to steady things or at least to take evasive personal action. In cold climates there's much to be said for wearing oilskins while cooking in heavy weather, but in the tropics this is simply not feasible and about the most one can stand is a plastic apron.

Some yacht stoves may not have a rail and gimbals. Even when they do exist they may be inadequate in bad weather — ocean gales can last for days, and you can't always put off eating until it moderates. A cheap but effective version can be made from strip aluminum about 1.5in (40mm) wide, shaped to surround the entire stove-top (see Fig 10). Deep notches take slot-in clamp bars, which can be moved around according to the pans in use. Flying stoves were one of the causes of damage and injury aboard yachts in the 1979 Fastnet Race, and since

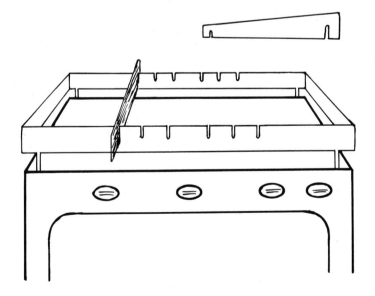

Fig 10 Slotted aluminum rail and bars around stove

then the ocean racing rules have required closed gimbals which will hold a stove in place even if the yacht should turn turtle. Remember we are discussing an angular piece of hardware probably weighing at least 40lb (18kg) so take this to heart. A bolt or wedge to lock the stove steady in harbour is also useful.

Happily I have never crashed against *Wrestler's* crash bar (I should probably break my hip) but the logic of setting a protective bar, which also makes a conveniently grabable handhold and is a great place for drying dish towels, in front of the stove is unassailable. Ours was fabricated by a local engineering workshop from 3/4in (19mm) stainless steel tube with neatly flanged ends and cost about $40, though a stainless offcut of suitable length with the ends set into hardwood blocks would doubtless have been cheaper. For maximum effectiveness it should be just at the height of the fuel valves, but not so close as to make reaching them difficult. Some cooks like a sling to provide support and leave hands free when the boat is on the 'wrong' tack. Personally I don't use one, on the basis that if something is going to jump off the stove I want to be able to leap out of the way — fast.

The cabin sole in the galley area must provide a safe non-skid surface not only when dry but also when wet or spattered with food or cooking oil. Few surfaces beat plain scrubbed teak for both grip and an ability to absorb punishment, and though softwoods may need to be painted I have never understood the fashion for varnishing cabin soles. Unless whole handfuls of grit are added — and do the crew never go barefoot? — varnish still becomes lethal when wet. Plenty of convenient handholds are also a must, and the odd angle into which an elbow can be tucked is often handy. If handholds are not already incorporated into bulkheads or other solid parts of the boat's structure, ready-made teak grab handles can be bought for less than $5 each and bolted in place where required. However, note the word 'bolted' — a flimsy or poorly attached handhold is worse than nothing at all. Rapid acceleration as the yacht falls off a wave may create a shock loading equal to several times the normal weight of an adult.

Finally both a fire extinguisher and fire blanket should be situated where they can easily be reached by the cook. Actually galley fires are quite rare with gas stoves, though much more common with kerosine, and if you do have a pan flare up it makes a lot of sense to go for the fire blanket in preference to the extinguisher. The latter makes an appalling mess and will certainly write off the rest of the meal whereas a quickly smothered pan may still have edible contents, but don't forget to TURN OFF THE GAS SUPPLY while you collect your thoughts.

Cooking fuels

For many years one of the hallmarks of the cruising yacht was her kerosene stove, and I respect the feelings of those who cite the safety angle and will cook on nothing else. However at least 90% of yachts built during the last 25 years use bottle gas systems, and for some very good reasons:

1. At one time kerosine was obtainable almost everywhere while gas refills could be difficult to find. Now that bottled gas is the norm for cooking ashore in much of the world the scales have tipped the other way. Incidentally, in southern Europe and the Atlantic islands kerosine comes in two grades — high grade from the chemists, which is much too pricey for cooking, and low grade from service stations which will cover the deckhead with soot.
2. Even devotees of kerosine stoves admit they are fiddly to operate. Pricking, priming with alcohol, keeping the pressure pumped up — all are things one can do without when the motion is lively.
3. From the safety angle, we all know the dangers of bottled gas but neither is kerosine immune. While it does not explode, one lapse of concentration and it can flare most alarmingly. I have spoken to four people who have experienced serious kerosine fires, but have yet to meet anyone who has suffered a gas explosion aboard or even witnessed one first-hand on another boat.

The ultimate in safe fuels is undoubtedly alcohol, which does not need to be pressurized but is both expensive and desperately slow. In any event, a good alcohol stove is the Origo, which may be had in various sizes from a single burner at $120 to a two-burner with oven at $700.

Bottled gas safety

Even though explosions aboard yachts are rare, one can't overstress the need for safety precautions. Being heavier than air, any escaped gas will collect in the bilges, and though one may normally expect to recognize the distinctive 'rotten cabbage' smell, this is added artificially and in some countries gas can be virtually odorless. Various types of gas sniffer are available, from the basic detector unit with audible alarm at around $40 to the sophisticated system with audio/visual alarm and automatic gas shut-off valve at $160 or so. However all need sensors installed low down in the bilge to do their job properly, and although these units are advertised as splashproof nearly all specify that they 'must not be immersed'. Sooner or later your bilges are likely to fill at least partially, but however innocent the cause it will not only write off the gas detector but also leave you confidently relying on a safety device which is no longer operational.

All newer yachts have self-enclosed gas bottle lockers which vent overboard, but in practice this is very seldom the part of the installation where leaks actually occur; far more often the stove is to blame, either due to a blown out flame or through a valve being turned on by accident (easier than it might sound, though a crash-bar at valve height helps). The only truly reliable way of keeping gas where it is supposed to be is to have the bottles readily accessible, and *turn them off* when not in use. The fact that this method also happens to come for free is a bonus.

Aboard *Wrestler* the bottles sit in an ordinary cockpit locker which drains into the bilges — frowned upon now, though standard in 1968 when she was classed 100A1 at Lloyd's. However this is more than compensated for by the fact that the cook can reach them through a small access hatch in the back of the galley, and it has become second nature to turn the gas ON at the bottle only seconds before striking the match, and turn it OFF again immediately after turning off the flame — even before pouring the kettle. Any looseness in the fitting of regulator hose to the cylinder would also be felt immediately. If you have to go out into the cockpit to reach your cylinders I would strongly advise fitting a ball valve with right-angled shut-off handle where the piping enters the yacht's interior, for use on those occasions when the gas will be wanted again in a few minutes and would otherwise inevitably be left on.

Standard practice in most cruising areas outside Western Europe is for cylinders to be refilled rather than exchanged (Camping Gaz in the French West Indies is an exception) so make a point of setting off with bottles which are in good condition. Refills usually take two or three days, and in most places gas is cheaper than it would be at home. In warm climates cylinders should not be filled to more than 70% capacity to allow for heat expansion, so take this into account when citing how long your gas supply should last. (In practice we have found that the higher ambient temperature generally compensates for slightly less gas.)

Butane and propane

Life is considerably complicated by the fact that a foreign cruise may take you from a propane area at home to a butane area in the Azores or Europe and then back to propane. I am indebted to Jonathan Barker of Calor Gas Ltd* for much of the following information. (There's an excellent section on bottled gas in Nigel Calder's *Boatowner's Mechanical and Electrical Manual*; International Marine.)

Briefly, the complete installation consists of four parts — gas, cylinder, regulator and appliance, plus connecting pipework. Most appliances (in this case the stove, though it could also be a cabin or water heater) are approved for use with both butane and propane, and careful examination will generally bring to light a manufacturer's plate confirming this. Pipework standards are also identical, leaving only the cylinder and regulator not interchangeable between the two types of gas.

It cannot be stressed too strongly that butane cylinders must *never* be filled with propane, which is stored at considerably higher pressure. Propane cylinders (usually red) have pressure release valves; smaller butane cylinders (usually blue) do not, while release valves on the larger butane cylinders will be set to the wrong pressure for propane. Ignore this and you risk an explosion on board. The brighter side of the coin is that butane cylinders can be directly exchanged for propane ones before departure (my local Calor Gas supplier told me that they are often in short supply, so several weeks' notice is advisable) and that a propane regulator is relatively inexpensive at around the $15 mark, depending on capacity. Butane and propane cylinders use very different connectors (butane has a male fitting on the regulator and corresponding female on the bottle, propane the exact opposite) so either new connectors will have to be fitted to the old cylinder/regulator connecting pipe or preferably, on the principle of not putting new wine in old bottles, the whole lot should be replaced.

Approved LPG hose can either be bought ready made up complete with end fittings, or by the metre with the fittings separate.

Ideally one should set off with propane cylinders (which will of course be filled with propane) connected to a propane regulator, but with a butane regulator in reserve. If gas bottles need to be refilled before crossing the Atlantic you can be fairly certain of receiving butane, and though at a pinch this can be run through a propane regulator the result will be more gas of a higher calorific value arriving at the burners than they were intended to handle, which can produce flame 'lift off' with the resulting unburnt gas ending up in the bilge. Far better to take the trouble to replace the old propane regulator with the new butane one, swopping the hose fittings around as necessary, before returning to the propane regulator on reaching the Caribbean. $15 spent before leaving, plus a few minutes fiddling with connectors from time to time, is vastly preferable to going up in flames.

So much for Calor Gas, but what about yachts built to take Camping Gaz cylinders? Here there is a greater problem, as Camping Gaz has no direct propane equivalent and few lockers intended for the standard 1.9kg Camping Gaz bottles are large enough to take the 4.5kg Calor butane or 3.9kg propane cylinders (which are the same size). Primus end fittings are quite different from those of other makes, and it might be difficult to get bottles refilled abroad. The problem of fitting bottles to the source of supply does in any case crop up from time to time, particularly in less frequented cruising grounds, so it's well worth carrying a selection of end fittings and joints for production if necessary. Any yacht fitted with gas which plans to spend much time in France or the Mediterranean would be well advised to add at least one Camping Gaz cylinder plus the appropriate regulator and connectors to the armory, as there are many areas in Europe where Camping Gaz exchanges are routine but getting even butane bottles refilled will prove next to impossible.

Stoves and other equipment

The most important single item of galley equipment is the stove itself, and I have already remarked that I consider a gimballed stove with oven to be a high priority for long-term living aboard. This may present a problem if buying an older yacht, since in the 1960s ovens were seldom fitted as standard in boats under 35ft (10.8m) or so and a galley intended for two burners is unlikely to provide room for an oven to gimbal. A standard two-burner and oven affair such as the Force Ten Gourmet costs around $600, and measures 22in high by 20.5in wide by 14.6in deep. Apart from the obvious advantage of being able to bake bread or scones we find tinned pies a marvellous convenience food in bad weather, while the occasional roast chicken is a relatively inexpensive luxury. Various stove-top oven substitutes are available, but I have yet to meet one which I could recommend.

There's a lot to be said for carrying some form of reserve cooking apparatus, should you encounter problems either with getting gas cylinders refilled or with the stove itself. A small one-burner kerosine stove such as the Force Ten FTP-201D, at about $65, will keep you in tea or coffee and simple meals and might be useful for the occasional picnic. Alternatively the one burner alcohol Ovigo at about $90 might make sense for a back-up. Another idea is the one-burner, self-contained, propane-canister Seacook gimballed stove that mounts on a bulkhead bracket. This also makes a good heavy-weather stove. Cost: $110 and $15 for a second bracket. The latest in galley equipment is the 12 volt Microwave. However it looks like being a long time before they reach the budget market, so worrying about where to fit one, or the amount of power they consume can be left to others. Defender Industries* has a wide selection of stoves.

Whatever kind of stove or oven you use, make an effort to keep it clean but *never, never* wash it with salt water. This is a quick way to become the owner of a heap of useless rust. The average stove can be stripped down a long way without recourse to screwdriver or wrench and an occasional thorough scrub on the dockside will improve its appearance, but it's more important to wipe up spots and spillages as they occur, particularly if the burners themselves are affected. Carry an aluminum baking tray with a deep rim to catch possible overflows inside the oven (relatively firm pies often become much more liquid as they heat up) and be careful not to chip the enamel or once again rust will creep in.

Most galley equipment lists include implements I've never even heard of. I work on the basis that you'll probably want much the same tools aboard as at home, though one exception to this is the old-fashioned mincer, totally superseded ashore by electric food processors but still of occasional use aboard (among other things it's about the only other way to make a decent gazpacho soup). Another heavyweight item I would not wish to be without is a pressure cooker, as much for its solid clamp-on lid as its fast cooking abilities, though these can be useful for producing economical bean stews or reducing cheap local meat to an edible consistency. Cooking at high pressure should be avoided in heavy seas, as too much movement will cause it to blow off steam like the *Flying Scot*, waking those off watch and covering the deckhead with a fine spray of masticated contents. Those unfamiliar with pressure cookers should experiment at home or in harbour first, being very careful to follow the instructions regarding minimum liquid quantities.

Refrigerator, ice-box or warm beer?

Having cruised *Wrestler* in the tropics both with and without a means of keeping food and drink cold, I can confirm that not only is a refrigerator or icebox a very pleasant luxury but should actually save you money. This is particularly true of a boat with only two people aboard, since food is usually sold in packets intended for four or more people and unless you can find another yacht willing to split a purchase the spoilage rate will be high. On several occasions during our 1984/5 cruise we experienced problems with fish or meat bought in the early morning market being of questionable freshness by evening. The second possible saving comes from the fact that most people are partial to a cold drink from time to time, and in many areas this will cost three or four times as much if bought in a bar ashore than if purchased in bulk in the local supermarket for consumption on board. Time after time during our 1987/8 cruise, by which time I had constructed a small but well insulated ice-box, we were able to resist the high prices ashore in the knowledge that a cold beer awaited each of us in the ice-box on board.

Both refrigerators and ice-boxes have their drawbacks, of course. Few refrigerators are designed to cope with the high ambient temperatures of the tropics, most are poorly insulated, and current drain will be high — typically 3 to 4.5 amps. Neither are they cheap, generally starting around the $400 mark. The only really cheap model on the market appears to be the small portable Koolatrons sold by Defender Industries from $65 for a 7qt size to $200 for a 36qt, but continuous use in a tropical climate would inevitably put a severe strain on the cooling mechanism. Like all other electrical equipment that finds its way aboard, a refrigerator may fail, particularly if allowed to come in contact with too much salt, but the more likely problem is keeping it supplied with power. A 3 amp drain, even if intermittent, is more than the average battery bank will be able to handle without either regular charging via the main engine, which gets expensive in diesel, or help from wind or solar power, themselves costly options.

The dependence on finding ice is the chief and obvious disadvantage of the foolproof ice-box, together with the fact that ice, where available, may sometimes be expensive. It tends to come in two types: ice-box quality, ie rather dirty, which one can often beg either free or at nominal cost from fish-processing plants; or drinks quality, which comes as either cubes or a block and can cost up to $2 for a 3lb (1.4kg) bag. The first type is more common on the European side of the Atlantic, while the American influence is to be seen in the Caribbean where ice cubes can often be bought from garages as well as supermarkets, marinas and fuelling docks. Another possibility is to arrange for a local person to make some for you in their freezer.

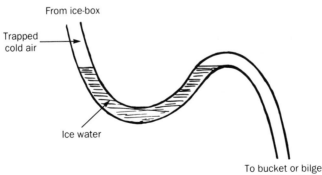

Fig 11 Reverse swan neck

Weight for weight block ice will last much longer than cubes, but what really makes the difference is the amount of insulation around the box and the care taken of the ice itself. If building an ice-box into an existing locker — *Wrestler's* is in the chart table seat — think in terms of a minimum of 4in (102mm) insulation and preferably 6in (152mm). The closed-cell insulation board sold by builders' merchants and intended for lofts and garages is best for the job though expanded polystyrene sheeting will do at a pinch, with the interior box either built of plywood and coated with epoxy resin to make it watertight or actually moulded from glassfibre using a male mould. While calculating insulation and interior capacity take care to allow for the lid, which should be just as thick as the box itself and have a good seal to keep the cold air in. Lastly do not forget that water, even cold water, is a much better heat conductor than air and that your ice will last noticeably longer if the box drains efficiently. Ours has a small flexible tube which either drains into a basin or directly into the bilge, and ideally this should incorporate a reverse swan-neck (see Fig 11) to prevent the chilled air also draining away. Each time the box is opened the life of the ice will be reduced, but we have found that even in the tropics a 3lb bag can be made to last up to 60 hours with a little care, and far longer in a cooler climate.

Fresh water and tankage

> Water, water, every where,
> And all the boards did shrink,
> Water, water, every where.
> Nor any drop to drink.
>
> (Samuel Taylor Coleridge, *The Rhyme of the
> Ancient Mariner*)

Carrying sufficient fresh water on long passages has long been a problem for the smaller yacht. We have found the oft-quoted figure of 'half a gallon per person per day' (about 4.5 litres per day for two) to be generous in northern climates but insufficient in hotter areas unless supplemented by plenty of other liquid such as beer or soft drinks, even without allowing for the most basic of washing. Remember when calculating water supply to allow a safety factor of at least half as long again as the passage is expected to take, in case of calms, or delays caused by sail, rigging or mechanical failures.

Integral tanks can and certainly should be supplemented by plenty of smaller containers; not only does this provide a reserve supply but could be vital should the main tank become contaminated or the boat have to be abandoned. (Don't fill spare cans quite full so that they will float in an emergency.) We prefer 5 litre (1 gallon) cans to larger sizes, and have collected a dozen or so free from bars and restaurants who get them filled with soft drink concentrates. Coming alongside to fill water tanks is not always possible abroad and we have sometimes walked a mile or more with a couple of cans each, looking for a tap when supplies had run low. On other occasions there may be a handy water supply convenient to the dinghy landing, when a dozen cans can be filled in one ferry-load. Apart from other considerations, water from a public tap ashore is generally free, whereas filling water tanks while alongside taking on fuel will often be charged for.

Few smaller yachts boast pressure water systems, but if yours is one of them you *must* fit a manual pump for back-up. Not only are electric pumps one more thing to fail, but they are inevitably wasteful of water and often noisy enough to wake anyone who may be asleep (knowing the frequency with which cups of coffee or soup tend to be consumed during night watches this may be more important than it sounds). If we had a pressure system aboard I would seriously consider keeping it permanently turned off at sea, certainly on longer passages.

Any fresh water hose which has been unused for a while should be run for long enough to clear away water which may have been sitting in it, and always check for quality before adding local water to the tanks. In some areas — the island of Porto Santo off Madeira is a prime example — the tapwater is distinctly brackish, while in others it may be heavily laced with chlorine. Some people like to add chemicals in the name of purity, but personally I cannot stand the taste and until one of us actually goes down with a bug which can be traced directly to the water supply we shall continue to drink our water unadulterated.

We are lucky that *Wrestler*'s main tank has large inspection hatches, and on the occasions when the tapwater has started to taste a bit musty close inspection usually reveals a fine crop of algae on the inside. For those who do not have access to the interior of their tanks with a scrubbing brush I am told that the bottle-cleaning products sold for home wine-makers work well and do not leave a residual taste provided the tank is flushed out thoroughly. If you are genuinely worried about water quality, boiling for ten minutes will kill all germs and bacteria but will do nothing to get rid of chemical impurities. Ice bought ashore will certainly be made from local tapwater, and freezing doesn't kill many bugs. Very often the best, and cheapest, water is that which comes straight out of the sky, when a good awning comes into its own not just to keep you dry but also as your own personal catchment area (see Section 6C). The first few gallons may be a little dusty and should be collected separately for washing (marvellous for hair!), after which the hoses can be fed directly into the water tank. During the deluge depicted in Photo 11 we collected something over 20 gallons (91 litres) in less than half an hour.

B. FOOD: YOUR LARGEST REGULAR EXPENSE

Eating habits

> How good one feels when one is full — how
> satisfied with ourselves and with the world!
> People who have tried it tell me that a clear
> conscience makes you very happy and con-

tented; but a full stomach does the business
quite as well, and is cheaper, and more easily
obtained . . .

(Jerome K. Jerome, Three Men in a Boat)

Few events in the sailing day are as directly influenced by individual shorebased habit as mealtimes. Though the majority of larger crews stick to the usual two or three meals a day at much the same times as at home, many couples and probably most singlehanders appear to eat only one main meal each day, supplemented by numerous snacks — very often a style of eating they also favour ashore. Couples or established crews who are already familiar with each other's eating habits should have no problems here, but assembled crews may need a few house rules so that the cheese earmarked for the next day's lunch does not become someone's midnight feast in the meantime.

As most calculations of quantity are based on the 'x people for x meals for x days' basis, the first thing is to establish how many meals you will expect to eat each day and the types of food that will be consumed at each meal. Will you and/or your crew expect a cooked breakfast? This will obviously have a bearing on the egg calculations and probably those for tomatoes and baked beans, while extra tins of cold meat will need to be included for consumption after the fresh bacon or ham runs out. Whether you prefer your main meal at lunchtime or in the evening will not affect the catering too much, but a preference for cooked puddings over fresh fruit certainly will. Most cruising yachtsmen take pleasure in sampling regional produce, and if buying something unfamiliar in the market I never hesitate to ask one of the local women how best to cook it — certainly flexibility in diet makes for economy as well as variety. However if you simply must start your day with a particular brand of cereal take this into account when storing up, and of course any allergies or specific dietary needs must also be catered for.

Calculating quantities

There are few places visited by the cruising yacht where food is cheaper than in the U.S., or where the variety is better. Thus it makes good financial sense to stock up with as much as the boat can reasonably carry before leaving home, where one has the advantage of familiar shops and brands and probably the use of a car. Most supermarkets will sell whole cases if warned in advance and it's certainly worth enquiring about discounts, though prepare to be disappointed. In fact buying by the case is seldom worthwhile for two, the exceptions tending to be ingredients rather than main items — canned tomatoes and meats are possible examples. Unfamiliar brands should always be tried out before buying in bulk — corned beef in particular varies dramatically from the excellent to the quite inedible. One thing the budget cook cannot afford is wastage, whether it stems from buying twelve cans of 'X Brand' stewed steak which the crew refuse to eat even when curried, or giant tins of baked beans which begin to

Photo 11 Tropical rain cascades off *Wrestler*'s awning into a strategically placed basin. It was falling too fast for the small diameter drain pipes to cope with, and on this occasion we collected over 20 gallons (91 litres) of free water in under half an hour.

bubble and grow scientific cultures before they can be finished. Notes on individual items and the storage of perishables follow in the next section.

It's well worth appointing a chief caterer with responsibility for buying stores both before leaving and *en route*, stowing them, and keeping a tally as they are used; a good book devoted to this subject alone is worthwhile. This becomes even more important if cooking duties are shared, and yet more so again if the original storing-up was done with one eye on the checkout cash register. Whether the caterer chooses to draw up actual menus for each day of a passage and then buy exactly what they will require (impractical unless one person is doing all the cooking), or prefers to lay in calculated amounts of meat/fish/eggs/ cheese, vegetables and potatoes/pasta/rice for main meals, plus fruit, cereals, crispbreads, etc for lesser meals, will vary according to individual choice and how the cooking roster will be organized.

A generous margin for an unexpectedly long passage must be included whatever method is used. One of the more practical formulas is: one-third extra of non-perishable stores (ie cans and freeze-dried foods), one-third extra of boring but cheaper items (ie rice, dried vegetables and grains, supplemented by a few cans) and one-third extra of 'subsistence' foods (mostly grains and beans plus herbs and other flavourings). The only problem here is that the last third need most water for preparation, at just the time when this may also be in short supply. In extremis, a healthy adult can live for several weeks without food with no long-term ill effects, and should you lose the mast or otherwise anticipate a much longer passage than expected, your first thoughts should be of your water supply. High protein foods require more liquid for digestion than carbohydrates, but cooking water (provided it is not heavily salted) can either be saved for re-use or become the basis for soups and stews.

Unless the yacht is equipped with a freezer (hardly in the budget bracket) the actual food consumed on a long passage will obviously be limited by the 'keeping' factor, but the importance of variety and particularly the occasional surprise treat must not be forgotten. Pride of place here goes to the friend who amazed his crew of five by making a delicious lemon meringue pie, from scratch, half way across the Atlantic. His wife swore he never cooked at home — he said he'd never had time before.

Sailing cookbooks vary in their relevance to ocean sailing, let alone to ocean sailing on a budget. Like any other cookery book they tend to be written by people who take their food seriously, are willing to pay for the best, and perhaps genuinely do start their weekly shopping list with: 'Artichoke hearts, asparagus . . .' forgetting that for many of us these are the sort of snack encountered about twice a year, usually provided by somebody else. However, there are a few books which do cover catering, storage and cooking on long passages in a sensible way. Maralyn Bailey's *The Galley Handbook* (Nautical Publishing) is probably the most useful, particularly regarding unfamiliar fruits and vegetables. Unfortunately it has long been out of print, but is worth looking for in second-hand bookshops. A good book that is available is *The Care and Feeding of the Offshore Crew* by Lin and Larry Pardey (W.W. Norton). It's not a book of recipes, but tells you what to buy, how to store it, how to make life on board more bearable, and how to cope in foreign ports.

Provisioning and storage

> A medley of damp tins of various sizes showed
> in the gloom, exuding a mouldy odour. Faded

> legends on dissolving paper, like the remnants
> of old posters on a disused hoarding, spoke of
> soups, curries, beefs, potted meats, and other
> hidden delicacies.
>
> (Erskine Childers, *The Riddle of the Sands*)

Buying in quantity before departure generally turns into a compromise between what one would like, what one can stow, and what one can afford. The initial reaction is usually to over-cater on non-perishables on the basis that any remainders can be used after getting home, and so far as stowage space allows this makes good sense. The problems arise with dated stores such as dried milk which goes stale in time, further complicated by the fact that most people will buy fresh whenever it's available. Any form of wastage is anathema to the budget caterer, who is left in the unenviable position of either buying short and possibly having to ration the more popular and expensive foodstuffs, or over-estimating and if necessary throwing stale food away.

The chances are that if you're sailing on a budget you're already used to eating cheaper foods and are fully aware of the value of pastas, grains, beans and other relatively low-cost bulk items. Fortunately these are readily available almost everywhere, so stocking up can be confined to things which are either markedly cheaper, better quality or only available at home.

Canned foods

While canned cold meats such as corned beef, ham and Spam are available pretty well everywhere, you may not be able to replenish stocks of 'cooking' meats such as stewed steak or minced beef outside the U.S. Only canned frankfurters appear to be widely stocked (and many would dispute whether these qualify as meat anyway). Canned fruit and vegetables are generally available even when the fresh equivalents are growing outside. The same is true of canned fish, with heaped stacks of tuna and sardines in Iberian countries, often at very low prices.

A 'blown' can is fairly unmistakeable — usually rusty, distended at the ends, and if not already leaking there will be a distinct hiss on piercing it with the opener. Blown cans can harbor botulism and all kinds of other nasties, and should be consigned to the deep without hesitation. Along with canned desserts, we have found acid fruits such as pineapple, apricots and tomatoes to be poor long-term keepers, while fish and meat are among the best. Experience seems to confirm that varnishing cans really does improve their survival qualities. Before our departure in 1984 we varnished all our cans and lost very few. Time was shorter in 1987 and they were stowed as is, with a noticeably higher failure rate. In both cases paper labels were removed and the contents marked on the top with indelible pen.

We no longer bother with canned butter when sailing in hot climates. The problem is not so much the quality or even the price, but the fact that once opened it keeps no better than ordinary butter (the same is true of long-life milk). This would be less of a problem for a large crew or a yacht with a refrigerator or freezer, but the budget boat equipped only with an icebox is trapped by logic — if you can buy ice you can almost certainly also buy fresh butter; if you are away from an ice supply then butter, fresh or canned, will turn into oil within hours. An alternative to buying canned butter is to preserve your own in smaller quantities. Wash glass jars in very hot water, cool, and either pack as solidly as possible with fresh butter, topping off with a layer of salt at least 1/4in (6mm) thick, or drop individual scoops of butter into the jar and then submerge it in brine (*clean* seawater is fine), screwing the lid on so that no air is trapped inside. We have had mixed results with both these methods, but they do seem reliable for at least a month or six weeks.

Margarine keeps much more readily than butter; large tubs will remain good for many months if stowed in the bilges and only disturbed in order to refill the ready-use pot. Incidentally there's a handy trick for measuring out margarine when baking, assuming you don't carry scales but do have a graduated measuring jug — displacement: 4oz of margarine will displace near enough 4oz of water, making it rise that much higher inside the jug.

Bottles and jars

These seldom contain staple foods, more often being employed for 'extras' such as jam, honey or marmalade, savoury pastes and patés, ketchup, mayonnaise, pickles and other sauces, as well as herbs and spices. At one stage we tried to enforce a total ban on glass containers, but as many foods will not keep indefinitely after opening and are only supplied in glass bottles this proved impractical.

Cooking oil is generally sold in plastic bottles, and though I have come across a few cooks who buy it in gallon cans to decant as necessary, I personally feel this is not a worthwhile economy for the small crew. One good spillage and any savings are not only lost but will form a lethal slippery patch for months afterwards.

Dry stores

The most obvious in terms of carrying from home are tea and coffee, plus cocoa if you drink it. Though you can buy ground coffee in most places it's usually either expensive or of inferior quality, while straightforward tea (without added rosehips, lemon grass or other exotic additions) is seldom available, let alone in bags. Instant coffee, if available at all, is often very expensive. Fortunately all lend themselves to fairly accurate quantity estimation, though laying in enough ground coffee for a one-year cruise is distinctly pricey.

Rice, pasta and flour are available pretty well everywhere, often forming the basis of the local diet. Quality seems to have improved markedly since the early 1970s, and today one seldom finds weevils or other intruders as was once standard. If you do find that something else has got to your stores first don't throw them overboard — some advice on coping with invasions follows in a few pages.

Perishables

Storage of hard fruit and vegetables is mainly common sense, and if care is taken most will keep for weeks or even months *provided they have never been chilled.* This is likely to be more of a problem in 'civilized' areas than in local markets — I work on the basis that the larger the shop, the more likely they are to buy in bulk and the higher the chance of refrigeration somewhere along the line. The only place I have encountered where it was virtually impossible to buy non-chilled fruit and vegetables was Bermuda. All fruit and vegetables *must* be dry for long-term storage, but there's much to be said for rinsing before departure — at the very least, it will help get rid of fly or cockroach eggs, should they be present. Scrubbing 20lb of potatoes under a dockside tap and laying them out to dry in the shade of the awning is much less effort than cleaning them in ones and twos as needed, and will do great things for the caterer's halo in bad weather or when others are doing the actual cooking.

Soft fruit and vegetables present more of a problem. In theory careful selection, from more than one source if necessary, should provide a range of ripeness from rock hard to almost ready which will keep delicacies such as tomatoes, mangoes and avocados on the menu for most of the passage. In practice one tends to swoop from none at all to surfeit and back again, and there's absolutely nothing to be done except tuck in and enjoy. That stalk of bananas on the backstay, long one of the hallmarks of the true cruising yacht, is probably the worst offender. They will all ripen at once (those which aren't ruined by too much salt water), severely testing the cook's resources — banana bread, banana cake, banana kebabs, banana chutney *et al* — not to speak of the crews' stomachs. If you want your bananas to ripen at intervals by all means tie them to the backstay for a photograph, but then separate the hands and keep them below, only bringing them out one at a time to ripen in the sunshine.

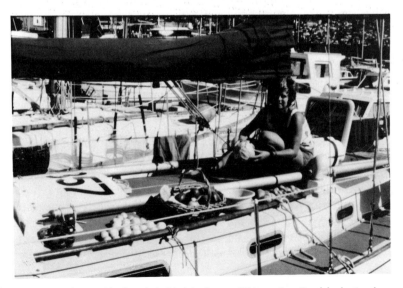

Photo 12 Fruit and vegetables bought in Madeira for our 1984 crossing. Careful selection from market stalls — more than one if necessary — should produce a stock which will ripen at intervals during the passage.

Careful inspection of all fruit and vegetables at regular intervals is essential if wastage is to be kept to a minimum. If one piece begins to go bad it will quickly infect its neighbours and the rot will spread like wildfire. Individual wrapping in paper is one solution, but has the disadvantage that inspection is much more difficult and therefore less likely to be attended to. Better to get into the habit of checking over the entire stock whenever you want just one – often only a small part will show signs of decay and you can make use of the remainder.

Eggs cannot legally be chilled in EC countries, but for long-term keeping they should not have been washed either. Try your local free range farm. If you have no alternative other than to buy them chilled, allow them to warm up to cabin temperature with the boxes open, drying them at intervals as condensation forms. If stored damp the shells will soon grow mouldy and while the egg itself may not be bad it will certainly taste odd. We have never bothered with flash-boiling or vaselining eggs; this is only to prevent the top of the shell drying out and letting in oxygen, which then allows the egg to go bad more quickly. Turning twice a week has exactly the same effect, is much less effort and costs nothing. After a month or more the eggs may begin to taste a little stale, but they will still be fine for pancakes or baking. There is a world of difference between a stale egg and a bad egg – the latter can be tested by immersion in fresh water (a bad egg floats, good ones sink) but I find it easier to break each egg into a cup, ready to chuck hurriedly if it fails the nose test.

Non-consumables

It's usually simplest to include housekeeping stores with general provisioning. Principal among these are toilet paper, paper towels, detergent and washing powder, but general cleaners, bleach, disinfectant and head cleaners (being careful what you use on a marine toilet with neoprene gaskets) are all likely to be called upon from time to time. Locally made toilet paper is not always up to scratch, while imports are usually expensive. Life aboard will be miserable if any of these basic stores is rationed, or even worse runs out.

A specimen stores list

As is obvious from the preceding sections, this list of long-term edible stores carried aboard *Wrestler* on leaving Falmouth in August 1984 at the start of our first one-year Atlantic circuit can only reflect our own tastes and eating habits – light breakfast, snack lunch, and cooked evening meal followed by a dessert or more often fruit. Unfortunately I have no complete record of the stores we loaded before leaving in 1987, but other than learning that there's no point in loading up with pasta if you'll be visiting Spanish territory, and that you can buy white flour (but not wholemeal) almost anywhere, it probably differed little.

Cans		Dry stores	
Cold meats	18	Dried milk	190pt
Cooking meats	28	Filter coffee	24lb

Frankfurters	6	Instant coffee	8lb
Meat pies	14	Tea bags	320lb
Chicken pies	6	Chocolate powder	1 tin
Fish	18	White sugar	3lb
Vegetables	14	Brown sugar	3lb
Tomatoes	32	White flour	6lb
Pasta	6	Brown flour	12lb
Fruit	24	Oats	2lb
Fruit pie filling	5	Cornflour	2 pkt
Sponge puddings	4	Yeast	3 boxes
		Rice	14lb
Bottles, jars etc		Pasta	6lb
Fruit squash	4	Dried fruit	2lb
Jam	7	Soya beans	3lb
Marmalade	3	Dried peas	4 pkt
Honey	1	Dried onion	1 pkt
Golden Syrup	1	Oxo cubes	1 pkt
Bovril	3	Instant soups	60 cups
Marmite	1	Dried meals (2 person)	6
Paste & paté (assorted)	8	Stuffing mix	2 pkt
Cheese spread	6	Breadsauce mix	2 pkt
Margarine	9lb	Breadcrumbs	2 pkt
Chutney	2	Parmesan cheese	4 drums
Sweet pickle	3	Curry powder	1 pkt
Mustard	1	Assorted herbs, spices & seasonings	
Ketchup	12	Savoury cookies	20 pkt
Mayonnaise	2	Sweet cookies	10 pkt
Salad dressing	3	Wrapped chocolate cookies	10 pkt
Jif lemon	2	Cakes	3
Cooking oil	4pt	Boiled sweets	lots!

Living off the land and fishing for food

Unfortunately no means of feeding for free should ever be relied upon. So far as local produce is concerned one has no more right to take fruit off a tree in a foreign country than one would have to enter an orchard at home and start picking apples. The tiny minority of yachtsmen (seldom British, I might add) who used to shoot goats and other domestic animals in the Caribbean and Pacific did vast harm to friendly relations, not least because a small herd of goats might well be a family's sole possession of value.

Living off the land in the more general sense of buying what is available locally is quite different of course, and an excellent way to keep food costs down. However, few people who are accustomed to European or American food would be satisfied for long with a diet of sweet potato, breadfruit and yams, even if their digestive systems did not rebel. As a general rule locally grown fruit and vegetables are cheaper where rainfall is plentiful, outside tourist areas and in temperate climates; if you want inexpensive local food stick to mainland Europe or the islands of the eastern Atlantic, though parts of the eastern seaboard of America are also relatively cheap, while Venezuela has a reputation for offering extremely good value in food as well as fuel. Much of the Caribbean is horrifically expensive as far as locally-grown produce is concerned, particularly in the case of the more exotic tropical fruits. Many of the islands are relatively dry, and an insatiable demand from hotels and charter boats catering for high-paying guests has forced prices up astronomically.

Fishing is a resource that we have never managed to tap consistently. True, we have landed the occasional fish, usually when close to land, but unlike some yachts have had no success at all with ocean fishing. I strongly suspect there is more skill involved than is immediately apparent, and most of the crews we have met who regarded fresh fish as a regular part of the diet turned out to include at least one keen fisherman among their number. In addition they often sported a serious looking rod nested in a holster on the pushpit, the price of which would have kept us in food for months. By all means equip yourself with a heavyweight trolling line and from time to time you will probably be rewarded, but don't rely on catching fish as a necessary part of your food supply.

Hospitality and alcohol

> I entertained on a cruising trip that was such
> fun that I had to sink my yacht to make my
> guests go home.
>
> (F. Scott Fitzgerald, *Notebooks*)

The cruising lifestyle is nothing if not sociable, particularly in warmer climates where the sun sets early, but providing drinks and nibbles to accompany an evening's conversation can be a drain on the cruising budget, particularly if one clings to shorebound habits. 'When in Rome drink what the Romans drink' was never more true. Some larger yachts take on bonded stores before leaving, but these are available in relatively few major ports and usually come only by the unmixed case, which presents a major stowage problem for the smaller boat. Mixers are also bulky to carry and expensive abroad, while the appeal of a gin and tonic drops sharply when served at blood temperature. Incidentally it is considered very bad manners in blue water cruising circles to ask your host for spirits, and in particular whisky, unless they're specifically offered.

In certain areas, including much of southern Europe and the Mediterranean, wines and beer are cheap. If a specialty such as sherry, madeira or port is produced locally there may be free tasting sessions (though I always feel duty bound to buy a bottle — a fine excuse!) and in the Caribbean rum is, of course, the staple. Even the best brands are seldom more than $5 per bottle, and a little goes a fairly long way where punch is concerned. The memory of some particularly nasty concoctions on various yachts prompts me to include the following classic recipe:

> 'One of sour, two of sweet,
> Three of strong and four of weak.'

('Sour' is freshly squeezed lime juice, 'sweet' is sugar syrup made by boiling a cup of sugar with two cups of water, 'strong' is golden rum, and 'weak' is water, ice or a combination.) This makes a delicious but pretty potent drink, so refills are best watered down if you want everyone to get home safely. For true authenticity, grate some fresh nutmeg onto the top of each glass.

Beer is expensive in the Caribbean even when bought by the case, and at least three times as much when served chilled in a glass. The truly budget conscious who also like a regular beer should stock up at duty free islands such as St Barts and St Maarten and then ration the supply. We made six cases of twenty-four 9oz cans last the two of us from St Barts in late March all the way to the Azores in early July, but not without considerable self discipline.

Regarding nibbles, the familiar potato and corn-based varieties tend to be expensive, sometimes stale, and in the case of peanuts all too often bug-infested. Good old American popcorn makes an excellent cheap substitute, with the advantage that it could hardly be more compact to carry.

Some skippers run a totally dry ship at sea though most allow a beer with lunch and a limited happy hour in the evening, but everyone should be aware of the potential dangers of alcohol affecting balance and judgement, slowing down reaction time in a crisis and contributing to over-confidence. Never, never celebrate sighting land at the end of a long passage with anything stronger than coffee — the time to relax and pass the bottle round is after the yacht is tied up or the anchor down.

Pests and invasions

Pests — other than the human variety — come in various shapes and forms, which I mentally divide into the relatively immobile (weevils etc) and the distinctly active (cockroaches, other beetles and even rats). The former generally come on board, often as eggs, in the food in which one eventually discovers them, though fortunately not nearly so frequently as used to be the case. In the early '70s one expected to sieve locally-bought flour in southern latitudes as a matter of routine, whereas by the late '80s to find bugs looking back at you was the exception rather than the rule. We have tried various remedies such as wiping out boxes with vinegar and adding a few bay leaves to flour, but without being scientific and running a 'control' sample have never known whether the resulting absence of bugs signified a genuine success or merely a good batch in the first place.

To throw away large quantities of dry stores merely because a small, non-toxic creature has got there first is plainly uneconomic, and being a firm believer in the old adage that what the eye doesn't see the heart doesn't grieve over I firmly sieve suspect flour, wash rice (rice sinks, bugs float) and shake pasta until residents fall to the bottom. I have never quite brought myself to tap biscuits as they did in Nelson's day, but otherwise only muesli remains a real problem — either feed it to the fish or rejoice in a little extra protein.

So far as active pests are concerned, this is one occasion where the budget skipper who lies out at anchor rather than coming alongside is at a definite advantage. I cannot believe that the most active rat is going to swim out and climb an anchor chain out of choice, and though cockroaches can fly at an early stage in their development they do not come buzzing around in swarms like locusts. If you are forced to lie alongside for any length of time in a suspect area, such as an old commercial harbour where refuse and therefore probably rats abound, use an anchor to hold the boat off and fit your lines with rat-guards made from large funnels or buckets (see Fig 12).

Cockroaches have two favourite methods of embarkation — on local produce and in the cracks of cardboard boxes, particularly the corrugated variety. As a general rule we avoid bringing boxes aboard, either taking our own bags or transferring produce loose from the dinghy, but who would forgo the pleasure of local fruit and vegetables just because of the threat of a few beetles? Inspect all fresh produce carefully as it comes aboard and if in doubt leave outside in the shade for a day or two before bringing it below. Don't follow the common advice to dip everything in seawater — in my experience all you end up with is a lot of rotten food very quickly. Our main stowage for fresh fruit has always been a fine wicker basket kept in the forepeak, where the occasional extra case of beer may also be stowed until room can be found for the individual cans. It may therefore not be entirely coincidence that the only cockroach we have ever seen aboard was also in the forepeak . . .

Before you dismiss my flippancy as disregard for a problem I have never encountered, I should point out that I sailed for a year aboard a yacht with a cockroach problem which bordered on infestation — a torch flashed onto her galley surfaces at night revealed a seething sheet of bodies, and they regularly ate their way into plastic packets and storage bins. A wooden yacht with plenty of crevices in which cockroaches could hide and lay eggs, she had been in the tropics for quite a few years and even fumigation was unable to control them effec-

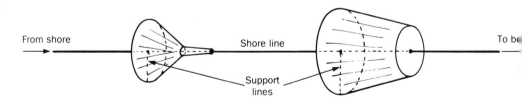

Fig 12 Simple rat guards

tively. Her owner suspected that a winter in a cold climate might do the trick, but I left before this was put to the test.

Basic preventative measures to discourage crawlies moving aboard in the first place should include scrupulous cleanliness in the galley. A good non-toxic trap for any who do make it through your defenses is Combat; it's worth positioning a few of these little black items in the odd nook and cranny. I have met various yachtsmen who swear by a light sprinkling of bicarbonate of soda, boric acid, flour laced with plaster of paris (presumably they drop like stones!) or crushed bay or laurel leaves. One resourceful singlehander had obtained a supply of the Pill, crushed them up, and fed them to his cockroach colony in the hope it would stop them breeding. Unfortunately he was headed the opposite way to us so we never heard if it was successful. The less inventive can find roach pellets in most hardware stores.

8   ON THE MOVE

A.   SETTING YOUR OWN PACE

Timing the trouble-free cruise

> To every thing there is a season, and a time to
> every purpose under the heaven . . .
>
> *(Ecclesiastes 3.1)*

However important your shorebound schedule may be — perhaps your three months' notice doesn't end until mid-October, or you need to be back by the beginning of May — don't expect sympathy from the seasons. Only yesterday I read of a young singlehander who had been picked up from his liferaft 300 miles off Land's End, his boat having sunk under him after a series of gales. He had left Plymouth in the last week of October. On 1 November I said goodbye to a friend, also heading south. She had wanted to be in England during October for the birth of a grandchild, so had sailed her Contessa 32 down to the Canaries in August and left it there. This cost my friend modest marina fees and a return air fare — leaving too late in the year cost the young man his boat and nearly his life.

The climatic information necessary for planning your cruise with regard to the changing weather patterns will be found in the various publications discussed in Section 4A. Study these early on in the planning stages, and without attempting to absorb all the detail use them as a framework around which to plan the bones of your cruise. The detail can come later.

For calculations of speed and distance, the rule of thumb for cruising yachts on ocean passages has long been 100 miles per day (fractionally over 4 knots), but this takes no account of the size and type of boat, her sail wardrobe, crew strength, experience and energy, and the amount of fuel carried. Even more important it does not take into consideration either general climatic or local weather conditions. Both *Wrestler*'s east–west trade wind transatlantics averaged out at just over 110 miles per day (4.6 knots) — about the norm for her size. Only the much larger, racier, or hard-driven average more than 125 miles per day (5.2 knots), while few except the very small cannot manage 100. However her west–east passages from the Caribbean to the Azores (the second time by way of Bermuda) were an entirely different story. Both were dogged by calms which brought averages down to around 85 miles per day (3.5 knots), and though better light-weather sails and more fuel would have boosted progress significantly, *Wrestler*, like many another budget cruising boat, tends to be short on such inessentials.

The longer the passage, the longer most people spend at their first landfall. After an east–west passage lasting three weeks or so most crews seem to need a minimum of four or five days before they feel like moving on. A shorter passage needs a shorter readjustment period. My theory is that this has little to do with recovery from the rigours of the trip (it doesn't seem to vary significantly according to conditions encountered or even the number on board) but has much to do with acclimatization to a new area, and may have more to do with miles covered than actual time spent at sea. Whatever the reason, allow for it when planning your cruising schedule.

Many novices make the mistake of attempting to cover too much ground too quickly. Not only is it generally true that the faster you go the less you see, but it also means that any delay — repairs to make good, illness, or even just waiting for mail — can throw the schedule for weeks ahead. Time in hand will allow flexibility of the 'They're holding a regatta next week? Great, let's stay' variety. Other yachtsmen may praise a spot which you had planned to miss, but travelling at a relaxed pace will probably allow you to fit it in. We were reminded of this in 1984 when Danish friends in Bayona waxed so eloquent about Lisbon (which we'd had no intention of visiting) that not only *Wrestler* but about eight other yachts immediately made it their next port of call — it stands out in my memory as one of the highlights of that cruise. Leave time for the unexpected and don't try to account in advance for every day. At first this may go against the grain if you're used to a busy working life with not only every day but every hour pre-planned, but when tempted to rush frenetically onwards remind yourself that ulcers are virtually unknown amongst cruising yachtsmen!

Races and rallies

Long distance races and group cruises have become very popular over the last few years, and fall into several distinct categories. The really serious races, such as the single and doublehanded races across the North Atlantic organized by the Royal Western Yacht Club of England, are no place for either the relative novice or the budget yachtsman — apart from other considerations, the entry fees are enormous. The Bermuda One-Two, single-handed from Newport to Bermuda and double-handed back, covers a much shorter distance with a lower entry fee to match, and if you are one of those people who loves to compete this is probably the best deep water race in which to cut your teeth. This race takes place every odd year, both boat and crew must have covered a qualifying distance before their entry is accepted, and all yachts are thoroughly inspected before the start for both seaworthiness and safety gear.

Lower down the seriousness scale the line between race and cruise is less clearly defined. The ARC rallies organized each November by Jimmy Cornell for yachts crossing from the Canaries to Barbados appear to be growing more competitive, and are increasingly geared towards the larger cruiser-racers carrying a crew of five or six who expect to hand-steer under spinnaker for days on end, rather than toward small cruising yachts of the wind-vane steering and running sails variety.

Before setting your heart on taking part in one of these organized events, weigh up the pros and cons:

1. How much is the entry fee and what does it cover? They often run into hundreds of pounds, sometimes on a sliding scale, but may include a free marina berth at start and finish and possibly small gifts such as T-shirts for the crew. (Paid-up competitors in the more serious races may also be offered discounts by manufacturers of oilskins, equipment, food etc.) Find out in advance, to avoid sitting in a marina for a week or more assuming it's already paid for only to be presented with a large bill on departure.

2. If you carry insurance, check whether the company will require an additional premium or want to increase your deductible — if you haven't notified them that you are entered in a race or competitive rally and then need to make a claim it could be disallowed. Also bear in mind that if you take the racing aspect at all seriously you will inevitably put more strain on sails and gear than if you were cruising, which will shorten their working life.

3. Accept the fact that the popular 'hold hands across the Atlantic' theme is totally unworkable in practice, and you will be as much on your own as if the race or rally did not exist. If you carry ham radio your chances of talking to other yachts will admittedly be greater than otherwise, particularly if a schedule has been organized, but this is still a relatively expensive toy and most budget yachts will only be equipped with VHF. Even with a hundred or more yachts going the same way the ocean is too vast for them to stay within VHF range for more than a couple of days, and after that any conversation or actual meeting is pure chance. Neither do all races and rallies have well organized rescue facilities, usually relying on the help of other competing yachts to augment any facilities already available.

4. Organized events generally have a strong social side and are a good way to meet people, but by no means the only one — see Section 6D. However don't assume all the associated parties or dinners will be free, and remember that even if they're not the temptation to go along will be much stronger than usual.

5. Taking part in a race or rally can bolster the confidence of the relative novice, but for the slower boat or less experienced crew it can also risk turning a potentially satisfying first ocean passage into a very disappointing race.

6. Last minute repairs and modifications are a familiar sight before the start of every long race, but for the dozens of crews who are merely occupying spare time there will always be the few who actually leave with important jobs undone. If you are setting off on your first major ocean passage a predetermined departure date is one more potential problem you simply do not need. Also, the start may be at a far from ideal time weatherwise. In northern latitudes this usually means leaving into a poor forecast or even a gale, while

at least one ARC rally started in such calm conditions that yachts were still within sight of land after thirty-six hours. Not only is this hard on the crew psychologically, but in a small yacht able to carry only limited food and water it may play havoc with the stores. Both gales and calms are part of ocean cruising, but there's no point setting off into either.

This may have painted a rather more negative picture of organized ocean crossings than I had intended, particularly as I've generally enjoyed the events in which we've taken part. However while the deadline aspect may give a useful boost at the preparation stage and additional confidence on leaving, this should be by way of a bonus, not a prop. If you and your boat are not ready to cross an ocean unaided, you're not yet ready to cross in an organized event either.

B. OFFICIALDOM

Registration and certification

The paperwork necessary to see both yacht and crew legally on their way is surprisingly simple and relatively cheap. The crew will of course need valid passports, those for the United States currently costing $42 for the 24-page version which is valid for ten years. Although passport applications are often dealt with in a few days, the process can take weeks or even months, so this is not something to put off until the last moment. Details of current visa requirements should be available from any travel agent. Again, visa applications can take time, so start the ball rolling well in advance. In a few countries you may be asked to produce individual passport-sized photographs for immigration records, so lay in a few happy snaps of the coin-operated booth variety — it will be a great deal cheaper than having them taken locally.

As far the yacht is concerned, she must either be registered in the state where she is principally used or be documented with the U.S. Coast Guard. If registered, the applicable state regulations must be complied with, of course, involving fees and the display of the boat's registration number on the outside of the hull. Federal documentation involves considerably more paperwork than does state registration and a fee of $100. The documentation number is carved into a structural member below. For a yacht that cruises widely, documentation eliminates any confusion over which is the state of principal use. The boat's registration or documentation certificate should, of course, be carried on board.

Should you be skippering a yacht which is not your own you will still need to carry her registration papers aboard, together with an original, signed letter from the owner whose name appears on them stating that you have his permission to be sailing her in a given area between certain dates. This should at the very least be typed, and if it can be on headed stationery and carry photographs of both the yacht and yourself so much the better. A couple of counter-signatures from yacht club officials or local dignitaries may not mean anything but will make it that much more impressive.

Customs and immigration

Official dignity tends to increase in inverse ratio
to the importance of the country of which the
office is held.

(Aldous Huxley, *Beyond the Mexique Bay*)

In spite of this somewhat cynical observation, officials are rarely a problem if
approached in the right way. Try standing in the line behind someone who con-
stantly has difficulties with customs or immigration, and you'll nearly always
find they bring it on themselves. Remember that not only are you a guest in the
country, but you are also on holiday (or that is the way an official will see it)
and thus have all the time in the world. Impatience will be taken as rudeness
and get you nowhere. Several male skippers I've talked to who admit that patience is not their strong point always send their wives/girlfriends ashore to
complete the formalities, and I've long suspected we women skippers of being
at an advantage — chivalry is still strong in many parts of the world and I see no
reason why we shouldn't capitalize on it.

A few remarks about how pleased you are to have reached their lovely har-
bour/island/country and what good things you've heard about it from other
yachtsmen will generally get the surliest official smiling proudly. Attempting
at least 'good morning' and 'thank you' in the local language is always appreciated, while in the Caribbean during an England cricket tour I made a habit of
asking whether any men from that island were playing for the victorious West
Indian team. Sometimes it was hard to get away!

While on the subject of clearance and immigration laws, remember that if
clearing in with crew who will be departing by air it's essential to inform the
immigration officer (who will want to see the tickets) and ensure that he makes
an appropriate note on the clearance documents. Otherwise when it's time for
the yacht to leave they have only your word that x and y really did fly out last
week, resulting at best in argument and delay and at worst in a heavy fine.

Courtesy flags

The term 'courtesy flag' is a misnomer in many countries, particularly those
newer, smaller states very aware of their own dignity. If you are not flying the
correct flag on arrival the local customs officer will almost certainly be glad to
sell you one — at a price. Many ocean cruisers make their own, varying from
carefully sewn replicas to rough affairs which owe much to indelible markers.
Coloured cotton handkerchiefs make good bases and avoid too much hemming,
while suitably coloured scraps can be appliquéd on for the designs (for a short
stay glue works pretty well). Avoid either traditional bunting or lightweight
nylon — both are brutes to sew.

It can be difficult to keep up with changes in courtesy flags. A major consti-
tutional development such as independence will almost certainly mean a new

design, but unfortunately those countries which are most insistent upon the correct flag being flown are also quite likely to alter their design every time the government changes. Neither is Britain the only nation to have different maritime and national flags. The classic work on the subject is *Flags of the World* by Captain E.M.C. Barraclough and W.G. Crampton, published by Frederick Warne in 1978 and periodically revised. Most libraries hold a reference copy, but do make sure you are looking at a reasonably recent edition. Much cheaper is the pocket-sized *Flags* by Eric Inglefield (Prentice-Hall). However thirty of the more common ensigns, including those of all European countries, are shown in *Reed's Nautical Almanac*.

While in foreign waters a yacht is required to wear an ensign which indicates her nationality. In home waters, one may choose either the national ensign (50 stars) or the yacht ensign (13 stars around a fouled anchor), but in foreign waters only the national ensign is proper. I have never understood those who apparently take pride in reducing the flag to a tattered, dirty rag. Give it the occasional wash and mend the fly when necessary, and by the time you get home it'll probably be due for retirement as a nice memento to hang in the hall.

C. KEEPING IN TOUCH

The home agent

A reliable individual has already been mentioned in Section 5B as the best way of dealing with the payment of regular bills or organizing emergency transfers of funds. For this reason they should preferably hold full Power of Attorney, which will need to be witnessed by a Notary Public. This is one of the reasons why the best home agent is often a relative or close friend, and it will also be more convenient for all concerned if most of your regular contacts are already known to them. However there's no reason why all the responsibility should fall on one person, and like many younger blue water cruisers we receive invaluable support from both our parents − Father deals with the financial aspect while Mother, in addition to writing regularly, sorts and forwards mail, fields telephone calls and even sends newspaper clippings of national and local events. Between them they seem able to locate pretty well anything we or *Wrestler* require. The only drawback to this ideal system is that it temporarily falls apart when they visit us or take off in their own boat for a week or two.

A really conscientious home agent will not only discard junk mail but, provided they have *carte blanche* to open letters, also acknowledge the urgent ones and keep a record of what has been forwarded to where, so that should a package go astray the contents are known. It is of course your responsibility before leaving to make sure that anyone who may want to contact you has your agent's address and telephone number, and it's only fair to reimburse the latter for postage, and perhaps contribute something towards their phone bill if they've had to chase up equipment for you.

The obvious ideal is to choose back stops who are themselves sailing people, but if this is not possible try to enlist the help of a sailing friend to whom they can turn for technical advice should it be needed. In either case it's both unreasonable and courting disaster to expect those at home to locate spares and parts without full details, so carry several up-to-date chandlery catalogues and even if you decide not to order direct you can at least supply them with the correct part number and address.

Telephones and mail

Not every aspect of ocean cruising has improved over the last decade or so but a few have, and the telephone system is one. In the mid 1970s it was said that if you wanted to phone Guadeloupe from Antigua, 42 miles away, your call would be routed through London and Paris. Like any international call it needed to be booked, with a probable delay in the region of two to four hours. Now you can dial Guadeloupe, the U.S. and probably Moscow direct, paying either by credit card or in cash. Technical friends tell me that geostationary satellites can take much of the credit, but whatever the reason the benefit to the cruising yachtsman is obvious.

Not only have international calls become quicker and simpler, but very often cheaper as well. By using public phone booths one can make use of reduced evening rates and avoid the old 'minimum charge' trap, though not all coin-operated phones accept international calls or allow you to reverse the charges (call collect). In tourist areas country codes are often listed in phone booths, but off the beaten track it may be necessary to check them at a post office. If there's no answer from home and you haven't time to wait around don't forget the humble telegram (cable), particularly useful when details such as parts numbers or a forwarding address must be received accurately.

Cruising mail may take a little more effort, and if you want to receive it at fairly regular intervals you will need to keep your home agent informed of your intended movements at least a month before they happen. By far the most practical approach is to organize for mail to be forwarded only to the major harbours, leaving your route and schedule between these points flexible, but trying to estimate how long it will take for a letter to reach home, and how long again for outward mail to arrive, can prove difficult. Distance is no real indication; I recently received a card from Bali postmarked only four days previously, whereas mail sent from the Cape Verde islands to England took nearly a month. On the principle that letters are not going to go bad on the shelf it would seem sensible to allow at least two to three weeks. Uncollected mail will not usually be returned to the sender, but if using American Express (who only hold mail for card-holders) try to let them know if you get delayed as otherwise letters are returned after one month. A note on all envelopes along the lines of 'Please hold for yacht in transit' in the appropriate language can never do any harm.

The local yachtsman's guide will often include suggestions of reliable mailing addresses, though we generally use the main post office and have seldom been let down. A yacht club may be a good bet, but be wary of having mail sent care of marinas or boatyards — not only are some disorganized to the point of chaos, but there can also be problems if you decide not to use their facilities. Neither should banks or officials such as port captains be expected to hold mail unless by prior agreement. Post offices will sometimes want to see identification and may occasionally make a small handling charge, but I have heard instances of commercial concerns holding the mail of non-clients virtually to ransom.

Letters should be clearly addressed with both your own name and that of the boat, but avoid titles and honorifics as they may be misunderstood and cause all kinds of confusion. Keep it as simple as possible, eg: 'Tom Brown, Yacht SEAFOAM, Poste Restante, Main Post Office, Funchal, Madeira', substituting 'General Delivery' for 'Poste Restante' in American-influenced areas such as the English-speaking islands of the Caribbean.

If you're fairly certain there should be letters waiting for you and the postal clerk swears there's nothing, don't be too shy to press the point. Ask if they could have been put somewhere else 'by one of your colleagues' (a good face-saver) and if possible describe what you are expecting. Arriving in Bequia just before Christmas we could not believe there were no letters for us, but it took several minutes of questioning to elicit the fact that all mail addressed to yachts was held in a local bar. On another occasion, this time in the British Virgin Islands, a combination of sheer persistence and being able to describe the overdue item as a pale blue airmail lettercard addressed in blue ink finally persuaded the postal clerk to take another look. I was silently presented with two lettercards, both of which she had missed previously. It might even be worth priming your home agent to mark envelopes distinctively — bright yellow labels, stripes of coloured highlighter or something equally eye-catching.

D. WORK AND EARNING

Unless you have an applicable skill it's not as easy to earn money as you cruise as most people imagine. First of all a clear distinction needs to be drawn between those people who live aboard their boat in some exotic (or not so exotic) part of the world but spend most of their time working, and those who are actively cruising. The former may well be taking time out from a long-term cruise to replenish the kitty, but if your own time scale is more limited you will do better to earn your money at home, where in any case rates of pay are likely to be much better, and then be free to enjoy the sailing, exploring, swimming or whatever.

Working as you go along

Work can best be divided into that which you get paid for on the spot and that which may bring rewards at a later date, with the former the most likely to attract the impecunious yachtsman — and the worst misconceptions. The majority of popular cruising grounds are areas of high unemployment, and one generally has to sign a form on arrival agreeing not to accept gainful employment. If the local immigration department catch you flouting this they are quite likely to impose a heavy fine and run you out of town. In theory this should not apply in Europe (including the French West Indies) after 1992, but I wouldn't bet on it. However, even accepting that most work will have to be on the quiet there are still some possibilities.

Chartering

Most cruising sailors are visited at some time or another by friends or family who often contribute generously towards expenses, and this is by far the best way for the smaller yacht to dabble on the fringes of chartering. I feel it quite fair to point out to potential visitors that not only are there obvious day-to-day expenses such as food and fuel, but also the considerable costs involved in getting the boat to wherever they will join it. Without wishing to make a profit out of one's friends, there's no reason why one should subsidize their holiday either.

Chartering on a commercial basis is something else entirely. Even if your boat is suitable (ie large enough, with full safety equipment, ample snorkelling gear and unlimited ice), in very few areas can you simply appear and start touting for customers on the beach. At best you will have to pay a hefty fee for a charter licence, and at worst could be fined and given twenty-four hours to leave. If you are serious about taking day charters it may be possible to set up an agreement with a local hotel who will then help clear it with the officials, but they will naturally expect to take a cut on everything you earn.

A third option is to look for employment with an established company aboard one of their fleet. Crew — most often skipper and cook — are usually taken on for the whole season, but there's always the possibility that the company may have been let down, and if they decide you are suitable may even be desperate enough to square it with immigration. Make no mistake, this kind of chartering is hard work, particularly for the cook, and certainly cannot be considered as part of a cruise.

Making and selling

We have met more than one crew who helped finance their cruising by making and selling goods either ashore (risky) or to other yachtsmen. In alphabetical order these have included canvaswork, courtesy flags, dressmaking, jewellery, leatherwork, scrimshaw (engraving on whale ivory) and woodcarving. In most cases some outlay was needed on tools and materials, and with profits in direct relation to the number of hours put in, those who made more than pin-money admitted that it was often at the expense of active cruising.

Practical skills

In larger harbours there may well be carpentry, engineering, electrical or other work available on neighbouring yachts, but this cannot be expected to pay well unless the owners are themselves earning, possibly by chartering. Work aboard another cruising yacht is as likely to be paid for in kind as in cash. As soon as you attempt to expand ashore the problem of a work permit rears its head. A real specialist such as an experienced diesel engineer might be taken on by a yard who could steer this through, but they're unlikely to consider it worth the effort for someone who may not be around long. If you carry scuba gear there is the possibility of irregular earnings from the recovery of lost anchors, outboards and even prescription glasses, and we have met one or two divers who specialize in scouring popular harbours for abandoned anchors and other equipment which they salvage, clean up and sell.

Professional skills
One of the most lucrative 'mobile' skills appears to be dentistry, should you already be qualified in this line. Charter crews often distrust local dentists and may be willing to pay generously for peace of mind, though most of the dentists we have met do not charge for essential work on fellow cruisers. Doctors are less lucky in terms of earning power since they will usually be called upon only in emergencies, often by people who themselves have little money. However we have met one or two who've fostered excellent relations with local people by holding informal 'surgeries' for minor ailments. The same goes for vets.

A trained hairdresser also has an easily marketable skill, needing little more than a good pair of scissors and a suitable box or low wall. One girl I talked to in the Caribbean reckoned to make up to $50 per day (BIG money by cruising standards) and yet kept a low enough profile not to be bothered by the officials. We have also met teachers of all kinds, from those advertising lessons for cruising children to a few running classes on specialist subjects for adults, but this will tie you down to one area in a way which does not mesh with serious cruising.

One girl stands out in my memory for her unique way of contributing to cruising funds — she was a belly dancer! She told me she never had trouble getting bookings, and a few tickets slipped to the immigration department disposed of any problems on that front. The only drawback was that the entire forepeak of the family 46-footer was taken up by her costumes . . .

Earning at a distance

The most obvious way of earning at a distance is by writing, but this is not quite as simple as it might appear. Many cruising yachtsmen do manage to sell the occasional magazine article, but those who support themselves purely by writing can probably be counted on the fingers of one hand, certainly of both. You will have a head start if you know what a particular magazine requires in terms of length, content, accompanying photographs, etc, and most will be happy to provide a sheet giving just these details on receipt of a stamped addressed envelope. It is essential that submitted articles are typed as few editors will bother to read a handwritten manuscript. Unless something really dramatic happens and you find yourselves in the headlines forget the idea of writing a book — very few narrative accounts of voyages are published these days, and even if you should be lucky enough to find a publisher the time lag is such that you will not see any return until long after the cruise has ended. Unfortunately the same is often true of magazine articles.

Hand in hand with writing goes photography, the problem being that unless you get films developed on the spot (generally impossible with transparencies and often both below par and expensive for prints) it may be months before you see the results. Magazines need a regular supply of cover and other photographs and some pay quite generously, but each tends to have its own style and subject matter so it's essential to study your market before leaving. Unless professional photography is already your livelihood you would be most unwise to regard this source of income as anything other than a bonus. Photography as a hobby is covered in Section 8E.

E. HOBBIES AND INTERESTS

Blue water yachtsmen frequently complain of boredom on longer passages, and certainly in heavier weather the lively motion aboard a small boat will effectively limit activity to the basics of watchkeeping, navigating, cooking, reading and sleeping. However for a large proportion of one's time at sea the wind will probably be light, and most yachts cruising the Atlantic circuit experience at least one calm of several days' duration. Even the two-person crew will have time to spare provided the self-steering is doing its job. Added to this there will be many unoccupied hours in harbour or at anchor, and one of the luxuries of the cruising lifestyle is free time on a scale undreamt of ashore.

Obviously some of this time will be taken up by routine chores essential to either the boat or her crew, but a great many cruising sailors take advantage of the remainder either to teach themselves a new skill or to pursue a favourite hobby or interest. We have met a computer addict who spent his spare time writing programs, several people who were deeply into the more esoteric aspects of celestial navigation and astronomy, designers (on paper) of everything from yachts to bridges, and many amateur birdwatchers and botanists. Long distance cruising also offers an unrivalled opportunity to study or brush up on foreign languages, those of one's fellow yachtsmen as well as whatever is spoken ashore. Many ocean cruisers start collections — shells, coral, fossils, rocks and so on — and should storage become a problem lesser treasures can always be sent home by sea-mail to make room for more.

New hobbies often require basic equipment — reference books, binoculars or a magnifying glass (both of which should already be on board), notebooks or storage pots — so if you suspect any friends of wanting to give you nonconsumable departure gifts drop some heavy hints. The suggestions which follow (taken in alphabetical order) barely scratch the surface.

Astronomy, or simply star-gazing

> Mortal I know I am, short-lived; and yet, when-
> ever I watch the multitude of swirling stars,

then I no longer tread this earth, but rise to
feast with God, and enjoy the food of the im-
mortals.

(Ptolemy of Alexandria)

Although recognition of individual stars isn't necessary for celestial navigation
if using the pre-computed method, in the past many yachtsmen came to astronomy via celestial navigation and one hopes the increased use of satnav will not
deprive too many people of this pleasure. The middle of a dark ocean is an ideal
spot from which to study the heavens, though the sheer number of bodies visible can be awesome. Unless the sea is very flat detailed examination with binoculars will probably have to wait until you get into harbour, but it makes
sense to become familiar with the layout of the brighter stars and constellations before confusing oneself with a closer look. There are numerous books
which include star charts, drawings of the constellations, forecasts of the movements of the planets and the dates of regular meteor showers. Two good cheap
ones are: *The Friendly Stars: How to Locate and Identify Them* by Martha
Evans Martin and Donald Howard Menzel (Dover); and *The Stars: A New Way
to See Them* by H.A. Rey (Houghton-Mifflin).

Musical instruments

Music can be made anywhere, is invisible and
doesn't smell.

(WH Auden, *In Praise of Limestone*)

Anybody who can play an instrument well is a real asset to a cruising yacht,
and I shall never forget our meeting with a steel 40-footer which was literally
designed around an upright piano. Her skipper, who played at concert standard,
expected to practise for several hours every day even at sea. Except in the case of
a singlehander it's doubtful whether a yacht is a good place to teach oneself
from scratch, and while in harbour there are obvious limitations in time and
place for practising the louder instruments since sound carries well across still
water.

A guitar, though one of the nicest and most sociable instruments to have
aboard, can only be justified in terms of space if it will be played regularly and
fairly well. I am told that they don't always take to the salt air and high humid-
ity, so this is obviously not the life for a valuable and highly prized instrument
— the same would presumably be true of the violin family. Smaller, more robust, and very traditional at sea are concertinas and accordians, and I have also
heard saxophones, clarinets and trumpets echoing across various anchorages.
Much cheaper and more transportable are recorders and mouthorgans — both
capable of surprising feats in expert hands or simply providing fun for younger
crew members. The ultimate must be bagpipes, best heard over water from several hundred yards away and guaranteed to make you the centre of attention on
New Year's Eve!

Oceanography and marine biology
This might cover anything from a serious scientific interest in the geology of the ocean basins to simple curiosity as to which species of dolphin are playing under the bows. Whatever your level, this is one subject where a good reference book is essential. Heavy in both weight and subject matter but nevertheless one of my favourites is *Oceanography and Seamanship* by William G. Van Dorn (Adlard Coles, 1974). Though long out of print there must be some second-hand copies around. For identifying whales, dolphins, seabirds and plant life the Audubon Society Field Studies (Random House) are excellent and a more practical size. There are plenty of others on the same theme.

Photography, video cameras, etc
There must be few cruising yachts around without a camera of some sort aboard, though it has sometimes surprised me how little effort people often make to keep a pictorial record of what will probably be a 'once in a lifetime' experience. Whether or not you buy a new camera for the cruise will obviously depend on outlook, what you already own (or can borrow) and remaining funds, but any non-marinized camera should be stored in a sealed bag or case together with plenty of silica gel (see Appendix 1). Even then frequent use in a salty atmosphere may shorten its working life. I am currently on my fourth SLR camera in sixteen years, but that does include some 50,000 ocean miles, eight Atlantic crossings and nearly ten years of living aboard various craft. If funds can possibly stretch to it I would recommend buying a waterproof or at least weatherproof 35mm camera (I have found the miniature format 110 variety disappointing). My own underwater camera is a Hanimex Amphibian, while my sister has one manufactured by Pentax. Both have wide-angle lenses and can be used either in or out of the water, making them ideal for sailing shots on wet and windy days and expeditions in the dinghy. Neither do they suffer from long-term exposure to damp. Unfortunately waterproof cameras start the wrong side of $150 if bought new, but they frequently turn up second-hand.

Film is even more expensive abroad than at home, and though Kodak is on sale almost everywhere stocks may sometimes be well past the expiration date. It's best to take a good supply with you, and there's also the possibility of a discount if buying in quantity before departure. Further supplies can be sent out as needed by your home agent or brought by friends flying out on holiday. We store unused film in Tupperware* boxes or self-seal bags, again along with plenty of dried silica gel, and have never experienced problems with deterioration. Neither have we ever had film damaged by x-rays when airmailed home for developing. I would be wary of airmailing very sensitive film (more than 100 ASA/21°DIN) but with the excellent light conditions prevalent in low-latitude cruising areas either 25ASA/12°DIN or 64ASA/12°DIN are likely to be more suitable, with 100ASA/21°DIN for use underwater.

Video cameras are becoming increasingly popular among cruising yachtsmen. Again the possiblility of deterioration applies to standard models (the outdoor variety such as the Sony Handicam retail well into four figures) and secure stowage will need to be found to protect the camera in bad weather. I referred in Section 6E to the cruising friend who videos local scenes and then collects an audience to view the results on his portable television set, and have myself had great fun making ciné films of several of our Atlantic passages.

Reading and book swapping

> This is not a novel to be tossed aside lightly. It
> should be thrown with great force.
>
> (Dorothy Parker)

My idea of being on watch in mid-ocean is to crouch over the chart table with a good book, deserting it only to take a look around the horizon at regular intervals. Long quiet watches are an ideal time to tackle the kind of tomes that would take months to wade through ashore, and in rough weather a good novel (preferably set in a desert or halfway up a mountain) can serve to take one's mind off conditions outside. We always leave with lots of reading matter on board, divided into three definite categories. There are the reference books, the novels, biographies etc that we intend to keep, and the paperbacks to be read and then swapped. These latter may sometimes have been bought new or received as presents, but if the supply is short it will be augmented before departure from second-hand bookstalls.

Swapping is most often done on a 'one-for-one' basis, though in the case of thicker books it may be calculated in inches. One sometimes ends up with incredibly appalling books this way, but with time to dip into subjects and authors that would normally be rejected out of hand there is the occasional pleasant surprise. More and more harbours have official book-swaps; the one in English Harbour, Antigua, occupies an entire room. Not only is book-swapping an important source of free reading matter, it is also an excellent way to meet new people. Fill a carrier bag with a dozen paperbacks and half the crews in the anchorage will be clamouring to invite you on board.

Sewing/dressmaking

As noted in Section 6B, cheerful local prints are often good value and a great many cruising folk make their own clothes, with or without the aid of a sewing machine. I seldom use a pattern, but if you prefer them it would be wise to take a few adaptable favourites along rather than rely on finding something suitable on the spot. Brass rather than steel pins are another item to lay in before departure, but if a needle rusts a gentle rub with emery paper will usually restore it. Whether or not you enjoy sewing, clothes will almost certainly need to be patched from time to time, and while it may sometimes be possible to cannibalize (eg legs from one pair of jeans to patch the seat and knees of several others) a bag of assorted scraps will certainly come in useful. If time really drags you can always turn them into patchwork!

Shell collecting (conchology)

I started shelling on our last cruise in the mistaken belief that it would be a nice cheap hobby. I swiftly became hooked, started hankering after reference books and have even bought a few choice specimens since returning home. My collection grew slowly as I consider it wrong to take a live shell, and in any case I found it far more interesting to bring an unusual specimen back aboard for a few days' study and photography before returning it to its own habitat. However careful searching was rewarded with some very nice empties. On one memorable morning I saw a lovely pale pink murex sticking out of a hole at a depth of about 10 feet. I grabbed it, only to have it pulled out of view and replaced by several waving tentacles — I had obviously disturbed an octopus at lunch. Taking the line of least resistance I too went home to eat, and on returning a few hours later found a beautifully clean, empty shell awaiting me on his doorstep. Careful excavation revealed several others, all in equally good condition.

Many hundreds of books have been written on all aspects of conchology. A good cheap one to get you started is *The Complete Collector's Guide to Shells and Shelling* by Sandra Romashko (Windward). Alternatively, wait until you've reached your main cruising ground and then get a book which covers that particular area, such as *Collectible Shells of Southeastern US, Bahamas & Caribbean* by R Tucker Abbott (American Malacologists, 1984) — unusual in having a choice of paper or waterproof editions. If you absolutely must kill a live shell either boiling or freezing will do the trick, but the ecology of many popular cruising areas has already been upset by over-collecting, so at the very least avoid taking immature specimens. I found the best way to clean and de-pong my treasures was to soak them overnight in dilute bleach, then scrub with an old toothbrush and if necessary pick any detritus out with tweezers or a bent pin.

Snorkelling and diving

It's a moot point whether snorkelling gear — mask, snorkel tube, fins and possibly a weight belt — should not be classified under safety equipment. Certainly you will have a much better chance of clearing a fouled propeller or anchor if you can see what you are doing, so logically the best swimmer aboard should be equipped with the full kit even if you are not visiting waters where they are likely to use it for pleasure. However, to visit warmer waters and not carry snorkelling gear for each person strikes me as a crying shame and false economy — clear, shallow coral waters are quite literally another world of undreamt of beauty and interest, and best of all, they're free! Snorkelling is not difficult but there is a certain knack involved, particularly in clearing the air-tube on returning to the surface, so if you find yourself having problems ask a more experienced diver to demonstrate.

The equipment is cheapest if bought before leaving home, and with the sole exception of the tube itself must be bought to fit the individual wearer. An uncomfortable mask is not only painful but will generally leak, loose fins have a habit of falling off and sinking, while over-tight ones will either split or cause swollen, puffy feet. Lead weights (usually 2lb/0.9kg) can be bought individually and threaded on webbing for a do-it-yourself weight belt; long strips of Velcro make an excellent quick-release fastening. Underwater photographers in particular will find the additional stability and neutral buoyancy conferred by some extra ballast to be invaluable. Snorkelling under a tropical sun is a quick way to get a badly sunburnt back, so wear a T-shirt until you've built up a tan.

Few budget yachts carry full scuba gear, let alone a compressor to refill tanks. However if you do already own tanks you will find many hotels with beach facilities where they can be refilled (at a price, of course) and it is sometimes possible to hire the full equipment on production of a YMCA, or equivalent, certificate of competency. Scuba gear should *never* be used by the inexperienced without qualified supervision. There is also the possibility of making it pay for itself (see section 8D).

POST SCRIPT

On reading the manuscript a final time I was struck by the number of references to *Wrestler*, to my sister, and to the many friends we've made through ocean cruising. My first reaction was 'I should have kept it more impersonal', but I very soon realized that this would have been almost impossible. For me, the main satisfaction of long distance cruising lies in sailing a boat of which I am immensely fond (in addition to having been my home for the past six years she has carried us more than 25,000 miles without drama, fuss or major failures), in company with a co-owner and skipper with whom I generally see eye to eye, reinforced by the pleasure of meeting people from a far wider range of nationalities and backgrounds than I ever would ashore. Many lasting friendships have their origins in distant harbours, and though it's impossible to keep in touch with everyone we've met, each Christmas brings its quota of envelopes with stamps depicting angelfish or frangipani.

The variety offered by the cruising life is another of its attractions. The blue water sailor has to be able to turn his or her hand to almost anything, often at a moment's notice, and for many skippers it's a unique opportunity to take total responsibility for their own and even other people's lives. The experience of taking true life-or-death decisions — not that most wrong decisions are likely to be fatal, but it can sometimes feel that way — is a privilege seldom enjoyed ashore. Few first-time blue water sailors return home totally unchanged, and still fewer do not dream of setting off again.

I cannot claim that we have never wished we had more money — when it would have been fun to hire a car and go exploring, or to sample some regional delicacy in a local restaurant. Then I think of an open West Indian bus bumping its dusty way across the mountains of Grenada, and an impromptu supper with friends whose fishing was more successful than ours. Would we really have increased our enjoyment noticeably by spending twice the money? I doubt it. Too many of the rewards of ocean cruising — the achievement, the friendships, the widened horizons both literally and metaphorically — reflect an investment of enthusiasm, commitment and effort, not of coins.

APPENDIX 1

USEFUL ODDS AND ENDS

We find there are various small items which have uses aboard out of all proportion to their cost, and some have already heen mentioned elsewhere in the text. It must he stressed that all are in addition to the normal contents of the bosun's bag, spares, repair equipment and so on.

Lots of **1-gallon (5-litre) plastic cans** — useful for water, diesel and paraffin, and often available for the asking from restaurants and bars. Must be very clearly marked as to contents!

Odd bits of **plastic pipe** for use as chafing gear. Pre-cut lengths of 18in (0.5m) or so are best, with a hole drilled across one end and a thin string threaded through as a retainer (see Fig 13). Necessary for secondary anchor cable, and on mooring lines whenever they come in contact with stone or concrete quays. If slit lengthways they can be fitted to lines already in place.

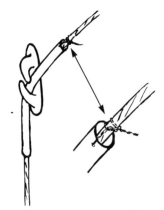

Fig 13 Chafe protector and retaining line

At least a dozen pieces of **thin line** about one yard one (lm) long. Melt, splice or whip the ends, preferably splicing eyes into some, and then keep them handy in pockets, cockpit side lockers, or a bag in the companionway. Their many uses include suspending deck blocks from the lifelines to prevent tapping, fashioning instant lanyards for sextants, cameras, sunglasses and other valuables, securing spare lines in tidy coils for stowing, and lashing anything which looks as though it might be about to go adrift.

Shock cord (bungee) of various sizes, plus **hooks** and **screw-in** eyes — it keeps storage tubs at peace with their neighbours, books in open-fronted bookshelves, containers upright in the heads, etc.

Plastic suction hooks — smaller sizes can usually be found in hardware shops, larger sizes are often sold on the knick-knack stands at boat shows.

Velcro Sticky Pads and double-sided tape are all invaluable whenever you want to attach something without permanently marking the boat. Available from stationers.

Velcro tape — has taken over where press-studs (themselves a useful thing to carry) left off. Stocked by fabric or furnishing stores, who may also have the even tougher industrial grade.

Plastic cable holders — from any electrical shop. Can be adapted for use as hooks, and if attached by a Sticky Fixer can later be removed without scarring surfaces.

Lots of **carrier bags** — particularly useful if you have no fitted garbage container in the galley, when a bag with handles can often be hung from hooks. Also necessary for shopping abroad where bags are seldom provided. Take care over disposal, and *never* dump plastic at sea.

Assorted **self-seal bags** — to keep small items under control, tools free of rust, clothes dry, cameras and film away from salt air, biscuits crisp. One of the most useful things aboard any boat, even those which don't leak.

Silica gel sachets — for use inside self-seal bags, particularly for storing film etc. Photographic shops have them by the hundred from camera packaging and will probably be happy to give you a few handfuls, particularly if you are buying film stocks for the trip. Dry them out thoroughly in a warm oven before use. Dried peas or beans are a non-toxic substitute for use in food storage.

Plastic boxes — unsurpassed for storing frequent-use galley items like tea and coffee. Also a range of plastic mixing bowls, measuring jugs and other galley equipment. A good brand is Rubbermaid.

Foam rubber offcuts — ideal for wedging crockery and bottles for silence and their own safety. Larger pieces make good no-nonsense cockpit cushions.

Empty wine box bags — particularly useful where a locker is gradually emptied over the course of a passage, as they can be inflated by degrees as necessary. I am told they also make passable cockpit cushions.

Old face cloths — make excellent galley cloths and save whole rolls of paper towels over the course of a cruise. Need regular rinsing and bleaching. Can be used damp to provide a non-skid surface for hot pans.

Old towels — as doormats and for general mopping up. Invaluable in the fight to prevent salt water soaking into furnishings and the cabin sole.

A **short drying line** — for gloves, socks, above-mentioned galley cloths and other small items. For the yacht without other heating, directly above the stove is the best place.

Ordinary **sprung clothes pegs** — not only for wash day or for keeping socks from falling in the soup, but as temporary closures for half-used packets, third hands on fiddly jobs such as soldering wires, and (dismembered) as ready-made wedges.

An **umbrella** — don't laugh! It does rain abroad, and festoons of wet shore-going clothes are a nuisance. The brightly patterned variety also makes a cheerful parasol.

APPENDIX 2

FURTHER READING

A surprising number of books have been written on the subject of ocean cruising, though nothing to the scores published on other aspects of sailing. Regretfully I have had to confine this list almost entirely to factual and reference works, but have included various technical books dealing with specific items of the yacht and her gear, many of which have already been referred to in the text. When far away from expert assistance the skipper must also be mechanic, electrician or whatever. A clear and comprehensive book on the subject is half the battle, and most will also be valuable during the preparation stage.

Unfortunately, books are expensive (though discount and second-hand book shops in sailing areas are a good source), heavy, and take up valuable space. Long distance sailors tend by definition to be individualistic and sometimes opinionated, often leaving the novice wondering who to believe, and some of the all-time classics are now out of date on certain points. The following vary in their relevance to budget ocean cruising, so try to borrow from friends or library before deciding which to buy. A few are currently out of print (OP), but may be available second-hand — see Appendix 3 for possible sources. The date generally refers to the edition I used, not always the most recent, but prices are those of the latest edition.

Advanced First Aid Afloat, Dr. Perry F. Eastman (Cornell Maritime, 1987, $11.95).

After 50,000 Miles, Hal Roth (W.W. Norton, 1977, $22.50).

Aground!, James E. Minnoch (John de Graff, 1985, $12.95).

Anchoring, Brian Fagan (International Marine, 1986, $9.95).

Anchoring and Mooring Techniques Illustrated, Alain Gree (Sheridan, 1984, $29.95).

The Atlantic Crossing Guide, Edited by Philip Allen (RCC Pilotage Foundation/International Marine, 1990, $32.95).

Atlantic Pilot Atlas, James Clarke (International Marine, 1989, $75.00).

Babies Aboard, Lyndsay Green (International Marine, 1990, $10.95).

Basic Astro Navigation, Conrad Dixon (Sheridan, 1985, $12.95).

The Big Book of Boat Canvas: A Complete Guide to Fabric Work on Boats, Karen Lipe (Seven Seas/International Marine, 1991, $18.95).

Boatowner's Mechanical and Electrical Manual, Nigel Calder (International Marine, 1990, $39.95).

The Care and Feeding of the Offshore Crew, Lin and Larry Pardey (W.W. Norton, 1980, $19.95).

The Care and Repair of Sails, Jeremy Howard-Williams (SAIL Publications, 1976, $14.95).

The Care and Repair of Small Marine Diesels, Chris Thompson (International Marine, 1987, $15.95).

Celestial Navigation, Tom Cunliffe (International Marine, 1989, $14.95).

Celestial Navigation for Yachtsmen, Mary Blewitt (John de Graff, 1967, $7.95).

Celestial Navigation Step by Step, Warren Norville (International Marine, 1984, $22.95).

The Circumnavigator's Handbook, Steve

and Linda Dashew (W.W. Norton, 1983, OP).

Comfort in the Cruising Yacht, Ian Nicolson (Sheridan, 1987, $29.95).

The Complete Collector's Guide to Shells and Shelling, Sandra Romashko (Windward, 1984, $6.95).

Cruising in Comfort, Jim Skoog (International Marine, 1986, $35.00).

The Cruising Multihull, Chris White (International Marine, 1990, $27.95).

Cruising Under Sail, incorporating *Voyaging Under Sail,* Eric Hiscock (International Marine, 1986, $22.95).

Cruising with Children, Gwenda Cornell (Sheridan, 1986, $27.50).

The Fiberglass Boat Repair Manual, Allan Vaitses (International Marine, 1988, $29.95).

Fine Yacht Finishes for Wood and Fiberglass Boats, Paul and Marya Butler (International Marine, 1987, $22.95).

Flags, Eric Inglefield (Prentice-Hall, 1979, $8.95).

The Friendly Stars: How to Locate and Identify Them, Martha Evans Martin and Donald Howard Menzel (Dover, 1964, $3.50).

From a Bare Hull, Ferenc Maté (W.W. Norton, 1983, $29.95).

The Galley Handbook, Maralyn Bailey (Nautical Books, 1978, OP).

Heavy Weather Sailing, K. Adlard Coles (John de Graff, 1981, $22.50).

Living on 12 Volts With Ample Power, David Smead and Ruth Ishihara (Rides, 1988, $25.00).

Marine Diesel Engines, Nigel Calder (International Marine, 1987, $22.95).

Marine Inboard Engines, Loris Goring (Sheridan, 1990, $27.50).

Northwest By North, Dora Birtles (Beacon, 1987, OP).

Ocean Cruising Countdown, Geoff Pack (David & Charles, 1988, $29.95).

The Ocean Sailing Yacht, Vols 1 & 2, Donald M. Street, Jr. (W.W. Norton, 1973, $38.95, and 1979, $27.95).

Ocean Voyaging, David M. Parker (John de Graff, 1983, $3.95).

Oceanography and Seamanship, William G. Van Dorn (Van Nostrand Reinhold, 1974, OP).

Osmosis and the Care and Repair of Glassfibre Yachts, Tony Staton-Bevan (Sheridan, 1989, $19.95).

Repairs at Sea, Nigel Calder (International Marine, 1988, $12.95).

A Sailor's Guide to Sails, Sven Donaldson (Putnam, 1984, $8.95).

Seaworthiness: The Forgotten Factor, C.A. Marchaj (International Marine, 1987, $34.95).

Sell Up and Sail, Bill and Laurel Cooper (Sheridan, 1987, $29.95).

Sensible Cruising: The Thoreau Approach, Don Casey and Lew Hackler (International Marine, 1986, $24.95).

The Sextant Handbook, Bruce Bauer (International Marine, 1987, $20.95).

Shipshape, The Art of Sailboat Maintenance, Ferenc Maté (W.W. Norton, 1986, $29.95).

Skene's Elements of Yacht Design, Francis S. Kinney (Putnam, 1989, $29.95).

Sky & Sextant, John P. Budlong (Van Nostrand Reinhold, 1978, OP).

Spurr's Boatbook: Upgrading the Cruising Sailboat, 2nd Edition, Dan Spurr (Seven Seas/International Marine, 1991, $34.95).

The Stars: A New Way To See Them, H.A. Rey (Houghton-Mifflin, 1973, $16.95).

Start with a Hull, Loris Goring (David & Charles, 1986, $39.95).

Surveying Small Craft, Ian Nicholson (Sheridan, 1984, $19.95).

This is Rough Weather Cruising, Erroll Bruce (SAIL Publications, 1980, $19.95).

This Old Boat, Don Casey (International Marine, 1991, $34.95).

Total Loss, Jack H. Coote (Sheridan, 1985, $29.95).

The 12-Volt Bible for Boats, Minor Brotherton (International Marine, 1985, $12.95).

Upgrading and Refurbishing the Older Fiberglass Sailboat, W.D. Booth (Cornell Maritime, 1985, $24.50).

What Shape Is She In? A Guide to the Surveying of Boats, Allan Vaitses (International Marine, 1985, $13.95).

Wiring 12 Volts For Ample Power, David Smead and Ruth Ishihara (Rides, 1990, $18.50).

World Cruising Handbook, Jimmy Cornell (International Marine, 1991, $69.95).

World Cruising Routes, Jimmy Cornell (International Marine, 1987, $37.50).

Your Offshore Doctor, Dr. Michael H. Beilan (Putnam, 1985, $12.95).

APPENDIX 3

ADDRESSES

Armchair Sailor Bookstore
Lee's Wharf
Newport, RI 02840
• Books and charts, store
and catalog

Autohelm America
New Whitfield St.
Guilford, CT 06437
800-833-4663
• Automatic steerers

Avon East
30 Barnet Blvd.
New Bedford, MA 02745
508-990-2700
Avon West
1851 McGaw Ave.
Irvine, CA 92714
714-250-0880
• Inflatable liferafts and
dinghies

Bacon Associates, Inc.
112 West St.
Box 3150
Annapolis, MD 21403
301-263-4880
• Used sails, buy and sell

Blake and Sons
(Gosport) Ltd.
Box 15
Sunbeam Works
Park Rd.
Gosport
Hants PO12 2HG
U.K.
• Baby Blake and Lavac
toilets/spares

Bluewater Books
and Charts
1481 SE 17th St. Causeway
Fort Lauderdale, FL 33316

305-763-6533
FAX 305-522-2278
• Well named, store
and catalog

Boat US
884 South Pickett St.
Alexandria, VA 22304
• Chandlery and books,
catalog, membership

Bondo Marine Products
Dynatron/Bondo Corp.
Atlanta, GA 30331
800-241-3386
• Cleaners, fiberglass repair
products, putties, etc.

Continental Marine
Box 330
Little Cove Lane
Old Greenwich, CT 06870
800-922-4872
FAX 203-698-0861
• Good selection
of electronics

Davis Instruments
3465 Diablo Ave.
Hayward, CA 94545
FAX 415-732-9188
• Plastic sextants and more

Defender Industries
255 Main St.
Box 820
New Rochelle,
NY 10802-0820
914-632-3001
FAX 914-632-6544
• Chandlery, catalog,
widest selection of all
gear, including fiberglass
materials, maintenance
products, paint

Defense Mapping Agency
Office of Distribution
Services
6500 Brooks Lane
Washington, DC 20315
202-227-2816
• Pilot charts, Universal
Plotting Sheets

Edson Corp.
460 Industrial Park Rd.
New Bedford, MA 02745
508-995-9711
FAX 800-338-5021
• High-capacity pumps

Force 10
23080 Hamilton Rd.
Richmond, B.C.
Canada VGV 1C9
• Stoves

Thomas Foulkes
9A Sansom Rd.
Leytonstone
London E11 3HB
U.K.
• Second-hand sextants

Goldberg's Marine
201 Meadow Rd.
Edison, NJ 08818
800-262-8464
• Chandlery, stores
and catalog

Hub Nautical Supply
200 High St.
Boston, MA 02110
617-426-9471
• Charts and navigation
publications

International Association
for Medical Assistance to

Travelers
417 Center St.
Lewiston, NY 14092
• Membership

International Marine
Publishing Co.
Division of TAB Books
Blue Ridge Summit, PA
17294-0840
800-822-8158
• Books, catalog

Koolatron
56 Harvester Ave.
Batavia, NY 14020
• Portable, 12-volt coolers

Henri Lloyd
86 Orchard Beach Rd.
Port Washington,
NY 11050
800-645-6516
• Foul weather gear

Marine Data Services
Box 2394
Woodland, CA 95695
• Crew and boat match-ups

Marine Vane Gears Ltd.
Northwood
Cowes
Isle of Wight PO31 8NA
U.K.

• Aries wind-vane
self-steering gear

Minn Kota
1531 Madison Ave.
Mankato, MN 56001
800-227-6433
• Electric outboard motors

National Association of
Marine Surveyors
305 Springhouse Lane
Moorestown, NJ 08057
800-822-6267
in New Jersey,
609-722-5515

Origo
1121 Lewis Ave.
Sarasota, FL 33577
• Alcohol stoves

Pacific Seacraft Corp.
1301 East Orangethorpe
Fullerton, CA 92631
714-879-1610
• Small, seaworthy
cruising boats

Practical Sailor
Box 819
Newport, RI 02840
• Bimonthly periodical,
objective boat and
gear evaluations

Raytheon Marine Co.
46 River Rd.
Hudson, NH 03051
603-881-5200
FAX 603-881-4765
• Electronics

Scanmar Marine Products
298 Harbor Dr.
Sausalito, CA 94965
415-332-3233
• Monitor and Navik wind-
vane self-steering systems

West Marine Products
Box 1020
Watsonville, CA 95077
800-538-0775
in California, 800-283-6070
• Chandlery, catalog

Wilcox-Crittenden
699 Middle St.
Middletown, CT 06457
203-632-2600
• Marine hardware

Zodiac
Thompson Creek Rd.
Stevensville, MD 21666
• Inflatable boats

INDEX